66 WEEKEND WOOD FURNITURE PROJECTS

By Lewis H. Hodges

TAB BOOKS

Blue Ridge Summit, Pa. 17214

FIRST EDITION

FIRST PRINTING—JANUARY 1978
SECOND PRINTING—APRIL 1978
THIRD PRINTING—MAY 1979
Copyright © 1978 by TAB BOOKS

Printed in the United States
of America

Library of Congress Cataloging in Publication Data

Hodges, Lewis H.
    66 weekend wood furniture projects.

    Includes index.
    1. Furniture making—Amateurs' manuals. I. Title.
TT195.H6 684.1'042 77-11402
ISBN 0-8306-7974-X
ISBN 0-8306-6974-4 pbk.

Cover photo courtesy NuTone Division, Scovill Mfg. Co.

66 WEEKEND WOOD FURNITURE PROJECTS

Preface

This book is designed for the typical home craftsman who possesses the basic hand and machine woodworking tools and wants a variety of quality projects from which to choose. The author has intentionally avoided large, time-consuming, complicated projects that become a bore before they are completed.

It is assumed that the craftsman has at least a nodding acquaintance with the tools and techniques referred to in this text. Chapters 1 and 2 will help bolster these acquaintances.

As a building and furniture material, wood is, by far, the best understood. It is part of our heritage, and Yankee ingenuity has made the most of it.

Perhaps until recently, we have taken wood for granted. But even today wood is probably the greatest bargain around. Unlike oil, coal and gas, lumber is a *renewable product.*

There is no other material, natural, or formulated by man, that has more desirable characteristics.

Considerable emphasis has been placed on Early American pine projects. The simplicity and humble beauty of Early American and Colonial pine furniture and accessories have fascinated and delighted Americans for well over two hundred years. The early craftsman designed objects of charm and grace, each one reflecting the individuality and genius of the maker.

Pine was used by the early pioneers for two reasons: it was abundant and it was easy to fashion into useful objects. In the subdued light of the log cabin it developed a rich orange-red patina without using any finishing materials. White pine was the favorite wood as it was soft and durable and comparatively free of knots. The few knots that existed simply added to the overall distinctive beauty of the piece.

The early folk-art pieces fitted in surprisingly well with early decor consisting of hand-hewn beams, wide stone fireplaces, rough-hewn logs and wrought-iron hardware.

The reader of this book does not necessarily have to copy any project verbatim. Any amateur or professional with creativity and imagination can, by using basic principles of design, come up with projects as pleasing as the ones depicted in this manuscript.

This book should give the home craftsman many new and practical ideas. In addition, 4-H Club members, Junior Achievement workers, industrial arts and vocational education teachers and others will find this ready reference a valuable addition to their library.

May the endearing qualities and humble characteristics of Early American pine pieces continue to give joy to the beholder and user for at least another two hundred years.

Lewis H. Hodges

Contents

Index 371

Chapter 1
General Related Information

GENERAL RELATED INFORMATION

To enable the home craftsman to become more familiar with all aspects of his raw material—wood—the first pages of this chapter are devoted to the development of lumber, methods used to obtain it, and factors affecting lumber grade and quality.

The remainder of the chapter is designed as a handy reference for the experienced woodworker to brush up on seldom used products or for the novice to become acquainted with the variety of tools, finishing materials, adhesives, hardware, etc., available today.

Also, detailed drawings and text remind the craftsman of the variety of joints and their particular uses for later reference when working on the projects of Chapters 4 and 5.

HOW WOOD FORMS

Trees grow vertically (above and below the earth's surface) and horizontally (to form the trunk). Each layer formed within the trunk and root system serves a vital purpose in the total development of the organism.

Man takes note only of the particular layers within the tree that serve his needs for lumber production. These layers—found in the trunk—and the cutting methods used to obtain them should be of concern to the home craftsman. Any wood project depends not only on the skill of the craftsman who fashions the finished product, but on the quality of the wood itself and the care taken when the wood was harvested.

How a Tree Grows

A tree grows much the same way as an onion—one conical layer on top of another.

Commercial lumber comes only from trees of some size; in other words, trees that have reached full growth or nearly so.

A tree consists of the trunk, branches of different sizes, and a root system. The top of the tree is usually referred to as the crown.

In size, the root system is about the same as the crown. The higher portion of the crown generally is the predominant portion because it receives more sunshine and rain, and that portion becomes the trunk. The secondary branches become just that, secondary, and many of the small ones wither, die, and drop off.

Growing takes place in two places: at the very tip of the elongated cone, which increases the height of a tree and, in the *cambium layer* (Fig. 1-1) which is between the bark and the wood.

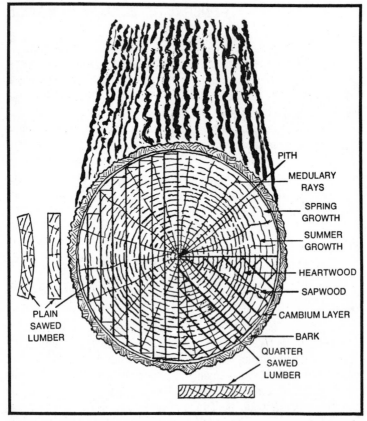

Fig. 1-1. A cross section of a tree demonstrating methods of sawing lumber.

This growth contributes to the thickness of a tree. Figure 1-2 is not drawn to scale. If drawn to an accurate scale, the height would be many times higher in proportion to the diameter of the trunk.

Ordinarily, the age of a tree can be ascertained by counting the annular rings—spring growth plus summer growth. Usually the summer rings are counted because they are denser, darker, more pronounced, and then the spring growth is added. Trees that grow in the tropics and are not regulated by seasons, but grow continuously throughout the year, do not have well defined growth (annular) rings.

Counting the rings on the stump or on the end of a log does not always give the correct answer. Take a look at Fig. 1-2. If we count the annular rings, we get an age of ten years, not fifteen. It took the tree between four and five years to reach the stump height. Only by cutting a tree off next to the ground and counting the rings do we approach the correct answer.

Tree Cross Section

A further explanation of the major parts of a tree follows.

The *pith* serves no useful purpose in a tree. Pith is the very center of a tree. It is generally soft and is apt to rot, which leaves a hollow. Sometimes honey bees take advantage of these cavities and deposit their honey there.

The wood that encircles the pith is called the *heartwood*. It is the main portion of the tree trunk and gives it strength and stability. It is no longer in the growing stage and it does not aid in carrying moisture and food to the rest of the tree. The heartwood is generally darker than the sapwood which surrounds it. The cells in heartwood are dead and are frequently clogged with dark-colored waste materials which give it some of its characteristic color. Some heartwood turns darker when exposed to the air while other heartwood turns lighter. The spring growth and summer growth rings are more condensed in the heartwood than in the sapwood.

Sapwood is made up of spring growth and summer growth. The spring growth is generally wider than the summer growth because of more favorable growing conditions (moisture, etc.). The summer growth takes place more slowly and is apt to be darker in color and denser in texture, although sapwood in general is lighter in color than heartwood. The sapwood is important as a conductor of food and moisture to the rest of the tree.

The *cambium layer* is between the sapwood and the bark. It is a semi-liquid, cohesive substance. The main function of the cambium

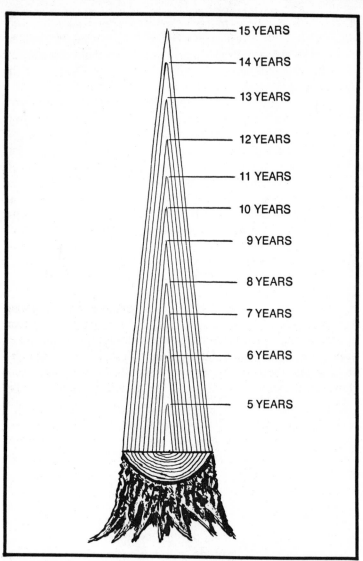

Fig. 1-2. The cambium layer at different stages of the tree's growth.

layer is to create cells which divide. Some of the cells form new wood while others form bark.

Identification of Wood Cuts

Each wood has characteristics which differentiate it from all other woods. Color, weight, density, grain configuration, odor, and taste are only a few of these characteristics. Burl walnut and bird's eye maple and crotch wood are woods with unusual configurations.

Methods of sawing or machining of wood may enhance the beauty of the finished product. Wood turned on a veneer lathe and quarter-sawn wood, for example, are quite attractive.

Quarter sawing of wood is accomplished by cutting a log into four parts, longitudinally, so that the end of the log is a 90-degree pie-shaped segment. Then, the quarter log is cut in such a manner that the saw cuts are parallel—or nearly so—to the medullary rays. Medullary rays conduct sap across the grain in both softwoods and hardwoods by strips of cells that run at right angles to the fibers (Fig. 1-1).

This sawing produces large flakes on the surface of the wood, particularly in oak. Quarter sawing is used with many other woods besides oak to prevent or retard shrinking, twisting, and to prevent small checks from appearing in the surface.

Wood cut in this manner will wear longer than woods cut in other ways.

Plain sawing of wood is the most common way of sawing lumber. There is not as much waste and it is much faster than quarter sawing (Fig. 1-2). Actually, when a log is plain-sawn, two or three pieces in the center of the log (the widest pieces) are quarter-sawn in that the saw cuts are parallel with the medullary rays. However, the outside pieces do not fare as well. When the wood is drying, the tension in these outside pieces is tremendous. In the drying process the internal forces in the wood apply along the annual rings. With the strength of thousands of rubber bands the annual rings try to contract (that is, to become straight lines). As a result, the board has a tendency to "cup" to the outside. See the demonstration of Fig. 1-1 labeled "plain sawed lumber." Naturally, the board the greatest distance from the center of the log will warp the most.

Classification of Wood

Wood is classified in two categories—*softwoods* and *hardwoods*. Traditionally, softwoods have come from the evergreens, or trees whose leaves do not fall. Trees that shed their leaves annually are called hardwoods. There are certain discrepancies in this method. For example, basswood classified as a hardwood is much softer than some of the pines and firs which are classified as softwoods.

Wood is also classified as *open* grain and *close* grain. Walnut, oak, and mahogany are open grain woods and in the finishing process require a paste filler. Pine, basswood, birch, maple, poplar, and redwood are only a few examples of close grain woods.

WOOD CELL STRUCTURE

Wood texture, color, and strength are important to the quality of the finished product. The structure of the cells within the tree determines whether it's open- or close-grain wood or the amount of shrinkage to expect with a particular type of wood.

Texture

An important physical aspect of wood is the texture. Texture pertains to the relative size and amount of variation in the size of *wood cells*. Texture is referred to as coarse, fine, even, and uneven. Timbers in which the vessels are wide are said to be of coarse texture. The woodworker commonly refers to woods of a coarse grain structure as *open-grain woods*. When vessels (a tubelike structure found in porous wood caused by a combination of cells in a longitudinal row) are narrow and rays thin, the timber is of fine texture and is referred to as *close-grain wood*.

Color

The color of wood is of considerable importance to the woodworker. Color is caused largely by various substances which filter into the *cell wall*. The color of these materials is dependent upon the type and content of the soil the tree grows on.

Strength

Wood has greater strength with the grain than across the grain because of the way the cells are oriented in the tree (parallel to the axis of the tree).

The decrease or increase of moisture within the cellular structure causes shrinking and swelling of wood. See Fig. 1-3.

LUMBERING

In the United States there are close to 200 different tree species that are commercially important.

Care is taken to see that trees are mature before cutting. They are carefully inspected and marked only if they are ready for harvest. Logs are kept in a millpond until sawing starts. This prevents early seasoning and thus prevents checking of the wood. Band saws with teeth on both edges are used which permit the cutting of lumber in both directions while the carriage passes the saw.

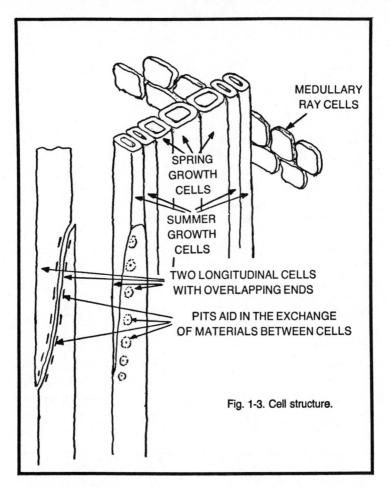

MEDULLARY RAY CELLS

SPRING GROWTH CELLS

SUMMER GROWTH CELLS

TWO LONGITUDINAL CELLS WITH OVERLAPPING ENDS

PITS AID IN THE EXCHANGE OF MATERIALS BETWEEN CELLS

Fig. 1-3. Cell structure.

Sawing of Lumber

There are two methods of sawing lumber. *Plain sawing* is the simplest and most common. Lumber is cut tangent to the annular rings. Wide boards are possible with this method and plain-sawn wood dries easiest.

Quarter-sawn lumber is produced by cutting the log into quarters and sawing the lumber off at right angles to the annular rings. This produces a pattern of more-or-less parallel straight lines. Quarter-sawn lumber shrinks, twists, cuts, checks, and splits less than plain-sawn lumber.

Hardwoods are not cut to standard sizes as are softwoods. They are cut in random lengths and widths and sold in this fashion as they come from the sawmill. Hardwood is cut to rough thicknesses and is not planed unless specified. Rough thicknesses of lumber are specified by quarters of an inch as follows:

$$1 \text{ in.} = 4/4$$
$$1 \text{ } 1/4 \text{ in.} = 5/4$$
$$1 \text{ } 1/2 \text{ in.} = 6/4$$
$$2 \text{ in.} = 8/4$$

Softwoods are cut to standard thicknesses, widths, and lengths, and are surfaced on four sides (S4S).

The standard lengths of lumber start at 8 ft. and increase by increments of 2 ft. up to 20 ft. (8, 10, 12, etc.) Thicknesses usually found are 1 in., 2 in., and 4 in. (before surfacing). Any lumber thicker than 4 in. is called a *timber*.

Widths of lumber run from 2 in. to 10 in. in increments of 2 in. (2 in., 4 in., 6 in., etc.).

Standard commercial softwood lumber has the following dimensions before and after surfacing.

RGH (Rough Dimension)	S4S (Finished on 4 Sides)
1×2	3/4 in. ×1 1/2 in.
1×4	3/4 in. ×3 1/2 in.
1×6	3/4 in. ×5 1/2 in.
–	–
–	–
–	–
2×10	1 1/2 in. ×9 1/4 in.

The craftsman should keep in mind that when he wants lumber 3/4 in. ×1 1/2 in. he orders 1 in. ×2 in. lumber. It is designated at 1 in. ×2 in. regardless of whether it is RGH or S4S.

SEASONING

When a hardwood log is cut in its green stage it consists of 33 1/3 percent to 50 percent free water or sap. The water must be eliminated from the wood before it can be used for furniture or for any other wooden object used indoors. *Seasoning* is the term we use for the process of removing the water.

The cellular structure of a tree has a capacity for retaining water. The cavity and the permeable wall of the cell are the retainers. Wood, in the process of drying, gives up its water, first from the cavity and then from the wall. The cell shrinks after the water escapes from the cell. Since wood is made up of a multitude of cells, it, in turn, shrinks. On the other hand, if the cell after it is dry absorbs moisture, the cell will expand (swelling). Thus, we have both the shrinking and swelling (contraction and expansion) of wood.

There are two techniques for eliminating water from wood: air drying and kiln drying.

Air Drying

Air drying is the process of piling lumber in a protected place or in the open with sticks between the boards, so that air can circulate around the boards. The evaporation of moisture into the air causes the lumber to dry. Air seasoning provides a minimum moisture content of 15–18 percent. Air drying is a slow process requiring months or even years with some species of wood.

Kiln Drying

To dry lumber to a point where it may be used as furniture, it must be placed in a dry kiln to remove still more of the moisture. *Kiln drying* is used to reduce moisture below 12 percent.

Dry kilns are huge ovens. Within the kiln, humidity, air circulation, and heat are meticulously controlled and adjusted during the drying process. Lumber is placed on cars (trolleys) with sticks between each tier of lumber and the trolley is pushed into the kiln. Each car load is called a *bunk*.

Heat, humidity, and circulation are necessary for kiln drying. By applying heat, moisture is evaporated from the faces and edges of the lumber. This process draws moisture out of the wet center toward the outer surface of the wood because moisture in wood has a tendency to transfer itself from moist parts to points that are drier. This continues as long as the speed of surface evaporation and transfer of moisture from the center continue to balance. *Case hardening* may result if the ouside is dried too fast. Moisture will remain in the core while the outside is dry. If such a board were run through a planer, the outside dry part would be removed, and the remaining board would warp and check in a few days.

Humidity is added to the warm air used for drying by means of steam-spray pipes. This keeps an adequate balance in the removal of moisture between the inside and outside of the board.

Moisture-filled air is continuously eliminated by circulation allowing fresh air to be brought into contact with the wood to evaporate more moisture.

There are three factors in kiln drying:

1. Warm air has the capacity to contain more moisture than cold air.
2. As warm air picks up moisture it becomes cooler.
3. Warm air rises as cool air falls.

There are three stages in kiln drying:

1. Steam high (softens fibers), heat low—wood green.
2. Steam reduced, heat increased—wood drying.
3. Little steam, high heat—wood seasoned.

LUMBER GRADES

Grades of lumber are listed below in order from poorest quality to highest quality.

Hardwood

Shorts
> Narrow in width and short in length.

No. 3 Common
> Not often listed.

No. 2 Common
> Considerable waste.

No. 1 Common
> Probably the most economical for the home craftsman. There are a few defects but most of the lumber can eventually be used in small projects.

Selects
> Permits some defects on one face.

FAS (First and Seconds)
> These two grades are generally combined into one. It is the best grade of hardwood and mqst produce at least 80 percent clear cuttings.

Softwood

Common Boards
> There are four or five grades of common softwoods ranging from #1 (the best). However, only two or three grades of common are generally available. These are used quite extensively for building purposes.

Select
> A—The very best grade
> B
> C
> D

The lower grades (C and D) may not be clear on both sides and may contain small knots and other minor defects.

KINDS OF MACHINE TOOLS

The machine tools listed below are those that would normally be found in small custom wood shops, small pattern shops, school shops, and home workshops. The list does not include large machines found in heavy woodworking plants such as furniture manufacturers or wood-milling shops.

Sawing Tools (Straight Cutting)

Straight-cutting saws serve a variety of functions and have become almost a necessary item for home workshops. The straight cutting saw serves ripping, cross-cutting, mitering, beveling, grooving, rabbeting, dadoing, and molding operations.

Universal Circular Saw. The universal circular saw has two saw arbors, making it possible for a crosscut or ripsaw to be used without changing saw blades. This saw is seldom found in the small school shop and never found in a home workshop.

Variety Circular Saw. This saw does a variety of operations: ripping, crosscutting, mitering, beveling, grooving, rabbeting, dadoing, and molding. Most modern variety saws have tilting arbors. Blades must be changed to switch from ripping to cross-cutting.

Bench Circular Saw. This is similar to a variety saw, but smaller. The bench saw must be fastened to a table, stand, or bench.

Radial Saw. The radial saw differs from the variety saw in that the saw pushes into the wood on most operations. It is easily set for cutting angles. The radial saw has become a very popular saw in recent years.

Motorized Miter Box. This is a rather specialized tool that greatly speeds up mitering. The miter box is a valuable tool for the carpenter, builder, and contractor. It would be one of the last motorized tools to buy for the home workshop.

Combination Woodworker. A combination woodworker is a tool designed specifically for the home craftsman. Sawing is only one of the operations performed on this machine. Other operations (with attachments) are disc sanding, jointing, jigsawing, drilling, and turning. Only one motor is needed.

Curve-Cutting (Sawing) Tools

Curve-cutting saws are designed specifically to handle all curved cuts on your finely crafted wooden products. The band saw is almost universal in its applications and the jigsaw is able to cut very small curves.

Band Saw. The band saw is the most universally used tool for cutting outside curves. When used with narrow blades, it is sometimes called a *scroll saw.*

Jigsaw. The jigsaw is also called a *scroll saw.* It cuts much slower than the band saw in that the saw cuts only on the downward stroke (up and down action). It cuts much smaller curves than a band saw, and it will also cut inside curves. You might say that a jigsaw is a motorized coping saw, because it uses coping saw blades. The jigsaw is a much safer saw to use than the band saw.

Planing Tools

Planing tools are used for exactly what the name implies, smoothing the surface of the wood. They ready the wood surface for scrapers or they are applied to a board to lessen its thickness.

Jointer. A jointer is used to straighten the edges of boards in the same manner as a hand plane (fore plane or jointer plane). The bench jointer is usually smaller than those purchased with a stand.

Planer or Surfacer. For planing the surface of lumber and cutting boards to lesser thickness the planer or surfacer is used. It is a rather expensive machine for the home workshop, but will be found in many.

Shaping Tools

Shaping tools shape wood for specialized functions. They are planer-type tools for cutting moldings, panels, etc., having irregular shapes.

Shaper. The single-spindle bench shaper is the shaper most often found in the basement shop.

Combination Shaper/Router. A router, mounted like an inverted shaper on a stand, has in many ways displaced the conventional shaper.

Boring Tools and Turning Tools

The *drill press* is the most common boring tool for the home craftsman. It can drill in metal as well as bore in wood. With certain attachments, it may also be used as a mortiser, shaper, router, and cylindrical sander.

The standard woodworking *lathe* can do faceplate work and spindle turning. It can also be used as a disc sander, a buffer, a drill press, or as a grinder.

A specially designed lathe for faceplate work only is a *face* or *bowl lathe.*

Sanding Tools

A variety of sanding tools make it possible to finish any surface. They are used as part of the initial sanding procedure, with a follow-up of hand sanding.

Belt Sander. A long strip of cloth-backed sandpaper passes over two pulleys some distance apart in a *belt sander* or *belt stroke sander*. Sanding is done by pushing a block on the back of the belt until it comes in contact with the work to be sanded.

Disc Sander. A large circular piece of sandpaper is glued to a large circular disc mounted to a motor. An adjustable table provides a supporting shelf for the work.

Oscillating Spindle Sander. This sander is a cylindrical, oscillating-rotating spindle with quick-changing, different diameter spindles. It is equally effective on inside and outside curves. The table tilts 45° both left and right.

KINDS OF PORTABLE MOTORIZED TOOLS

The popularity of portable, motorized tools is growing daily. They adapt well to apartment or townhouse quarters, store easily, and can be readily transported to locations outside the home.

Portable Electric Handsaw

This portable tool has the greatest use of any. It is the major tool of the carpenter and builder. There are many sizes with many trade names which can saw lumber from 15/16 in. to 2 7/8 in. thick. The better models are equipped with a kick-proof clutch and telescoping saw guards.

Bayonet Saw

The bayonet is essentially the same as the saber saw. In general, the bayonet saw carries a larger blade and might be considered a motorized handsaw. It often makes straight cuts in places that the portable electric handsaw cannot reach. The craftsman should always keep in mind that both the bayonet and saber saw cuts on the upstroke and splintering takes place on the top side of the work.

Saber Saw

The saber saw is used for cutting both inside and outside curves. It might rightly be called a portable electric jigsaw.

Portable Electric Router

The portable electric router is a high-speed (up to 22,000 RPM) portable electric shaper, and in many ways has displaced the shaper. Sanding is practically eliminated when using this extremely smooth, chip-free routing, molding, planing, and shaping device.

The portable electric router is made more versatile by the many attachments available, such as the dovetail template, shaper table, and router edge guide.

Portable Belt Sander

The portable belt sander is designed to sand flat surfaces. Its function is similar to the belt stroke machine used in industry. It sands much faster than the orbital and vibrating sanders and, in general, is used with the coarser grades of sandpaper. Most portable belt sanders are equipped with dust collectors.

Portable Finishing Sanders

The finishing sanders are of the oscillating, orbital or vibrating types. They are used most times after the portable belt sander. The finishing sander is seldom equipped with a dust collector.

Portable Disc Sander

The disc sander is used most often where a stationary disc sander can not be used (auto bodies, exterior house siding, etc.). The disc is flexible rather than rigid, as is the case with the stationary disc sander.

Portable Drill

The drill is a handy gadget to have in the home workshop even if there is a drill press available. The portable drill can be used in many situations where the drill press would be useless.

Portable electric drills vary in drill bit capacity from 1/4 in. to 2 in. The small, pistol grip drills of 1/4 in., 3/8 in., and 1/2 in. capacity are the most popular.

Cordless, battery-operated portable drills are now used extensively where electricity is not available and where the cord would interfere with the operation.

ADHESIVES

A properly constructed glue joint will form a bond stronger than the material being bonded. With glue, or any other quality adhesive, failure will not occur at the adhesive line.

Most adhesives fall into four categories according to the material or function that increases its sticking power:

1. Water or liquid solvents (e.g., animal glue)
2. Pressure sensitive (e.g., Mastic Tape, Velco, etc.)
3. Hot melts (e.g., bread wrapper)
4. Chemically cured (e.g., epoxy).

In most cases, adhesives must set in order to hold. In the case of animal glue, the water must evaporate. This principle does not hold true, however, with pressure-sensitive adhesives.

Hot melts are also called thermoplastics. Application of heat causes the material to be plastic and the cooling process causes setting.

Types of Natural Glue and Adhesives

Although a large variety of adhesives are currently on the market, only a small percentage are useful to the wood craftsman. The following list contains glues obtained from natural sources.

Animal Glue. Animal glue is a gelatin like substance made from hide trimmings and other portions of animals. Cattle hides make the highest quality glue. The glue is prepared in a double boiler or in an electric glue pot. Animal glue works best when it is steaming hot and applied to wood that has been warmed.

Casein Glue. Casein is a water-resistant glue that is made from the protein (curd) in milk. The powdered substance is mixed with water and works best if stirred with an electric mixer.

Fish Glue. Fish glue is made of fish scraps and kept in a liquid state by adding an acid. Most liquid glues that come in a tube are of this type. It is a rather low quality glue.

Starch Glue. Starch glue is made of cassava starch. It is not used to any great extent by the craftsman.

Soybean Glue. Soybean glue is similar to casein glue and is used for gluing veneers.

Synthetic Resin Glues and Synthetic Adhesives

Contact Cement. Contact cement remains somewhat elastic after it cures. It must be applied to both surfaces before bonding. It is used primarily with plastic laminates (e.g., Formica). Great care must be taken in gluing parts together as there is an immediate, strong bond upon contact. Contact cement is water resistant.

Polyvinyl Acetate. Polyvinyl acetate is white in color and ready to use (liquid). It is used a great deal in furniture construction because of its strength and the rapid setting action at room temperature. It is commonly called Elmer's or white glue and generally comes in squeeze bottles. Polyvinyl acetate is not to be used where there is excessive heat as the glue will soften. It is not water resistant.

Urea Resin. Urea is made of synthetic urea crystals and formaldehyde. It usually comes in powdered form and is used a great deal in the manufacture of plywood. Urea can be made into glue by adding water and a catalyst.

Phenolic Resin. Phenolic resin is used to glue exterior plywood. It is waterproof and thus is used in boat hull construction. Phenolic resin comes in three forms: paper film, dry powder, and in water or alcoholic solution.

Resorcinal Resin. Resorcinal resin is a dark reddish liquid with either a powdered or a liquid hardness. It will withstand high humidity for long periods of time.

Epoxy Resin. Epoxy resin is probably the strongest of any of the adhesives and will bond together almost all materials including metals. It does not require very high pressure to bond and it is very stable with moisture. The resin and the catalyst come in equal size tubes making it very convenient for the home craftsman to use. Equal parts of the resin and the catalyst must be mixed thoroughly before using.

Polyester Resin. Polyester resin is similar to epoxy but not as strong and requires a catalyst. It is used with fiberglass and is waterproof.

Melamine Resin. Transparent melamine resin is used to bond layers of plastic laminates (e.g., Formica).

ABRASIVES

Abrasives are of two types: natural and manufactured. Each are found in a variety of forms, and each serves a particular purpose. For most woodworking activities, manufactured abrasives have taken the place of the natural varieties.

Natural Abrasives

The following natural abrasives are applied to a cloth or paper backing. Although most have been replaced by higher quality synthetic materials, garnet sandpaper remains one of the best for the home craftsman.

Flint Sandpaper. Flint sandpaper is an off-white, creamish color. It is a natural substance that comes from quartz. This abrasive has been used for a long time, but has been replaced by other abrasives of greater quality and life.

Garnet Sandpaper. Garnet sandpaper is made from the jewel mineral and is the best of the natural abrasives. It is probably the best all-round abrasive for the home craftsman. Garnet sandpaper is reddish in color.

Emery Cloth. Emery cloth is blue-black in color and is generally used on metal. Emery cloth is not a very high quality abrasive.

Manufactured Abrasives

Synthetic abrasives have, for the most part, replaced the natural because of higher quality and longer wear. These too are applied to a cloth or paper backing.

Aluminum Oxide. Aluminum oxide, used for abrasives, is the result of many ingredients (bauxite, coke, sand, salt, sawdust, aluminum oxide, etc.) fused at very high temperatures. Aluminum oxide paper and cloth are hard and tough and the wearing qualities about the same as garnet.

Silicon Carbide. Silicon carbide is a very hard, abrasive substance, much harder than any other abrasive. Silicon carbide is often used with liquid (Wet-or-Dry Paper) smoothing finish materials. Sand is the basic substance for making silicon carbide.

Abrasives Not in Paper or Cloth Form

Not all abrasives, natural or manufactured, are applied to a backing. The following examples are generally used in the finer stages of finishing.

Steel Wool. The finer grades of steel wool (No. 000 is the finest) are extensively used for rubbing finishes, particularly where sandpaper would undergo hard use (carvings, turning, moldings, etc.). Steel wool is commonly used before pumice stone and rottenstone.

Pumice Stone. Pumice stone is a powder which is derived from lava. Pumice is mixed with either water or a rubbing oil. When it is mixed with water it cuts faster, although the surface is somewhat dull. When mixed with rubbing oil, a glossier finish is obtained that does not have to be followed up with rottenstone. For convenient use, pumice stone powder is often kept in a large salt shaker.

Rottenstone. Rottenstone, about the same consistency as powdered sugar, is made from limestone. It often is used on finished surfaces after pumice stone has been used. When mixed with water to form a paste, it produces a high gloss, piano finish.

When rottenstone is mixed with oil it produces a more subtle, eggshell-like, velvety finish—more desirable for many kinds of furniture.

Rubbing Compounds. Special rubbing compounds in paste form are often used on lacquer. Care has to be taken as rubbing compounds cut faster than rottenstone.

Sanding Belts

The belts for belt sanders are aluminum oxide on cloth. They range from 3 in. to 6 in. wide and from 21 in. to 48 in. long. Extra fine, fine, medium, coarse, and extra coarse are the grades available.

Sanding Discs

Sanding discs of aluminum oxide paper or fiber-backed abrasives are used for wood, metal and plastic. The fiber-backed discs last longer. Discs come in 4 in. to 10 in. diameters. Fine, medium and coarse are the grades available.

Sizes and Grits

Most sandpapers come in sheets 9 in. × 11 in. Usually the sheet is divided into 4 parts for convenient use with a sanding block.

An old worn-out handsaw is an excellent device for tearing sheets into the four parts. For the ordinary woodworking surface, after planing and scraping where slight scratches and tool marks are left, a No. 2/0-100 or a No. 3/0-120 grit is the first one used. If the surface is free from all defects, the starting grit can be No. 4/0-150 or No. 5/0-180.

When moving from a coarser to a finer sandpaper, do not jump more than two or at most three grades. Otherwise, it will be almost impossible to remove the scratches caused by the coarser sandpaper.

Note: If you are using electric sanders, the straight-line (back and forth) sander is best for the final sanding with very fine sandpaper.

KINDS OF JOINTS

Each of the joints listed below serves a specialized need. A description is accompanied by a detailed drawing to aid the craftsman in both the selection and implementation of the joint to best serve his purpose.

Butt Joint

The butt joint is one of the easiest joints to make since butting one member against another and fastening with glue, nails, brads, screws, or other fasteners is all that is necessary. However, the butt joint is the weakest joint and should be avoided if strength is a factor.

Butt joints must be square and straight. See Fig. 1-4.

End-Lap Joint

An end lap is used on corners where a joint stronger than a butt joint is needed. There are, however, many joints that are much stronger and should always be considered when making a corner joint. See Fig. 1-5 for an end-lap joint.

Cross-Lap Joint

This joint is used a great deal in furniture making and is stronger than either of the joints mentioned above. The cross-lap joint is used in joining the faces of two members. See Fig. 1-6.

Edge-Lap Joint

An edge-lap joint is similar to the cross-lap joint except the edges are joined together rather than the faces. It is a strong joint that needs only glue and clamping for fastening. Refer to Fig. 1-7 for an edge-lap joint.

Middle-Lap Joint

This joint is used when the end of one member is fitted into the middle of another member (Fig. 1-8).

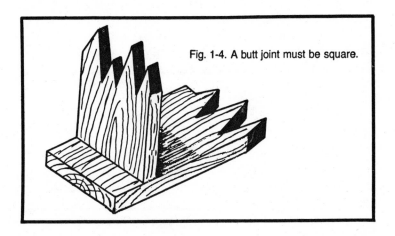

Fig. 1-4. A butt joint must be square.

Fig. 1-5. An end-lap joint is used on corners.

Half-Lap Joint

A half-lap joint is often used when it is necessary to make a long piece from two shorter ones.

It should be noted in the construction of the lap joints above that one half the thickness of the stock is cut away in both members. As a result, the final joint is only as thick as one of the members. See Fig. 1-9 for a half-lap joint.

Blind Mortise and Tenon Joint

The blind mortise and tenon is one of the most used—if not the most used—joints, particularly in the leg-rail construction found in tables. However, it is the most difficult to make. The mortise is generally made first as it is easier to fit a tenon to a mortise than vice versa. Figure 1-10 shows a 1 1/2 in. square leg and a 3/4 in. ×2 1/2 in. rail. The mortise is never made in the center of the leg because the inside corner material would be too small and would be liable to break. This, of course, means a narrow shoulder (1/16 in. to 1/8 in.) between rail and leg which has a much better design appeal. It also provides a longer tenon.

The blind mortise and tenon shown in Fig. 1-10 is in two parts, a top view and a front view. A few general rules of design are:

Fig. 1-6. A cross-lap joint joins the faces.

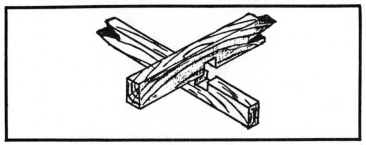

Fig. 1-7. An edge-lap joint joins the edges.

1. The material between the top of the mortise and the top of the leg should be at least 3/8 in. (more for softwood) to assure that the top of leg does not break out.
2. In order to keep the tenon as wide as possible, make the lower shoulder cut between 1/16 in. and 1/8 in. This is especially true with narrow rails.
3. A tenon should never be thinner than one-third the thickness of the rail. A tenon of one-half the thickness of the rail is probably the best size.

Through Mortise and Tenon

The through mortise and tenon joint is a strong joint that can be used in many situations where the end grain of the tenon is not objectionable. It is a very easy joint to make in that three passes of a dado head (one for the mortise and two for the tenon) are all that are needed. See Fig. 1-11.

Haunched Mortise and Tenon Joint

The haunched mortise and tenon joint is a blind mortise and tenon designed for a specific function. It is a corner joint and is most

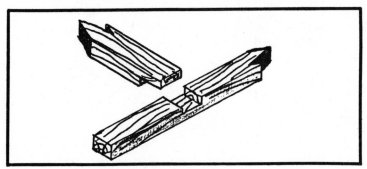

Fig. 1-8. A middle-lap joint joins a middle and an end.

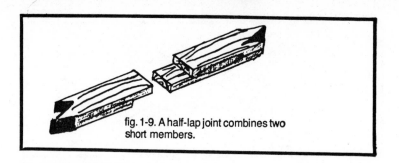

fig. 1-9. A half-lap joint combines two short members.

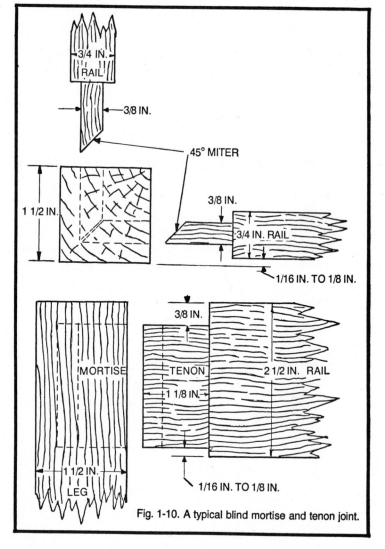

3/4 IN.

RAIL

3/8 IN.

45° MITER

1 1/2 IN.

3/8 IN.

3/4 IN. RAIL

1/16 IN. TO 1/8 IN.

3/8 IN.

MORTISE

TENON

2 1/2 IN. RAIL

1 1/8 IN.

1 1/2 IN.

LEG

1/16 IN. TO 1/8 IN.

Fig. 1-10. A typical blind mortise and tenon joint.

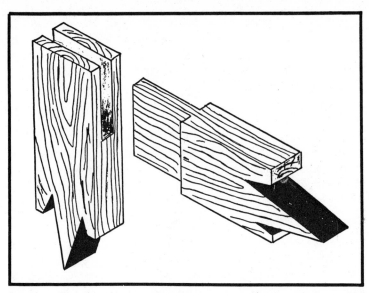

Fig. 1-11. A through mortise and tenon joint is used when the end grain is not objectionable.

Fig. 1-12. A haunched mortise and tenon joint was designed for specific purposes and is used most often on paneled doors that are grooved.

often used on paneled doors that are grooved. The shoulder, or haunch, of the tenon fits into the groove and the rest of the tenon fits into the mortise. This way, the haunch fills the open groove space that would otherwise be unsightly. Figure 1-12 demonstrates a haunched mortise and tenon joint.

Dovetail Joint

The dovetail joint is the strongest for mating the front and sides of drawers. It is also used in chests and wooden containers. The dovetail joint is a slow, tedious process to do by hand. A router and a dovetail template will do the job much faster and better. See Fig. 1-13 for an example of a dovetail joint.

Combination Rabbet, Dado and Tongue Joint

This combination joint is used in about the same fashion as the dovetail. Joints are made even faster than the router/template method and are nearly as strong because of the large amount of gluing surface. All that is needed to cut this joint is a dado head for the circular saw. Figure 1-14 demonstrates a combination rabbet, dado, and tongue joint.

Tabletop Fasteners and Joints

1. *Block and screws*
Block and screws is an easy and inexpensive joint to make because it can be made of scrap wood. However, it is not a very good fastener as it provides little freedom for the top to contract and expand.
2. *Angled Screw*
It is rather difficult to bore a hole at an angle. Furthermore, it requires some gouging (carving). Therefore, the angled

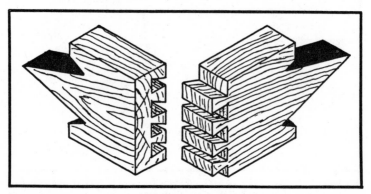

Fig. 1-13. A dovetail joint is made most efficiently with the use of power tools.

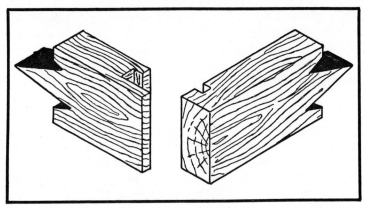

Fig. 1-14. A combination rabbet, dado, and tongue joint is strong because of the large amount of gluing surface.

screw is a rather mediocre method of fastening tops to rails.

3. *Counterbored Screw*

    A counterbored screw is an easier joint ot make than the angled screw, but not much better for effective fastening.

4 *Block and Groove*

    A block and groove is probably the best of all tabletop fasteners and can be made from scraps. It allows consider-

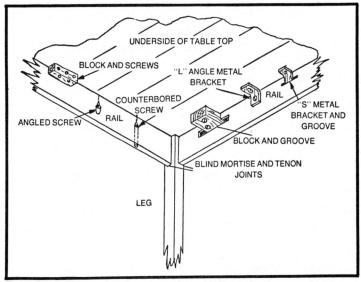

Fig. 1-15. A demonstration of a variety of tabletop fasteners and joints.

able room for expansion and contraction, although the top remains tight and firm.

5. *"L" Angle Metal Bracket*
   The "L" angle metal bracket is an easily attached fastener, but one of the least effective.

6. *"S" Metal Bracket Groove*
   The "S" metal bracket groove can be a fastener that is nearly as effective as the block and groove. It allows plenty of room for expansion and contraction. Fastener/groove combinations are better tabletop fasteners than fastener/nongroove varieties. Figure 1-15 offers a demonstration of all varieties of tabletop fasteners described above.

FINISHING MATERIALS

It is doubtful that any home craftsman would have all of the materials and equipment listed here. However, a comprehensive listing gives the craftsman some of the options available.

Clear Furniture Finishes

Clear furniture finishes introduce no color to the completed project. They vary in their effectiveness, strength, and frequency of application.

Shellac. Shellac is one of the oldest finishes known. It is sometimes called *spirit varnish* as the solvent is alcohol. Untreated shellac is orange in color. White-treated shellac is used the most, but a mixture of the two colors produces a beautiful and unique finish on some woods. A craftsman should purchase only the dewaxed type as it is the only type that sands to a smooth finish.

The largest drawback to shellac is its lack of durability. It is affected by water and other liquids and will turn white if subjected to heat. A few coats of wax will help alleviate this fault. Shellac works best as an undercoat for other finishes such as varnish or lacquer.

Shellac comes in a liquid identified as 4 lb (sometimes 5 lb) cut, which indicates that 4 lb of solid shellac flakes are dissolved in one gallon of alcohol. For general use, the 4 lb cut shellac is diluted with alcohol.

Shellac is seldom, if ever, used directly from the container.

A fairly satisfactory synthetic shellac of phenol and vinyl products has been developed.

Varnish. There are two types of varnish: the *natural* varnish and *synthetic resin* varnishes.

The original varnish or *natural varnish* was made of linseed oil and fossil gums. Later, tung oil was added which improved it somewhat, but it was slow drying and was not very durable.

Synthetic resin varnishes have, in general, taken over the role of a superior clear finish. They are far more durable and dry much more quickly. Phenol-formaldehyde (Bakelite), alkyd, polyurethanes, and epoxy synthetic resin finishes are a few of the most common.

Gloss varnish can be turned into flat (dull) varnish by the addition of stearate.

Lacquer. Lacquer comes close to being the best clear furniture finish. It is quick-drying, moisture-resistant, and exceptionally hard. Lacquer is also available in colors.

Clear lacquer has been used in the manufacture of furniture for many years. The big drawback for the home craftsman is the fact that lacquer is hard to apply with a brush. Spray equipment is needed to apply lacquer to large pieces, and the cost of exhaust fans and a spray booth are almost prohibitive. Of course, portable spray equipment can be used outdoors if the weather permits.

The aerosol spray can of lacquer is one of the most convenient ways of finishing small and medium-sized projects. It goes on professionally smooth and dries rapidly.

Lacquer (as varnish) comes in gloss and dull (flat). Flat lacquer is used only as a last coat. The earlier coats are gloss lacquer. Gloss lacquer builds up faster than flat lacquer.

Lacquer thinner is used to thin lacquer. Only use lacquer thinner manufactured by the company that makes the lacquer.

Sanding between coats is held to a minimum because all lacquer coats and sealer merge into one. Lacquer sealer is used under lacquer to prevent oils of fillers and stains from "bleeding." Shellac can also be used, but lacquer sealer made by the same manufacturer that makes the lacquer is recommended.

Lacquer should never be applied over varnish or other oil base finishes.

Rubbed-In Finishes. Rubbed-in finishes are penetrating finishes—they do not lie on the surface. They create a highly durable finish that protects the wood. Rubbed-in finishes are used extensively on teak, walnut, and cherry to bring out the natural grain. They are readily available under trade names such as Miniwax and Sealacell.

Stains

Stains are used to imitate the color of other woods (e.g., on gum to make it look like walnut), to put grain into a plain grainless wood, to give the appearance of age, and to increase color contrast.

The trend today, however, particularly in modern/contemporary projects, is to use little, if any, stain on woods that have a beautiful natural color such as mahogany, walnut, cherry, red cedar, redwood, rosewood, birch and maple.

Water Stain. Water stain is a low-cost stain because of the solvent (water) used. Water stains are permanent (very little fading) and contain a brilliance not found in other stains. They are easy to apply and non-bleeding under other coats.

The biggest disadvantage is that water stain raises the grain, but this can be eliminated by applying a sizing coat (hot water and animal glue) before the stain is applied.

Oil Stain. Oil stain is probably the most widely used stain by the home craftsman and in school shops. Oil stains are not as permanent as water stains, but they do not raise the grain, are inexpensive, and do not affect veneer glue lines as does water stain.

Bleaches. Bleaches are not true stains but they do affect the color of wood—they eliminate all color and the wood becomes a uniform white. Care should be taken to use all bleach materials before further toning or staining takes place.

Spirit Stains. Spirit stains (alcohol stains) are seldom used for the basic staining of wood. They are used mainly for distressing, touch-up, padding between coats, tinting coats of shellac, and applying French polish after repairs have been made by burning in stick lacquer and stick shellac.

N.G.R. Stains (Non-Grain-Raising). N.G.R. stains are widely used by furniture manufacturers. They have the brilliance and durability of water stains, but they do not raise the grain. They are seldom used by the home woodworker because they can only be applied by a spray gun and are high in cost. Retail finishing stores seldom, if ever, carry N.G.R. stains.

Pigmented Wiping Stains. These stains are used widely by the home woodworker because they are so easy to apply. They are brushed on, allowed to stand a certain length of time, and then wiped off. Pigmented wiping stains are generally used with close grain woods (woods which do not require a filler).

Combination Stains and Filler. Stain and filler is sometimes applied in one application. This combination is used primarily in refinishing. It is a type of make-do, shortcut method that is much inferior to applying stains and fillers in separate applications.

Glazes. Glazes are not true stains in that they do not affect the wood directly, but are applied after a number of finish coats have been applied. Glazes, particularly on traditional furniture, enhance the overall beauty and appearance more than any other finishing material.

Fillers

Fillers are used extensively on open-grain wood to fill up the pores. *Silex base* filler is considered the best. On woods such as walnut, mahogany, and butternut, the filler used is colored considerably darker than the wood itself after it has been stained.

General Supplies

Linseed oil comes in two varieties. Raw linseed oil is used with exterior paints. Boiled linseed oil is used with interior oil-base finishes.

Turpentine is used mainly with oil stain, wood filler, varnish, enamel, and paint.

Mineral spirits may substitute for turpentine.

Denatured alcohol is used with shellac and spirit stains.

Water may be used with water stain and glue size.

Lacquer thinner acts as a thinner for lacquer and lacquer thinner.

Benzine is used with oil stain.

Naphtha is the best thinner to use with a filler.

Japan drier may be used to hasten drying in varnish and other oil base materials.

Tung oil (or tung oil base transparent finish) is mainly used on bar tops, tabletops, and gun stocks but may be used on metal as well.

White vinegar is mixed with hot water, one to one, for removing wood bleach.

The home craftsman may use *pumice stone* of at least two of the following grades:

FFFE, extra fine; FFF, fine; FF, medium; and F, coarse.

Rottenstone is used for an extra high gloss surface.

Lacquer rubbing compound is used for lacquer and lacquer-based finishes.

Colors ground in oil (in tubes) are found in the following:

Black, blue, brown, raw sienna, burnt sienna, raw umber, burnt umber, Van Dyke brown, chrome yellow, and Venetian red.

The craftsman will need a variety of *brushes*:

A graining brush made from ox hair, a Fitch brush for varnish, a stiff brush for fillers and a number of inexpensive brushes for shellac and glue.

Rubbing felt is used with pumice stone, rottenstone, and rubbing compounds.

Masking tape may be used for masking parts between sections having different finishes and for covering parts that are to be glued.

A *tack rag* is a chemically treated rag to remove the finest dust particles before varnishing or lacquering. A homemade tack rag may be constructed with turpentine to which a few drops of varnish are added.

Clear or *colored paste waxes* are used as a final finish over varnish or lacquer. Colored waxes are used to add another dimension (depth) to the finish. Colored waxes must be compatible with the colors underneath (stain, filler, glazes, etc.).

Patching and Surface Repair Materials

Stick shellac is used on shellac base finishes to repair small nicks, bruises and scratches by burning it in with a burning knife. It is available in about 5 dozen colors.

Stick Lacquer is used in the same fashion as stick shellac but on lacquer-base finishes.

Plastic wood is used on large nicks, bruises and scratches. Colors are limited.

A *burning knife* is used for burning in stick shellac and stick lacquer.

A *knife heater* is for preheating a burning-in knife.

Non-inflammable remover may be used for removing an old finish.

Almalgamator is used to revitalize an old, gummy, crazed, "alligatored" or cracked finish.

Additional Equipment

For storing inflammable liquids *safety cans* are required.

Cloth and rags used around finishes may catch on fire due to spontaneous combustion. *Waste cloth* containers confine the fire inside the container. The container opens with a foot pedal.

FURNITURE HARDWARE

Hardware is a general term referring to the external, decorative items fastened to the surface of a finished piece. The examples listed below are particularly beautiful on Early American pieces.

Chippendale Hardware

The Chippendale period extended roughly from the third decade to the ninth decade of the seventeen hundreds. Chippendale

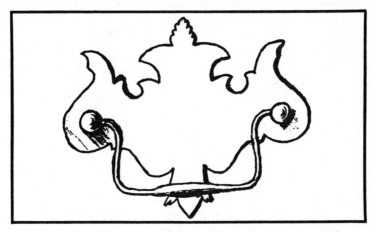

Fig. 1-16. A Chippendale pull designed in the seventeen hundreds.

pulls (handles) and Chippendale keyhole escutcheon plates were generally of the same size. The only differences were that the keyhole pierced the center of the upper part and escutcheon pin holes replaced the handle-post holes. Figure 1-16 is a sketch of the Chippendale pull.

Hepplewhite Hardware

The Hepplewhite period, and to some extent the lesser Sheraton and Adam brothers period, was at its peak during the last few

Fig. 1-17. An example of Hepplewhite hardware.

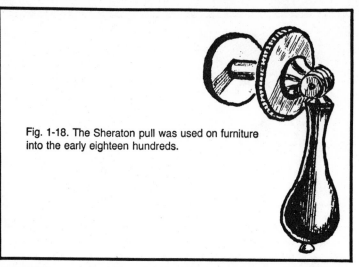

Fig. 1-18. The Sheraton pull was used on furniture into the early eighteen hundreds.

years of the seventeen hundreds and the early years of the eighteen hundreds. Pulls (handles) were of brass and were oval in shape. Round handles were also used. Refer to Fig. 1-17 for an example of Hepplewhite hardware.

Fig. 1-19. The Empire pull of the late seventeen hundreds.

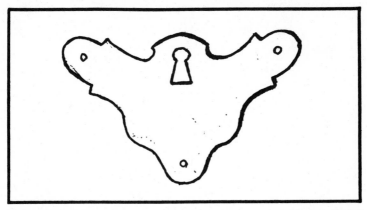

Fig. 1-20. The Queen Anne keyhole escutcheon plate was used in the early third of the seventeen hundreds.

Sheraton Pull

The Sheraton period extended into the early eighteen hundreds. The pulls were somewhat ornate as demonstrated by Fig. 1-18.

Empire Pull

Knobs of brass, wood and glass were very popular during the Empire period from the late seventeen hundreds into the third decade of the eighteen hundreds. Ring pulls were also quite common. See Fig. 1-19.

Queen Anne Keyhole Escutcheon Plate

Queen Anne period furniture was in vogue during the first third of the seventeen hundreds. Most all furniture hardware of this period was made of brass. Refer to Fig. 1-20 for an example.

Chapter 2
How To

To remind the more experienced woodworker and to instruct those new to the trade, this chapter offers detailed explanations of how to use the tools and materials listed in Chapter 1.

HOW TO USE MEASURING TOOLS

The term measuring tools encompasses more than a 12 or 36 inch straight ruler. A variety of measuring tools exist in woodworking to serve the large number of tasks encountered throughout the construction process.

Rules and Scales

Rules and scales are used for measuring flat surfaces. Each serves the particular need of measuring inside or outside surfaces or for measuring sections where the edge cannot be seen.

Folding Rules. The folding rule was the favorite measuring device used by home woodworkers and carpenters alike until the steel tape rule came into use. The three- and six-foot folding rule was small enough to slip into the pocket. Usually one side of the folding rule is divided into eighths of an inch while the other side is divided into sixteenths. Folding rules are made of hardwood or aluminum.

Steel Rules and Tapes. Steel rules vary in length from six feet to twelve feet in increments of two feet. Steel tapes—used extensively by builders and carpenters—are seldom used by the home craftsman. Steel tapes are generally 50 feet and 100 feet in length.

Some steel rules have a square corner case which makes it convenient for making inside measurements. Some have a push-button rewind and the blade can be stopped in any position.

Hook Rules. The hook rule has the advantage when the user cannot see the edge of the wood he is measuring. It comes in a six-foot length and the hook can be folded out of the way, or if the occasion calls for it, the hook can be removed.

Bench Rules. Bench rules are probably the most extensively used tools in the home workshop. They come in both one-foot and two-foot lengths. Bench rules are made of wood or steel. Wood bench rules are usually marked in both eighths and sixteenths of an inch, while the steel rule is graduated in sixteenths of an inch only. Some bench rules read from both left and right.

Steel Scales. Steel scales or rules are six inches to twelve inches long. The six inch length is the most popular as it can be carried in a shop apron pocket. The main advantage of steel scales are that many are graduated in sixty-fourths of an inch for very accurate measuring. Some scales come with a leather case with a clip to hold to the edge of a pocket.

Squares

Squares are used for measuring and laying out angles. They also are useful for constructing 90-degree (square) corners. A home workshop would be incomplete without at least one of the squares listed below.

Framing Square. The framing square is used by the home-craftsman to square wide lumber and for testing projects for square-ness.

For the carpenter, the framing square is an indispensable tool used for a multitude of purposes, and next to the hammer and saw is probably the most used tool. The carpenter uses the framing square to figure rafter lengths and angles, for measuring braces and for figuring board feet of lumber.

Try Square. The home craftsman will rely more on the try square than the framing square, mainly because the size of the framing square adds to the difficulty of handling. Try squares are available from 6-in. blades to 12-in. blades in increments of 2 inches. The smaller sizes are the most popular. The blades are made of steel and the handles are made of iron or rosewood.

T-Bevel Square. The T-bevel square is not really a true square for laying out 90-degree angles. It can be set for any angle and locked into position with a thumb screw on the end of the handle. It is used extensively to test and duplicate angles and check chamfers and bevels. Sizes generally run 6 in., 8 in. and 10 in. long. It is available in either iron or rosewood handles.

Combination or Bevel Square. The blade of the combination square is slotted and a head which measures both 45 degrees and 90 degrees slides along the slotted blade. The head also contains a level glass. The length of the blade can be read from left to right or from right to left. The combination square can be used in situations that the try square would find hard to handle.

Gauges

Gauges are used to mark lines on a piece of wood. They are also useful for insuring that pieces have the exact thickness required. They inscribe lines on the wood or, when this would be objectionable, the marking lines are penciled in place.

Marking Gauge. The marking gauge is used to make parallel scribed lines to an edge of a piece of wood which is straight. Marking gauges are made of both steel and wood, and can mark lines up to six inches from the starting straight edge. The beam, head, and spur are the main parts. A thumbscrew holds the head in place on the beam. Sometimes a short pencil is used in place of the steel spur where the inscribed line would be objectionable.

Mortise Gauge. The mortise gauge is essentially the same as the marking gauge except the mortise gauge has two spurs which are adjustable for distance apart and distance from the end of the beam. The mortise gauge assures that all mortises are laid out with exact thickness.

Panel Gauge. The panel gauge is simply a large marking gauge. It is particularly useful in laying out panels for doors. It usually is made of hardwood. Due to its size, both hands are involved in marking with this gauge.

Circle Scribers

Circle scribers are designed to do what the name implies, mark circles. They also mark arcs and help the craftsman transfer measurements from one piece to another. As with gauges, a pencil may be substituted when scribed lines are objectionable.

Dividers. Dividers are sometimes called wing dividers. Some dividers are equipped with a fine adjustment screw to insure accurate settings. Others have one removable leg which can be replaced with a pencil so that it can be used as a compass. Dividers are used to scribe circles, arcs and to transfer measurements.

53

Trammel Points. Large arcs and circles are scribed with trammel points. Trammel points are attached to a hardwood bar 3/8 in. thick and 3/4 in. wide. The maximum size of the circle or arc is determined by the length of the bar.

Marking Tools

Scratch awls and Sloyd knives mark the surface of wood by leaving a depression. A lead pencil is substituted for these marking tools when the depression would be noticeable on the outside surface.

Scratch Awl. The scratch awl (somewhat like an ice pick) comes in different length points. The shorter, but more pointed awl, is used for piercing leather. The larger one (the one ordinarily used in woodshops) is about 6 in. long. It is used primarily for indenting locations for holes that are to be drilled or bored. The drill bit automatically centers itself in the depression made by the awl. This inexpensive tool should be an integral part of every home shop.

Sloyd Knife. Sloyd knives are sturdy, short-bladed knives that will stand a lot of punishment and resharpenings. The knife blades vary in length from 1 7/8 in. to 3 1/8 in.

The Sloyd knife was first used in Scandinavian countries to teach whittling methods, and was later used in the United States in the early days of manual training for the same purpose.

The Sloyd is still used a great deal today for layout and marking purposes.

Lead Pencil. A hard lead pencil, with a chisel edge, is used a great deal for layout purposes, particularly where scribed lines in wood would be objectionable and hard to remove.

HOW TO USE SAWING TOOLS

In Chapter 1, sawing tools were described in some detail. From this description, the craftsman was able to select the correct tool for the particular task at hand.

The pages following review the brief description, add a little more detail, and instruct the home woodworker in the proper procedures for using sawing tools accurately and safely.

Handsaws

The term handsaw again refers to those tools whose movement depend upon you. No motorized saws are included in this category. Every home craftsman must develop skill with these hand-held tools to make small, delicate jobs easier and more accurate.

Ripsaw. The teeth on a ripsaw are like little chisels. They take out rather large rectangular chunks of wood. The ripsaw is used to cut with the grain, never across it. The channel or slit that is cut out by the teeth—as with all saws—is called the *kerf*. Alternate teeth are pointed in opposite directions to prevent the saw from binding in the cut. All saws have this characteristic.

Ripsaws have larger teeth than other saws, and the number of points per inch is usually 5 1/2. (There is one more point per inch than there are teeth) the recommended length of the saw blade is 26 in. Some handsaws are Teflon coated.

All saws should be well *sharpened* and *jointed* (teeth all even in height). Jointing is always done before sharpening. Sharpening is generally done more often than jointing.

Jointing a Saw. By looking down the blade of a saw from either end, it is readily ascertained if jointing is necessary. If the saw needs jointing or sharpening, it should be placed in a saw clamp. A substitute clamp can be made with two boards clamped on the saw with the teeth slightly protruding above the boards.

Jointing is done by pushing a flat mill file the length of the teeth. Check from time to time to see if all the teeth are even. When all the teeth are touched by the file, a small, shiny spot will appear on the points of the teeth. If it has been necessary to joint a considerable amount, it may be necessary to reshape the teeth to the same size and shape.

Setting a Saw. After reshaping teeth, the teeth are then *set*. Setting is done with a saw set. Each tooth is bent equally so that the saw will not bind in the wood. Not as much set is necessary when sawing dry and hard woods as when sawing wet or soft woods.

Sharpening the Saw. The ripsaw, compass saw and keyhole saw are all sharpened alike. The file handle is placed in the right hand and the point of the file is held with the left index finger and thumb.

Filing is done straight across the teeth. The file is held horizontally and at a right angle to the saw blade. Alternate teeth are filed in the first operation. Turn the saw around in the clamp and file the remaining teeth.

Be sure that the pressure on the file is consistent. The pressure should not be excessive. It is a good idea to practice on an old saw. Filing is done only on the forward stroke. Never drag the file across the teeth on the backward stroke.

Usually filing is started at the toe (the end opposite the handle) of the saw. File only those teeth that are bent away from you.

Use the same pressure and the same number of strokes for each tooth.

Ripping Stock With the Ripsaw. Large pieces of stock are placed on fairly low sawhorses. Sometimes only one sawhorse is necessary.

Sawing should start on the upstroke and the saw should be held at about 60 degrees to the face of the wood.

The layout line should be left on the surface by sawing close to the line on the surplus side. If the saw has a tendency to "wander" away from the line, a slight twist of the handle will bring it back in line.

Saw with long easy strokes. Let the saw do the sawing. Do not force it. When nearing the end of the cut change to short strokes to prevent the stock from splitting prematurely.

When ripping small pieces the stock should be held with the waste stock extending outside the vise. The heel should be held lower than the toe, about 75 degrees. Figure 2-1 sketches the contours of the hand-held ripsaw.

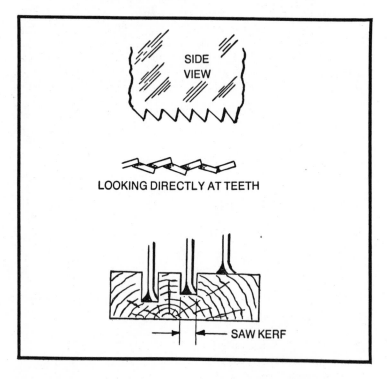

Fig. 2-1. A ripsaw showing a side view, shape of the teeth, and the kerf made.

Crosscut Saw. The crosscut saw is used to cut across the grain. The teeth are knife-shaped or wedge-shaped and the points are very sharp and pointed.

The crosscut saw has many more teeth(or points)per inch than the ripsaw. They range form 8 points per inch to 12 points per inch. The 10-point saw is probably the most used. In length, the crosscut saws run from 20 in. to 26 in. The crosscut saw is sometimes called the panel saw.

Sharpening. The crosscut saw is sharpened in a similar manner to the ripsaw, except the handle of the file is held about 15 degrees below the horizontal and about 62 degrees with the blade or teeth line. A slim taper file is used for both the ripsaw and the crosscut. An extra slim tape file is sued to file a dovetail and a backwas.

Cutting Into Wood. Two low sawhorses should be used in cross-cutting long stock, after the stock has been marked for length with a framing square and a sharp, hard lead pencil. The carpenter uses a special wide, rectangular cross-section lead pencil, but it is not suitable for fine interior and furniture cabinetmaking.

Sawing should be on the waste or surplus side of the line.

From time to time the saw blade should be checked with a try square to see if the blade is sawing perpendicularly.

Start and end the sawing with short strokes. The in-between sawing should be in long easy strokes. Again, let the saw do the sawing. The pressure should be moderate, not excessive. Short strokes at the end will prevent splintering off before the sawing is completed. Be sure to hold the waste or surplus near the end of the sawing, otherwise the weight of the piece will cause splintering near the end of the cut. Figure 2-2 demonstrates cuts made by a cross cut saw.

Backsaw. The backsaw is used for fine, accurate cabinetwork. It is called a backsaw because of a steel stiffener along its back opposite the teeth. The blade is very thin, and the teeth are smaller than the teeth on a crosscut saw. The length of the saw is generally 12 or 14 in.

Dovetail Saw. The dovetail saw is a specially designed saw to make the finest of all cuts. It is used extensively where handmade dovetail joints are called for. It can cut both with and across the grain. The dovetail saw has smaller teeth and a thinner blade than the backsaw. The handle on a dovetail saw is similar to a file or chisel handle, while the handle on a backsaw is identical with the handle on a rip saw or crosscut saw.

Compass Saw. The compass saw is designed to cut interior shaped holes after the blade is inserted through a drilled or bored

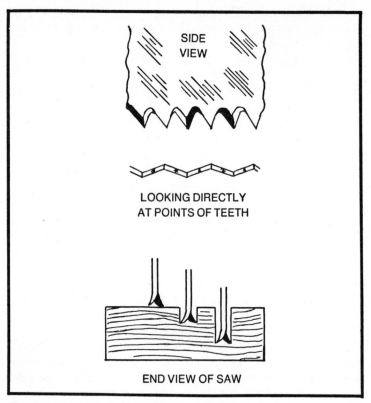

Fig. 2-2. The crosscut saw with side view, teeth configuration, and cutting pattern.

hole. It will cut interior curves of large radii, but the coping saw or saber saw is best adapted for that purpose. The compass saw can cut exterior curves, but certainly not with the efficiency of the band saw.

Compass saw blades are usually 12 in. long and the saw has a pistol grip. Some compass saws have interchangeable blades so that the saw may be used as a keyhole saw.

Keyhole Saw. The keyhole saw has a shorter blade (10 in.) and a sharper point at the end than the compass saw. Naturally, the saw was designed to do what its name suggests—to make keyholes. Some keyhole saws have a pistol grip while others have a handle similar to a file or chisel handle.

The keyhole saw will cut interior curves of shorter radii than the compass saw.

Coping Saw. The coping saw can cut short-radii, exterior and interior, curves by inserting the blade through a hole. However, the coping saw has considerable trouble sawing stock over 1/2 in. thick.

58

The blade in a coping saw can be turned from right to left without turning the handle. The home craftsman, as well as the student in a school shop or art and craft shop, uses the coping saw with the teeth pointed toward the handle. The work is held in a horizontal position on a "V" block and the sawing is done near the point of the "V".

The carpenter uses the coping saw with the teeth moldings which are placed in the corners of ceilings or floors in buildings.

Coping saw blades are of two kinds: the popular *pin end blade* (6 1/2 in. long with 10 to 15 teeth per inch) and the *loop blade* (6 in. or 6 1/2 in. long with 15 to 32 teeth per inch).

Power Saws

The home craftsman will find that most tasks can be accomplished most efficiently with motorized saws. They do the job of cutting large pieces of wood down to size and exact dimensions. Special units are designed to handle jointing cuts, dadoing, curve-cutting, and mitering.

Circular Saw. The stationary circular saw, variety saw and universal saw are used for the same purpose. *Circular saw blades* are of many sizes and types—*crosscut* or *cutoff, rip,* and *combination* blades. Combination blades are either flat-ground blades or hollow-ground planer blades. The hollow-ground planer combination blade is probably the best all around blade to use in the circular saw to avoid the changing of blades. It rips and crosscuts with equal ease and the cut is so smooth that in many cases it needs no sanding. The only disadvantage of the hollow ground blade is the near impossibility of cutting wet or warped wood without burning the blade.

Some blades are coated with Teflon for easier running and longer life. Other blades are carbide tipped and seldom need sharpening.

There are safety combination blades that practically eliminate any chance of dangerous "kick-back."

Circular Saw Operations. Circular saw operations involve ripping, rabbeting, dadoing, grooving, beveling, mitering, and molding. Each task involves special precautions and some require the use of attachments.

Ripping. Ripping long stock is a common operation on the circular saw. The width is established by using the ripping fence which is parallel to the blade. The blade of the saw should never extend more than 1/4 in. to 3/8 in. above the stock. The width of the stock to be cut need only be marked on the end of the stock, but the better way is to measure the width accurately from the right side of the blade to the left side of the ripping fence. (**Warning:** Never measure while the saw is running.) It is essential that the edge of the stock that rides against the ripping fence be made straight and square by running it over the jointer or by planing it with the fore plane of jointer plane. Cutting stock freehand on the circular saw is definitely a poor practice.

In guiding the last few inches, particularly if the stock is narrow, use a push stick and the guard. Keep hands at least 3 in. away from the saw blade. Figure 2-3 demonstrates proper procedure for using a ripping saw.

Crosscutting or Cutting Off. Crosscutting (cutting across the grain) is accomplished by using the miter gauge which fits into a slot in the tabletop and slides along the slot, allowing the stock to be moved into the saw blade. Large industrial saws allow a portion of the table to roll forward on bearings to accomplish this task. The miter gauge can be adjusted from a straight cutoff (0 degrees to 90 degrees on gauge) to 45 degree miter cuts.

If only a few pieces are needed, the stock is marked for length and cut off by holding it against the miter gauge with the left hand. The saw kerf is kept on the left side of the line.

When a number of pieces of the same length are needed, a stop attached to the miter gauge or a block fastened to the ripping fence is

Fig. 2-3. Ripping stock using a combination blade on a power circular saw and the ripping fence.

Fig. 2-4. Crosscut sawing to a specified length across the grain. Here a combination blade and crosscut fence are used to prevent pinching.

used. The stock should clear the block before the saw starts cutting. Figures 2-4 and 2-5 demonstrate proper use of a crosscutting saw.

Rabbeting. Rabbeting is the process of removing material along the edge or end of stock to form a joint. Rabbeting can easily be done

Fig. 2-5. Cutting a dado with a circular saw.

with the combination blade by making two cuts at right angles to each other, but the best method is to use the dado head. A dado head or dado set consists of two outside cutters 1/8 in. thick, plus a combination of inside cutters 1/16 in., 1/8 in. and 1/4-in. thick. For example, a 5/16 in. rabbet (or dado) would be made with two outside cutters and a 1/16 in. inside cutter. When more than one inside cutter is used the inside cutters are staggered. Two inside cutters would be placed at right angles to each other; three inside cutters would be 60 degrees apart. A special, wide-throated insert must be placed over the dado head due to its being wider than a saw blade.

Rabbeting can be done with either the ripping fence or the miter gauge, depending on whether the rabbet is on the edge or end of the stock. Figure 2-6 demonstrates cutting a rabbet with a circular saw.

Dadoing. Dadoing is the process of cutting a recess in stock, across the grain, away from the end of the stock. It is considered one of the best methods for constructing shelves. Dadoing can be done with the combination blade to make a series of cuts. The use of the dado head, however, is much faster and more efficient.

Grooving. Grooving is the process of cutting a recess or slot in stock, with the grain, away from the edge of the stock. As with rabbeting and dadoing, the combination blade can be used by making a series of cuts, but again the use of the dado head is much faster and efficient.

Fig 2-6. Cutting a rabbet with the grain of wood using a dado head on a circular saw.

Beveling. Most circular saws have a tilting arbor allowing bevel cuts to be made between 90 degrees and 45 degrees.

Mitering. Mitering is done by setting the miter gauge at the required angle.

Molding. Moldings can be made on the circular saw by making a special fence which angles over the blade of the saw. The depth can be controlled by raising and lowering the blade, and the width of concave cuts adjusted by changing the angle of the special fence. Concave and cove moldings can be made by this method. Push the stock over the blade very slowly to prevent undue strain on the blade.

Radial Saw. Practically all the operations done on the circular saw can be duplicated on the radial saw. Builders, carpenters and lumber companies use it a great deal because most operations allow the stock to remain stationary while the saw moves.

Many school shops use the radial saw as a cut-off saw for long boards and use the circular saw for all other operations.

If the home craftsman is to buy only one straight-line cutting saw, in all probability, the circular saw would be the best choice. The second best saw for straight cutting would be the portable electric circular saw.

Portable Electric Circular Saw. The portable electric circular saw is an indispensable tool for the builder and carpenter. In the home shop or school shop its use is very limited.

Some saws have an adjustable base so that bevels can be made. Layout marks are made for most cuts except when using a model of the saw equipped with a ripping fence or guide.

The saw is moved into the work after it reaches full speed. The left hand holds the stock in place and must be some distance from the saw. Always remember that the top of the saw is *moving toward you*. Be sure the guard is in good working order. Do not lay the saw down until the blade completely stops rotating.

HOW TO USE PLANING TOOLS

Planing tools are used essentially to smooth the surface of the wood. This smoothing process involves more than flat pieces or outside surfaces. Corners, edges, and inside surfaces all must be smooth and free from rough wood and splinters.

Hand Tools

The popularity of hand-held planes is due in part to the fact that they are inexpensive when compared to their motorized cousins.

Hand-held planes can serve the same purposes and do the job as well, but require more work and, perhaps, more skill on the part of the craftsman.

Block Plane. The block plane differs from other planes in that it is designed to be used in one hand. There are very few parts in this small plane, and the iron is set much lower than others. The bevel of the cutting edge is turned up instead of down. The block plane is used to plane the end grain. It would be the last purchase for the home workshop, because either the smoothing plane or the jack plane can do the same operation nearly as well.

Regardless of which of the three planes mentioned above are used for planing the end grain, certain precautions should be made to prevent splitting of the wood. Three of these precautions are listed below:

1. Plane toward the center of the end from both ways instead of clear across the end.
2. Cut a small 45-degree chamfer in the waste stock with a chisel.
3. Put a piece of scrap stock behind the piece to be planed. Secure both pieces at the same height in a vise. Thus, the splitting will take place on the scrap piece.

Jack Plane. The jack plane is an all-purpose plane that can be used for many tasks. You might call it the "jack of all trades" plane. If the home craftsman can only afford one plane, this is the plane to purchase.

The jack plane is usually 14 in. long with a 2 in. wide blade. There are eighteen parts to a jack plane as compared to only three for the block plane. The plane iron can be easily shifted so that it will not cut in too deeply on either cutting corner.

If the craftsman does not have power tools and wishes to square up rough lumber, he should follow these steps:

1. Plane a working face. Check with a square or straightedge to make sure that the surface is flat. Plane only *with the grain*. If the wood has a tendency to "roughen up," try planing in the opposite direction.
2. Plane a working edge square to the working face. Test squareness with a try square and straightness with the blade of a try square or straight edge.
3. Plane a working end square to the working face and the working edge. Check frequently with a square.
4. Mark the required length and square a pencil line across the board. With a backsaw or crosscut saw, cut off the

waste material close to the line just marked. Plane this second end square with the working face and working edge.

5. Mark the required width. If the required piece is fairly narrow (under 6 in.) use a marking guage. If the piece is wide, use a panel gauge. Cut off the waste stock with a rip-saw held close to the scribed line. Plane the stock to proper width. Check the width at both ends. This second edge should be square with the working face and the two ends.

6. Mark the thickness with a marking guage. Accentuate the line with a chisel edge and a hard lead pencil. Cut a chamfer on the second face on both the edges and the ends until the chamfer nearly meets the thickness line. The chamfer will act as a guide when planing the board to thickness. It will not be necessary to watch the line on every stroke of the plane.

Fore Plane. The fore plane is generally 18 in. long with a plane iron somewhat wider than those found on a standard jack plane. Boards are often jointed on the edges with the fore plane before gluing. It is also used on the face of large stock.

If the home craftsman is thinking about a second plane to add to his tool inventory, he is advised to select the longer jointer plane.

Jointer Plane. As its name suggests, the jointer plane is used almost exclusively for jointing edges of boards, particularly before gluing. The length of jointer planes runs from 22 in. upward to nearly 3 ft.

Smooth or Smoothing Plane. The smoothing plane looks like a "chopped off" jack plane. The bed is much shorter and extends only to the back of the handle. Smoothing planes are 8 in. or 9 in. long.

The smoothing plane—as its name suggests—is used for smoothing surfaces.

This plane is especially useful on small pieces. It should be kept very sharp and very close to the plane iron cap to produce a small, silky shaving almost of the same quality as produced by a well-sharpened scraper.

Router Plane. The router plane differs radically from all of the above planes. It has two round, identical handles and an oblong base with a narrow, adjustable knife extending through the base between the handles.

The router plane is used to smooth the bottom of rabbets, grooves and dadoes.

The home craftsman might better invest money in a power router which can perform many more operations. By purchasing an inexpensive accessory table, the router can be used as a shaper.

Rabbet Plane. There are a number of planes used for cutting rabbets. One plane can be used with either the left or right hand. The *bullnose rabbet plane* has the plane iron near the front, and extending across the whole plane. Thus, the plane may be used in corners.

There is a *combination plane* that can be used both for regular and bullnose planing. *Bullnosing* is the process of smoothing the bottom of a cut that does not extend clear across a piece of stock.

Spokeshave. As one would suspect, the spokeshave was originally used to make spokes for wheels. It can be used effectively for rounding corners of stock and for cutting chamfers. It can get into places that would be impossible for a plane.

The spokeshave has two wing-like handles. It has a plane iron and cuts in the same fashion as a plane.

The spokeshave and the cabinet scraper are similar in appearance.

Universal Plane. This tool is designed to do all kinds of planing jobs and works particularly well on moldings. A universal plane is a rather expensive tool and one that is hard to keep sharpened and adjusted. The biggest objection is the fact that it is very difficult to use. Money that might be spent on this tool might better be spent on a power router, which will do the same job faster and better.

Circular Plane. This plane has a flexible, steel-spring bed and is designed to plane both convex and concave curves of many sizes. It is a rather difficult tool to use, and the same operations can be done with other tools more efficiently.

Plane Iron Sharpening. All plane irons are sharpened in the same way. If a plane iron is very dull and nicked it will require regrinding as well as whetting.

When *grinding*, hold the bevel side down against the grinding wheel, and place the index finger on the under side to slide against the rest on the grinder.

Take a few passes across the edge of the grinding wheel to see if the correct angle has been established. If not, slide the index finger until the right angle is found. The bevel on most plane irons is about twice the thickness of the plane iron. During the grinding process, check often for squareness and for overheating. If the iron starts turning dark in color, dunk it in water.

When the grinding is complete a wire edge will turn up on the side opposite the bevel. This wire edge can be removed by rubbing the edge against a piece of wood or by subsequent whetting.

Start *whetting* on the coarser side of the oilstone. Use kerosene or light oil on the oilstone face to prevent the pores of the oilstone from clogging. Check from time to time during the whetting process to make sure that the heel of the bevel, as well as the cutting edge, is being whetted. Also check for squareness.

Turn the stone over and whet the iron on the finer side. Sight along the blade edge to make sure there are no shiny white patches which indicate dull spots. Run the thumb nail along the edge to check for minute nicks.

Honing is done after the whetting and imparts a razor-like edge. Honing is sometimes done on a leather strap, but the best method is to buff the edge on a buffing wheel using buffing compound or jeweler's rouge. When the plane iron removes the hair on the back of your arm you know it is ready to put back in the plane.

Power Planing Tools

Powered planing tools serve many of the same purposes of their hand-held counterparts discussed above. The router is particularly useful as it serves a variety of specialized needs. This one tool eliminates the necessity of having several hand-held planes.

Planer or Surfacer. The terms planer and surfacer are used interchangeably. This tool is a rather expensive item for the home craftsman. The smallest planer, which takes stock 12 in. wide and 4 in. thick, will run in the $600 to $700 range. There are many home craftsmen who own this tool however, because they can start with rough stock and plane any thickness needed down to 1/8 in.

The planer operator should go to the back of the planer to catch long pieces as they come through. Otherwise, the end of the board coming through last is apt to be thinner than the rest.

The grain direction should be checked before inserting stock into the planer or the surface may be badly checked and rough.

Short pieces of stock should be pushed through the planer—one piece close behind the other. Generally, slightly angled pieces will go through the planer easier.

Jointer. A power jointer can do many more operations than the planer, and from the home craftsman's standpoint, is much less expensive. They generally run in the $200 to $300 range for a 6 in. jointer.

The power jointer is especially valuable when it is necessary to rip a large number of long pieces. All stock must be jointed on one edge before ripping can take place safely.

When working with stock the width of a jointer or narrower, the jointer can do a good job of surfacing. By pushing the stock at a slow speed, a very smooth surface can be achieved.

The jointer is an excellent tool for tapering such things as table legs. A mark on the leg is made where the taper begins. The leg is placed across the top of the jointer blade, with the mark lined up with the front edge of the back-bed or outfeed table. For instance, if the taper starts at zero inches and ends up at 1/4 in., four cuts of 1/16 in. each would be made.

When thin, narrow strips are being jointed it is best to use a *feather board* (a board with a number of saw kerfs close together in one end to form a spring-type pressure against the fence) clamped to the infeed table to push the stock up against the fence and to prevent possible injury to the operator.

Router. The portable motorized router is a highly versatile tool. Its fast turning motor (up to 27,000 RPM) produces cuts that need no sanding. Motors are rated from 1/4 HP to 2 1/4 HP. Cutters are designed to make a variety of cuts (rabbeting, chamfering, corner rounding, beading, cove cutting, ogee cutting, fluting, "V" grooving and veining). In addition, there are cutters for making dovetail joints.

The router should always be moved from the left to right as the cutter moves in a clockwise direction in normal operation. The router should be moved at a consistent speed as too slow a movement will cause burning of the wood. Work should be securely clamped to the bench top or held in a vise so the router may be held with two hands. If a deep cut is to be made, it is best to take two or three passes, otherwise the motor will slow down with the increased load and it will not operate effectively.

There are many useful accessories that make the router more versatile. The *dovetail template* (together with the proper bits) can make drawer construction an easy and efficient task. There is a special bit and cutter attachment, with the necessary grinding wheels, which greatly facilitates the *sharpening* of bits and cutters. Another attachment permits *edge planing, parallel grooving, dadoing* and *slotting* operations. One of the more important attachments is a *shaper table* which changes the router into a shaper for more convenient handling of small parts. An auxiliary guard is available which provides safer operation.

Electric Plane. The electric power plane is, in essence, a motorized router mounted on a plane bed. It can do both edge and surface planing. It can make cuts up to 1/8 in. in depth and 3 in. wide. In some ways the electric plane is like a miniature, upside down jointer in that it has both an adjustable infeed and outfeed table. It also possesses a fence.

The electric plane comes in handy when working on large pieces. When using this machine a person has a distinct advantage—he can take this highly portable tool to the work instead of vice versa.

The electric plane probably has its greatest use in trimming and fitting interior and exterior doors for buildings.

How To Use Curve-Cutting Power Tools

The following list of motorized tools enables the woodworker to cut any curved surfaces. Interior and exterior curves may be cut with these tools. They help the home craftsman add to the beauty of his finished product by adding that special, finely crafted touch of curved surfaces.

Band Saw. Band saws vary in size from the 10 in. and 12 in. (wheel diameter) with a 1/8 in. blade that create rather fine scroll work to huge 75 ft long blades with 16 in. wide blades. These huge saws have teeth on both edges of the blade for sawing giant logs in both the forward and backward passes of the carriage.

The 14 in. band saw is the most popular in the home workshop as well as in pattern shops, small school shops, cabinet shops, maintenance shops and small furniture shops. In vocational schools, technical institutes and large furniture plants, band saws vary from 36 in. to 42 in. in wheel diameter. The blades most commonly used are 3/8 in. to 3/4 in. wide. The gauge thickness of band saw blades varies according to the wheel size. The thinner blades are used on the smaller band saws. The skip-tooth blade is used to saw faster in certain kinds of woods, and due to its hardness will last longer. However, when it gets dull the blade has to be thrown away as it cannot be resharpened.

The band saw is a safer saw to use than the circular saw because there is no chance of a kick-back. There are certain precautions, however, that must be taken. Round stock must never be cut unless it is securely clamped to a "V" block. Irregular surfaces that rock on the band saw table should be avoided. Watch both hands at all times. The distance between the top surface of the work and the top guide should never be over 3/8 in.

One of the first things that a craftsman must learn is how to fold a band saw blade. There are many methods that may be used but they all arrive at the same result—a three-loop circle that can easily hang over dowel pegs when not in use. The best way to learn how to fold a band saw blade is from another craftsman. A movie or a series of photos do not seem to do the trick in most cases.

The major function of the band saw is to cut outside, irregular curves. There are, however, many other operations that a band saw can perform; the most important of which is resawing. *Resawing* is the process of placing stock on the edge and pushing it through the band saw. This method provides two thin boards in place of one thick one. A wider blade and a special fence are used for resawing.

In a pinch, the band saw can be used for ripping if a special fence is clamped onto the top of the table.

Before sawing on a band saw, turn on the switch and stand back a few seconds. Watch and listen for any unusual signs or sounds. Are there any clicking sounds that indicate a saw is about to break? Is the saw "wandering" or running erraticly in the guides, which might mean that the upper wheel is not tilted correctly?

When properly adjusted, the blade should run close to the guide wheels in the upper and lower guides at idle, but when the pressure of cutting is put on the blades the guide wheels should spin rapidly.

Jigsaw or Scroll Saw. The jigsaw is essentially a motorized coping saw, and for most purposes uses the same type and size of blades. The band saw cuts much faster than the jigsaw. The jigsaw cuts only on the downward stroke while the band saw blade cuts continuously. The band saw will also cut much heavier stock. The advantages of the jigsaw are the ability to cut curves with small radii, to cut fine lines, and to cut interior curves as well as exterior curves.

The teeth of a jigsaw should point downward, which assists in holding the work against the table. The spring hold-down should be leveling against the work. The work should be pushed slowly into the blade and if the work starts to chatter, ease up on the rate of speed at which you are pushing the work into the blade.

Cutting internal curves call for certain steps to be followed:

1. Bore or drill one or more holes large enough for the blade to be pushed through. These holes should be in the center portion of the part to be cut out. Keep the holes as far as possible away from the scribed lines.
2. Remove the blade from the jigsaw.
3. Place the hole just bored over the throat of the jigsaw between the upper chuck and the lower chuck.
4. Insert the blade through the hole in the wood (teeth pointed downward) and place the ends of the blade in the two chucks and tighten the blade.
5. Start sawing. The sawing should angle gradually toward the line to be sawed.
6. If it is necessary to saw sharp corners, it is best to cut clear to the corner and then back off and cut a well rounded corner into the part at right angles to the one already cut.

Run the saw to the nearest hole and cut to the corner from the opposite direction.

Saber and Bayonet Saws. The saber saw is like a miniature, upside down, portable jigsaw with only one chuck fastened to the motor. This feature means that the blades must be much stiffer than coping saw blades.

There are many types and sizes of blades available for the saber saw. Many of the blades will cut materials other than wood. The number of teeth per inch vary from six for wood to 32 for metal. When purchasing saw blades be certain to get those that will fit the machine. Saber saw blades will not fit all makes of saber saws.

If the home craftsman does not have any curve-cutting equipment, he should consider buying only the best quality saber saw which generally has the greatest versatility. The quality saws will have a tilting base for angled cuts, variable speed motor, and enough power to saw through a two-by-four if need be.

One distinct advantage of the saber saw is that it will cut internal (inside) cuts without drilling or boring holes. This makes working with paneling much easier. This type of sawing is called *plunge* sawing. The saw is tilted up on the front end, and the saw blade is slowly lowered into the work, thus cutting its own hole. It is best to try this procedure on waste stock first as this technique takes some practice.

The *bayonet* saw is the "big brother" of the saber saw. It is heavier, more powerful and has to be operated with two hands. The more expensive models have two speeds and also an option switch for selecting either orbital or reciprocating blade motion. The blade of the bayonet saw sticks out in front of the motor, while the blade of the saber saw points downward.

HOW TO USE DRILLING AND BORING TOOLS

Drilling and boring tools are used to make holes in wood where screws or other joining devices are needed. The size and depth of the hole drilled depends upon the type of drilling tool chosen and the size of the blade inserted.

Hand Tools

Hand-held drills are used a great deal in the home workshop. The craftsman must take care with the type of bit used with these tools to assure correct dimensions of the hole required.

Augur Bits. Augur Bits are used for boring holes in wood. Augur bits are available in sizes from 1/4 in. to 1 1/4 in. diameter.

Sizes are indicated by a number indented in the tang of the bit. This number designates the size in sixteenths of an inch. A number 6 on the tang identifies a 3/8 in. bit (6/16 in.).

The *tang* is the square part of the bit that fits into the brace. A small tapered screw (feed screw) on the tip of the bit pulls the bit into the wood so that the *spurs* (knife-like projections) can cut the outline of the circle. The cutting edges cut away the rest of the hole which follow up the twist of the bit.

Augur bits are of two kinds: the *single twist* and the *double twist.* The double twist is considered the best for easy boring and for making smooth, clean holes.

The depth of a hole can be roughly estimated by counting the number of turns that the bit makes. Each *turn* (revolution) of the bit will pull the bit into the wood approximately one sixteenth of an inch.

Drill Bits. Drill bits are used for drilling in both metal and wood. They are available in *fractional* and *letter* sizes. Fractional sizes run from 1/32 in. to 1/2 in. in increments of 1/64 in. Letter sizes are available in sizes from 1/4 in. to 1/2 in. where a fractional size is not applicable. Fractional-size drills are usually adequate for all wood drilling.

Drill bits used exclusively for wood drilling are sharpened to a finer point than bits used for metal.

Spade Bits. Spade bits are used exclusively for boring in wood. The flat, spade-shaped bits are available in sizes from 1/4 in. to 1 in. in increments of 1/16 in. The shanks of all spade bits are round (1/4 in. in diameter) so they can be used in portable electric drills. Spade bits bore faster and cleaner than many other bits. They are ideal for the home craftsman.

Expansion Bits. Expansion bits are available in two sizes: those that bore holes from 5/8 in. to 1 3/4 in. and those that bore holes from 7/8 in. to 3 in. in diameter. One model of expansion bits has a micrometer dial that gives precision boring to 1/1000 in. It also has a depth gauge which instantly shows how deeply the hole is bored.

The expansion bit is much more difficult to use than the spade bit. The expansion bit has a square tang which allows it to be used only in a brace. When boring the larger holes (2 in. to 3 in. in diameter) it is almost impossible to turn the brace. Therefore, it is not a very good buy for the home craftsman.

Multi-Spur Bit. Multi-spur bits are available in sizes from 1/2 in. to 1 in. in increments of 1/16 in., and in sizes 1 in. to 1 1/4 in. in increments of 1/8 in.

The multi-spur bit has a round shank of 1/4 in. diameter, so it can be used in a portable electric drill. It is a very fast, clean boring bit. It will bore a portion of a circle on the edge of a piece of wood. In addition, it will bore at an angle, overlapping or on close centers, without splitting the wood. It works well on veneers without tearing.

Forstner Bit. Forstner bits are available in sizes from 3/8 in. to 1 in. in increments of 1/16 in. Sizes stamped are the same as those stamped on augur bits. There are also Forstner bits available in sizes from 1 1/4 in. to 2 in. in increments of 1/4 in.

Forstner bits are used for counterboring and (as the multi-spur) will bore a hole close or on the edge of stock without tearing. It will bore nearly through wood without the spurs or feed screw coming through and puncturing the reverse side of the stock.

Dowel Bit. The dowel bit is simply a shortened augur bit for boring dowel holes. It is much easier to hold the bit perpendicular to the surface of the wood. It is also advantageous whenever a shorter bit would do the job better than the standard augur bit.

Router Drill Bit. The router drill bit can be used in a fashion similar to the saber saw. It cuts its own starting hole and can move from there in any direction. It is ideal for making small irregular shaped holes.

Combination Wood Drill and Countersink. The combination wood drill and countersink performs three operations at one time: it drills a *pilot hole* for the spiral part of a screw, it drills a *shank* hole, and *countersinks* so that the top of a flat head screw will fit flush with the wood. It is especially helpful where speed and mass production are called for. It would be a luxury and not a necessity for the home craftsman. It comes in sizes from 3/4 in. by No. 6 to 2 in. by No. 12. (The first number indicates the length of the screw, and the second number the wire size of the shank.)

Plug Cutter. The plug cutter is a short, hollow bit which cuts short dowels to cover the heads of counterbored screws. It is available in 3/8 in., 1/2 in. and 5/8 in. diameter sizes. The advantage of the plug cutter is that short dowels of the same wood as the project can be made, rather than having to rely on the standard commercial birch dowels.

Countersink Bit. The most commonly used countersink is sometimes called the rose countersink because it has many flutes around the conical point which bores a recess for the screw heads.

This bit has two types of shanks: one with a square shank to use in a brace, the other with a round shank to use in a portable electric drill or the drill press.

Circle Cutter Bit. The circle cutter is a tool for cutting holes in thin metal, plastics, or wood up to 8 in. in diameter. A small drill bit starts the hole and a cutter on an adjustable arm cuts the outside circumference. The circle cutter is available with either a square shank or round shank. It is a highly specialized tool that would be used very little by the home craftsman.

Automatic Drill Bit. The automatic drill bit is an accessory of the automatic drill that works on the same principle as the Yankee screwdriver. It drills a hole only on the forward or downward stroke of the automatic drill. The drill bits are available in sizes from 1/16 in. to 11/64 in. in increments of 1/64 in. All automatic drill bits have notched shanks. The automatic drill is a hard drill to use and has no useful purpose except in very close quarters. The hand drill is much easier to use, by far.

Augur Bit Brace. Augur bit braces can be used with a boring or drilling bit that has a square tang. Sizes available are 8 in., 10 in. and 12 in. (the diameter of the circle made by the turning handle). Present-day braces are equipped with a ratchet which allows them to be used in cramped quarters.

Hand Drill. The hand drill is built to handle round shank drill bits 1/4 in. in diameter and less. It is an indispensable tool for the home craftsman, particularly if he does not possess a portable electric drill.

Breast Drill. The breast drill is an oversized hand drill that will handle bits up to 1/2 in. in diameter. It has a breast plate for the operator to lean on to apply more pressure to the drill bit. The breast drill is a necessary tool where electricity is not available.

Drilling and Boring with Hand Tools. Center marks or layout marks for drilling or boring are generally two pencil or scribed lines at right angles to each other. Pencil lines should be used on visible surfaces as they can be erased.

Where the two lines cross, a hole is pricked with a scratch awl so that the bit will center itself and the bit will not "wander."

Material to be drilled or bored should be securely anchored with a vise or clamps.

Special precautions should be taken when drilling or boring a hole clear through stock, otherwise tearing or splitting will take place.

Two methods which *prevent splitting* are as follows:

1. When drilling through wood with drill bits 1/4 in. in diameter or smaller, place a piece of waste stock under the piece to be drilled. The only tearing or splitting will be in the waste stock.

2. When boring with an augur bit, place the left hand under the stock. As soon as the augur bit feed screw starts to penetrate the second side, take out the bit. Turn the board over and complete boring the hole using the feed screw hole as the center. Of course, waste stock can be placed under the location of the hole as in method Number 1.

Boring or *drilling to depth* requires a commercial depth gauge or a simple homemade device of wood. A square piece of stock should be drilled or bored through the long way. This block is cut to length and the bit is inserted in the hole. When the block touches the surface it will not be possible to drill deeper, and the hole will be the correct depth.

Boring at an angle can be accomplished by setting a T-bevel to the angle required and using it as a guide. The augur should be started straight in and gradually tilted to the angle as boring progresses. If a number of holes are to be bored at the same angle, it is best to make a jig to guide the augur bit.

Counterboring is related to countersinking. Counterboring is boring a hole straight in with a regular bit. The sides of a countersunk hole are at an angle. The angle is the same as the angle on the head of a flat-head screw. Many times a counterbored hole is necessary to sink the head of a bolt or nut below the surface of the wood. The most important thing to remember about counterboring is *counterbored holes* must be *bored* before *shank holes*. To bore the shank hole first would remove the wood into which the counterbore bit would have to center itself.

Sharpening augur bits is much more difficult than sharpening drill bits. A beginner should start on an old augur bit. Use only the special files designed for the purpose. The cutting lips are sharpened with the file pointed toward the tang. Do not oversharpen. The spur is *sharpened* on the *inside only*. Any filing on the outside of an augur bit will ruin it beyond repair.

Power Tools

Power tools accomplish the task of boring holes quickly and accurately. They are particularly useful when a large number of holes are required. Powered drilling tools are available in both stationary and portable varieties.

Portable Electric Hand Drill. Portable electric hand drills are available that drill from 1/4 in. diameter to a 2 in. diameter in wood, and up to 1 in. in steel. The larger models are controlled with both hands. The 1/4 in., pistol grip, one handle model is the most popular for the home workshop. Smaller drills operate at a higher speed than the larger ones.

Drill Press. Drill presses come in two models: the bench type and the floor type. Most drill presses have from three to six speeds made possible by different size pulleys. The six speeds vary from 350 RPM to 5600 RPM. One model has a variable speed motor and any speed between 450 to 4800 RPM may be obtained by simply turning a dial. This eliminates the dirty and time consuming job of changing belts on cone pulleys.

Drill presses are rated according to the distance over a board that it can reach. A 15 in. drill press will drill holes in the center of a 15 in. wide board.

The 15 in. drill press is the most popular for small industries, schools and the home workshop.

Slow speeds are used when boring and drilling holes with large diameter bits. High speeds are necessary for small hole drilling, shaping, routing and mortising. Augur bits can be used in drill presses only if the tang is cut off, and the threads on the feed screw are filed off.

Mortising can be done with a mortising attachment, hollow chisels, and hollow chisel bits. Sizes of chisels are 1/4 in. square, 5/16 in. square, 3/8 in. square and 1/2 in. square. The diameters of the bits are 1/4 in., 5/16 in., 3/8 in. and 1/2 in.

Cylindrical sanding drums and *sleeves* are available for drill presses. Drums vary from 11/16 in. in diameter and 2 in. long to 3 in. in diameter and 3 in. long. Sleeves are available in garnet and aluminum oxide and in different size grits.

It is possible to do shaping by boosting the speed with a special high speed motor, but it is a somewhat risky setup. The quill and spindle are not built for this rough usage and safety becomes a real problem.

Routing is sometimes done on the drill press, but when the speed of approximately 8000 RPMs is compared to the speed of a portable electric router of approximately 24,000 RPMs it is obvious that routing on a drill press would run a very poor second.

HOW TO USE CHISELS AND CHISELING TOOLS

Chisels and other cutting tools help the craftsman create carved surfaces. They are used to create beveled edges, grooves and cutouts on legs and mortises. Very often chisels are used in conjunction with motorized tools like the lathe.

Types of Chisel Blades

Each of the chisel blades listed below is used in conjunction with a specialized task. The thickness of the blade is dependent upon the chore it is required to perform.

Firmer Chisel. The firmer chisel is any chisel that has a straight cutting edge and the cutting edge face is perfectly flat.

Gouge. The gouge is any chisel with a rounded or U-shaped cross section. Hand gouges are inside and outside ground and are straight across the cutting edge. Lathe turning gouges are outside ground only, and the cutting edge is rounded.

Bevel Edge Chisels. The bevel edge chisel blade is easier to use because of the visibility it provides. It is also lighter in weight. Most firmer chisels have beveled edges.

Straight Edge Chisels. Straight edge chisels (as opposed to bevel edge chisels) are used where greater strength is needed.

Types of Chisel Handles

Chisel handles must stand as much abuse as the chisel blade. The craftsman should take care when selecting a handle to make sure it will stand up to the job at hand.

Tang Handle. Chisels with tang handles have a long, sharply pointed projection that fits into a handle with a metal ferrule. Mallets should never be used with tang-handle chisels or gouges.

Socket Handle. The socket handle chisel will stand considerable abuse and is quite often used with mallets (wood, rawhide, rubber, plastic, etc.). Most mallets are shaped like a hammer, but mallets used with sculptor's carving tools are shaped like a potato masher. Never use a steel hammer as a mallet.

Pocket Handle. Pocket-handle chisels are built for extremely hard usage. They are ideal for school shops. The blade and shank are forged in one piece extending through the handle to a steel cap on the noncutting end.

Types of Chisels According to Function

A home workshop would be incomplete without at least one of the chisels listed below. Care should be taken that these tools are used only for the purposes for which they were originally designed.

Butt Chisels. The butt chisel is a firmer chisel with a short blade. It is a general purpose chisel with both tang and socket handles. Most butt-chisel blades are bevel edge.

Mortise Chisel. The mortise chisel is a socket-handle, narrow, long, thick-bladed chisel for cutting mortises.

Turning Chisels to Use with the Lathe. The lathe turning tools are quite different from other chisels. The handles are much longer and smaller in diameter. All turning chisels are of the tang-handled type with the tang fitting into a ferruled handle.

Chisels used for turning are the full skew, half- and full-round nose, diamond point, parting tool and gouge.

Carving Chisels. Carving tools are used for surface decorating and sculpturing. The tools are the skew, the parting tool, the fishtail chisel, the firmer chisel, the corner chisel, the front bent chisel, the veining tools, the straight gouge, the "U" gouge, the medium gouge, the narrow gouge, the shallow gouge, the spoon gouge and the wide swing gouge.

Cutting with Chisels and Gouges

Cutting with chisels and gouges requires a very sharp edge. Sharpening is done in the same fashion as sharpening plane irons (grind, whet and hone).

The stock being chiseled must be securely held in a vise, with clamps, or against a bench hook.

The most common operations are cutting dadoes, tenons and cross laps.

The chisel is held in the right hand and the left hand is used to guide and keep the chisel under control.

Cutting with chisels and gouges involve the following steps:

1. Remove most of the wood with a socket-firmer chisel and mallet with the bevel side down. This can be done quite rapidly. Stop before you get to within 1/16-in. to 1/8-in. to the layout line.

2. Lay aside the socket chisel and use a sharp, tang-handled, paring chisel. Paring action requires the handle to be moved back and forth. Pare always toward the center; first from one side or edge and then from the other. The bevel side should be up for this step in the operation. Continue paring until the line indicating the depth has been reached. So far all the work has been cross grain and horizontal.

3. Pare from above (vertical) and across end grain. The bevel of the chisel should face away from the edge being pared. Start back from the line at least 1/16 in. and do not attempt to remove too much material at a time. Rock the chisel handle back and forth from side to side and keep the chisel blade firmly under control with the thumb and index finger of the left hand. Always strive for a shearing cut.

Note: Keep in mind that all of the above chiseling work on dadoes, tenons, cross laps and the like can be eliminated with a circular saw and a dado head.

The inside, straight edge gouge is used when cutting the edge of a curved line from above. The outside, straight edge gouge is used more frequently and is used for carving flutes and in cutting out recesses in trays. Use a mallet and socket-handle gouge for roughing out. Only thin shavings with a paring gouge should be taken as the layout line is approached.

Carving tools are used in about the same way as other chiseling tools.

Turning with Lathe Chisels and Gouges

The lathe is used to perform two basic operations: *faceplate turning* (salad bowl) and *turning between centers* (baseball bat).

The most common turning chisels are gouges, skews (two different sizes), a roundnose (two different sizes), a diamond point and a parting tool.

A pair of outside calipers and a steel rule or scale are necessary accessories to turning. *Never* use calipers on turning stock unless the stock has been turned perfectly round. Calipers caught by turning stock have caused serious injuries.

There are two basic techniques of turning: the *scraping* method and the *turning* method. The turning method is very difficult and takes a long time to learn. The highly skilled wood turner does most of his turning with the skew. It looks so easy, but it certainly isn't. The home craftsman should stick to the scraping method.

Each end of squared stock (turning between centers) should be marked diagonally across the corners. On one end, saw two kerfs about 1/8-in. deep. This end will be driven by the spurs on the live center. Where the two lines cross on the other end, drill a small hole for the center of the dead center. Then, take the two centers out of the lathe, place them over their corresponding ends on the stock, and tap the butt end of each center sharply with a mallet.

Place the stock in the lathe cut off the corners of the squared stock with a draw shave to form a rough octogon in cross section. Check to see if the tailstock is locked and force the dead center into the wood with the crank on the tailstock until it is firmly seated. Stock is turned over by hand.

Check the speed setting, stand to one side, and turn on the switch. If the lathe starts to vibrate, turn off the switch immediately and set for a lower speed.

The stock is turned to the round with a large gouge. A shearing cut should be used, moving to the right with the right corner of the gouge and to the left with the left corner.

When the stock is still oversize, measure the lengths between the square parts and round parts, as well as between beads, "V's", and other parts. It is best to mark the distances on a piece of scrap wood. Hold the piece about 1/8 in. form the revolving stock and mark with pencil.

At or near these lines, establish diameters with calipers and a narrow parting tool. Hold the calipers set at the right diameter in the left hand and the parting tool in the right hand. The handle of the parting tool should extend along the forearm. Turn and measure alternately until the correct diameter is reached. Never force the calipers or a false measurement will be read.

Remove all excess waste stock with the gouge; make the necessary tapers, coves, beads, concavesn convexes, flats, and V-shaped portions with the appropriate tool.

The home craftsman who plans on doing lathe turning should borrow library books or take a woodworking course in which the finer points of the craft are explained in detail.

HOW TO USE SCRAPING TOOLS

Scrapers are used after a surface has been planed. They help smooth the wood and ready it for sanding. Scrapers are tools of necessity for the craftsman who works with hardwood.

Hand Scraper

The hand scraper is a thin, rectangular piece of flexible steel, varying in size from 2 1/2 in. by 5 in. to 3 in. by 6 in.

Handle Scraper

The handle is a highly advertized commercial product that is held in rather low esteem by cabinetmakers. When in use it has two hooked cutting edges that can be reversed to form two more cutting edges. Blades are usually 2 1/2 in. wide. It is a rather difficult scraper to keep sharpened, although it is probably the most widely used of all scrapers.

Cabinet Scraper

The cabinet scraper looks like an enlarged spokeshave. The blade is usually 2 3/4 in. wide. It is the finest scraper to use on flat surfaces. Due to its solid frame, handles, and an established angle, more pressure can be put on the blade, thus providing faster cutting. It is a good investment for the home craftsman.

Scraper Plane

The scraper plane looks like a plane. It has great stability because of its large bed and the blade can be adjusted for different angles. It is a good scraper for heavy work.

Hoe Type Scraper

This scraper has a long handle like the handles on lathe chisels. It has a swivel type head and the blade can be adjusted to different angles. The blade sticks out in front so it can be used in corners that other scrapers can not reach.

Swanneck Scraper

The swanneck scraper has many curves of different radii similar to the French curve used in mechanical drawing. It can be used to scrape moldings or such concave surfaces as the bottom of a bowl or tray.

How to Sharpen a Scraper

The hand scraper is sharpened differently from other scrapers. The edge is draw filed with the flat mill file at 90 degrees to the two surfaces of the scraper. A machinist vise is used to hold the scraper, and the file is used in a horizontal position. The filing will produce a *burr* on each edge of the scraper and it is the modified burr that does the scraping. Sometimes it is necessary to remove the burr on an oilstone and produce a new hook with the burnisher. A *burnisher* is used to turn the burr into a smooth cutting edge. Start the burnisher in a horizontal position and on each stroke lift the handle. Continue gradually until an angle of 80 degrees to 85 degrees is reached. Turn the scraper around in the vise and use the burnisher for the other edge in the same way.

How To Sharpen Cabinet Scrapers, Scraper Plane Blades, and the Hoe Type Scraper

Be sure the edge is perfectly straight before putting the scraper in a vise. Remove the old burr by filing, with little pressure, on the flat side of the scraper.

File the beveled edge, with a flat mill file, at an angle of 30 degrees to 40 degrees. File only on the forward stroke and do not drag the file backward over the edge. Continue until a substantial burr (wire edge) has been formed on the flat side of the scraper opposite the beveled edge.

Take the scraper out of the vise and *hone* the beveled edge on a fine oilstone. Turn the scraper over and hone the flat side of the scraper.

Put the scraper back in the vise and start burnishing at about the same angle that was filed on the bevel side. At each stroke across the edge, raise the handle a few degrees until the burnisher is in a horizontal position at right angles to the two faces of the scraper. This process should leave a hook or scraping burr on the scraper.

How To Use the Hand Scraper

Both hands are used with the hand scraper. It can be either pushed or pulled. The hand scraper is not designed for heavy scraping. If the scraper produces fine sawdust instead of fine, thin, silky shavings the scraper is dull or it has not been properly sharpened. Several burnishings may be done before it is necessary to file and hone the edges again.

How To Use Other Scrapers

Cabinet scrapers and scraper planes are generally pushed. The handle scrapers and hoe type scrapers are usually pulled. The swanneck scraper can be either pushed or pulled. If the blade is held at a slight angle to the direction of the grain of cross-grained woods, it will cut better and will hold its edge better.

Scrapers are used on cross-grain hardwood or other uniquely grained woods (knotty wood, wood from burls, birds-eye maple, and wavy or curly grained woods).

The home craftsman who works with hardwoods can hardly do without one. Some woods are impossible to plane smooth.

HOW TO USE SANDPAPER AND OTHER ABRASIVES

Sanding should never attempt to take the place of cutting tools. An acceptable wood surface is one on which all blemishes have been eliminated. These blemishes come in the form of scratches, dents, machine marks, clamp marks, fuzzy grain and surface spots.

The process of eliminating blemishes is possible by using a sequence of successively finer grits of sandpaper. Each grit reduces the size of the scratches produced by the grit previously used.

The home craftsman must never assume that subsequent coats of finish materials will cover defects. It will only magnify them.

Defects too deep to be removed with abrasives must be filled with a filler material (Plastic Wood, Wood Dough, stick shellac, stick lacquer, etc.) A good, inexpensive, homemade filler is fine sandings, the same as the project being worked on, mixed with glue into a paste. Some shallow defects may be remedied by putting a few drops of water on the defect and applying a hot iron.

There are several factors which influence the quality of sanded surfaces. They are in two categories:

1. Those determined by the kind of abrasive and its use.
   A. The type of mineral used.
   B. The type of backing.
   C. The type of coating used.
   D. Size of particles.
   E. Amount of pressure used.
   F. The condition of sanding equipment.
   G. Speed of sanding.
2. Those factors pertaining to the wood.
   A. Moisture in the wood.
   B. Kinds of wood being sanded.
   C. Alignment of wood grain in relation to the surface.
   D. The direction the abrasive travels in respect to the grain of wood.
   E. The type of grain.

Heat is often generated by the action of the sandpaper, particularly if sanding machines are used. This has a tendency to deform and shrink the wood cells. When stain is applied the cells tend to return to their original size and shape. The causes raising of the grain which is detrimental to further finishing efforts. The condition can be avoided by applying glue size (10 to 13 parts of hot water to one part of animal glue). After the glue size is dry the wood is sanded with fine sandpaper.

Sanding a Flat Surface

Sandpaper is generally available for the home craftsman in sheets 9 1/2 in. by 11 in. The sheet should be torn (over the edge of an old saw blade is a good way) into 4 to 6 equal parts. A sandpaper block of appropriate size can be made of a piece of scrap wood. It should be 1 1/2 in. to 1 3/4 in. thick and the working face should be covered with a cushiony material such as felt, rubber, foam rubber or leather. Some commercial blocks are made entirely of rubber. An old blackboard eraser makes a fair sanding block, although a little too soft. Fold the sandpaper where the corners of the sanding block are located.

Fasten small pieces in the vise or anchor them with clamps to a flat surface. Grip the sandpaper and block with the thumb on the left side and the little finger on the right. The remaining fingers apply pressure to the top of the block. Very small pieces are sanded by rubbing the piece over a full sheet of sandpaper laid flat on the bench top. *Never* sandpaper across the grain.

Sand the entire surface with the same number of strokes and pressure, unless it is necessary to remove a particular blemish. Remove the sanding dust from time to time during sanding.

Start with coarse sandpaper and end with fine sandpaper. As a general rule, never skip more than three grit sizes in moving from coarse to fine sandpaper. Do not sand too close to the edge of the stock or the edge may be rolled. At least one half of the sandpaper block should be over the face of stock at all times. *Never* sand surfaces that are to be glued.

Sanding an Edge

Sanding an edge, particularly if it is narrow, is not an easy operation. After placing stock in the vise, with the edge to be sanded in the up position, take the sandblock in both hands and let at least one finger of each hand slide along the two surfaces at right angles to the edge being sanded. The fingers act as guides to keep the sanding block square with the sides.

Sanding Convex Surfaces

The sandpaper and the fingers are all that are needed when sanding small convex surfaces found on molding or molded edge. Large convex edges and surfaces are sanded in the same manner as flat edges and surfaces.

When sanding thin (3/8 in. or less) edges on convex surfaces, fold the sandpaper and bend it over the two ends of the thumbs as they are placed together. Hold the sandpaper with the thumbs and index fingers. Sand the convex edge with the major pressure on the center of the edge being sanded. The outside edges will take care of themselves.

Sanding Concave Surfaces or Edges

Place sandpaper over a cylindrical object. A piece of dowel works fine for smaller curves. The diameter of the cylinder must be somewhat smaller than the diameter of the concave surface or edge.

HOW TO ASSEMBLE AND GLUE

Assembling and gluing is usually done in three stages.

1. Assemble and clamp project together. Do not use glue. Mark all parts—if they have not already been marked—so

that pieces will go together again in the same arrangement in the final assembly.

2. Dissassemble project and apply glue to the joints. Care should be taken not to overglue as the "squeeze-out" will affect subsequent finishing operations. Be sure to know the assembly time of the glue you are using. Some adhesives require clamping within five minutes after glue is applied. Directions are usually printed on the can or container.

3. Reassemble the project and apply clamps. Clamps should have been opened only a little after the project was dissasembled to allow pieces to be reinserted. Be sure to have wood pads ready to put under the clamp jaws to prevent denting of the wood surface.

Subassemblies

Subassemblies are glued and clamped first and allowed to dry before the whole assembly is glued and clamped.

Glue Blocks

After the final assembly is made it is a good idea to use glue blocks to reinforce the project. Glue blocks are triangular cross-section shaped blocks from 2 in. to 3 in. long, with a right angle on two sides. They are used where two surfaces come together at right angles, and are usually in a concealed position.

Apply glue (animal glue is the best) to the two right-angle surfaces and place in the approximate position. Rub the glue block (about 1 in. strokes) back and forth applying considerable pressure. When the glue begins to "set-up" move the block to its final position and hold it there for about thirty seconds before releasing pressure.

Miter Joints

Miter joints present some troublesome problems in the gluing/assembling/clamping process. The best methods require special clamping devices.

One device, called the *miter and corner clamp*, glues up one corner (e.g. picture frames) at a time.

Another device requires that shallow holes be bored in the back of the frame to form recesses for round jaws of a special clamp. A hole is bored on each side of the miter joint. All four corners of a frame can be glued and clamped at the same time if four clamps are available. These clamps work well and are to be recommended if the eight holes are not objectionable on the back of the frame.

A very fine clamp for small frames has four right-angle clamps fastened together with threaded rods. Naturally, all four of the corners are clamped at the same time. This clamp may be used on highly finished materials.

A *band clamp* is made of one inch wide nylon and has four steel corners for gluing frames of any size. It can also clamp and hold objects of any shape. A special cam and wrench combination tightens and releases the band. The nylon band can handle loads up to one thousand pounds.

HOW TO FINISH

The finishing of a fine piece of furniture involves several steps beginning with sanding and ending with application of wax. No step in between should be skipped. Each step should be read carefully and the figures studies carefully before actual work is done.

How to Apply Quality Finish To Open-Grain Woods

Open-grain woods such as oak, walnut and mahogany require special treatment in the finishing process. The eleven steps illustrated in Fig. 2-7 through 2-10 emphasize the fact that the quality finishing of wood is a rather complex operation. But the beauty and depth of the finish is well worth the effort. These steps are essentially the same as used by manufacturers of fine furniture.

The home craftsman should note that the apparent depth of finish is due to very small amounts of color added to transparent finishes.

Step 1 of Fig. 2-7 depicts one enlarged pore of open grain wood. The finishing process generally starts after the wood is sanded with 2/0-100 sandpaper. Raw lumber direct from the mill or lumber company will require coarser paper. Unfinished furniture is usually sanded with 3/0 sandpaper.

Of course, the sanding should be done with the grain only.

The application of glue size (Fig. 2-7, *Step 2*) takes place after all planer marks, chip marks, clamp marks and other blemishes have been removed. It is permissible to leave shallow dents or depressions as the glue size will raise the surface. Ten to thirteen parts of hot water are added to one part of animal glue—Franklin's liquid glue will do. The water should be as hot as the hands will tolerate. The penetration of glue size into wood is probably greater than other finish processes due to the fact that it is hot. A natural or synthetic sponge is ideal for the application of glue size. On large, flat surfaces, sponging should be done with and against the grain. This is particu-

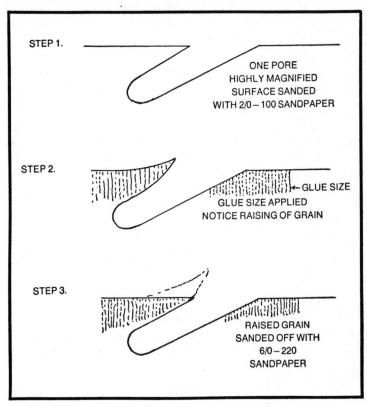

STEP 1.

ONE PORE
HIGHLY MAGNIFIED
SURFACE SANDED
WITH 2/0 – 100 SANDPAPER

STEP 2.

←GLUE SIZE
GLUE SIZE APPLIED
NOTICE RAISING OF GRAIN

STEP 3.

RAISED GRAIN
SANDED OFF WITH
6/0 – 220
SANDPAPER

Fig. 2-7. Steps 1 through 3 of the wood-finishing process.

larly important if water stain is to be used, as it will raise the grain not covered by the glue size. The sponge should carry enough glue size so that the wood is thoroughly moistened, but no puddles should be left standing on the wood. If it appears that the wood is too wet, wring out the sponge and go over the area.

The glue size causes the fibers of the wood to turn upward. Water will do the same thing. The advantage of glue size is that after twenty four hours of drying, the fiber is in a fixed position. Subsequent sanding (Fig. 2-7, *Step 3*) eliminates the raised fibers. If water alone is used, the flexible, hair-like fiber simply lays down when the sandpaper passes over it and springs right up again after the sandpaper passes over. Use 6/0-220 sandpaper for sanding.

During this step (Fig. 2-8, *Step 4*) a thin sealer washcoat of thin shellac or lacquer sealer is applied. At least twice as much thinner (alcohol for shellac, lacquer thinner for lacquer sealer) should be mixed with the finish material.

87

The purpose of the washcoat is twofold:

1. To provide a base for the stain; otherwise the stain will sink in more rapidly in some places than others causing a blotchy appearance.
2. To provide a casing around the filler. This prevents the oil in the filler from soaking into the wood too rapidly, which causes the filler to shrink away from the sides of pore, and causes many problems in subsequent finishing operations.

Stain, along with filler and glaze, add the most color to wood products. Stains used in furniture manufacturing are usually applied with a spray gun. Refer to Fig. 2-8, *Step 5*.

On most traditional furniture the filler is colored darker than the stain. Filler should be thinned with naptha, mineral spirits, or turpentine to about the consistency of coffee cream. Use a brush or air hose to get rid of all dust particles before filling. Brush the filler into the

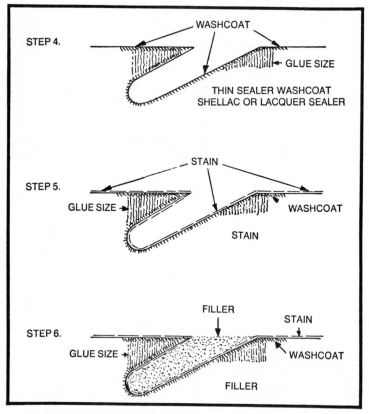

Fig. 2-8. Continued process of wood finishing for open-grained wood.

pores with the grain of the wood. Work the filler thoroughly into the grain or pores. When the filler starts to appear dull in appearance (about five minutes) rub the surface in all directions with the lower part of the palm of the hand. This further packs the filler into the pores. Use old rags or burlap to follow up the hand process. Rub back and forth across the grain to eliminate the possibility of removing the filler from the grain. Follow the rags with a clean cloth to remove the remaining filler and oil. With a rag over a sharpened stick, remove excess filler from carvings, moldings or other recesses. Allow filler to dry over night. Refer to Fig. 2-8, *Step 6* for the correct application of filler material.

Two thin coats of lacquer sealer or shellac (Fig. 2-9, *Step 7*) are applied over the filler. Lacquer sealer is best applied with a spray gun. Sand lightly with 8/0-280 or 9/0-320 abrasive paper. Use very fine steel wool on carvings and turnings. Shellac will have to be sanded a little more than lacquer sealer. Two coats of lacquer sealer actually merge into one coat, while shellac stays as two separate coats. Sand only enough to remove embedded dust particles and any runs or streaks in the finish. Add a small amount of color to these coats of sealer to add depth to the finish. The tint is barely visible but the overall effect is one of depth.

Glaze on traditional furniture does more to enhance the finish than any other process. Refer to Fig. 2-9, *Step 8* for the glazing process.

Apply one coat of shellac or lacquer sealer. This coat must be applied with a spray gun or aerosol can. Add a trace of color if a spray gun is used. If a spray is not used the glaze will smear as it is brushed. When the coat is dry sand with 9/0-320 sandpaper abrasive or rub with fine steel wool. Be careful not to sand through the sealer into the glaze. Fig. 2-9, *Step 9* illustrates this process.

Varnish or lacquer coats are applied next as in Fig. 2-10, *Step 10. Never* apply lacquer over varnish. Varnish coats are thicker than lacquer coats, but lacquer coats are harder and require less time for drying. Furniture manufacturers sometimes heat the lacquer so that it can be applied in heavier coats. Lacquer requires little sanding as all coats merge into one. Do not add any color to the last coat. If a flat or dull finish is desired, do not apply the flat varnish or lacquer until the last coat, as it does not have the body of gloss varnish or lacquer.

A straight-line sander used with Wet-or-Dry paper and a liquid works best to obtain a perfectly flat surface. Mineral spirits or water can be used as the liquid.

If a high gloss is wanted, use rottenstone or rubbing compound. If a flat finish is wanted, use coarse pumice stone or steel wool.

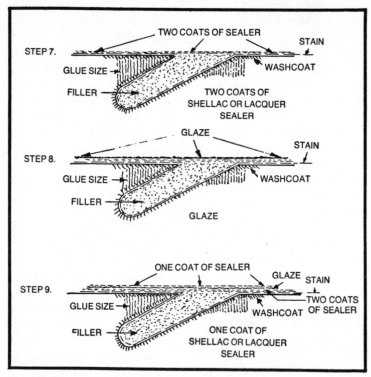

Fig. 2-9. The text should be studied carefully in relation to this illustration depicting the finishing process.

Waxing, Fig. 2-10, *Step 11*, is the final step although sometimes wax is omitted on flat finishes. For gloss finishes, use a good grade of wax. Waxes with a high percentage of parafin should be avoided. In a completely coordinated and matched system the colors should be consistent and compatible in all coats. This also holds true for wax. Some of the waxes used in the furniture industry look a little like shoe polish.

Buff the wax until a smooth and even polish is attained.

How To Apply Finish to Close-Grain Woods

On traditional furniture, follow the same steps as in "Applying Finish to Open-Grain Woods," except the filler will be omitted.

How To Apply Finish to Open Grain
Modern/Contemporary Projects

The process will be the same as already discussed except no color will be added to the filler. Little, if any, stain will be applied. No

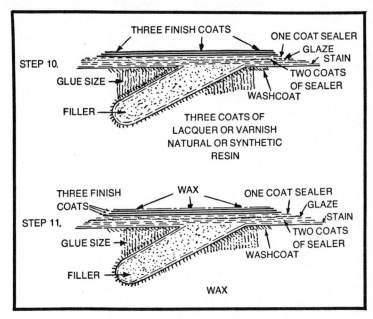

Fig. 2-10. The final steps in quality finishing involve three finish coats and wax.

glaze will be applied, and no color will be added to transparent finished or wax.

How To Apply Finish to
Close-Grain Modern/Contemporary Projects

Little, if any, stain will be applied. No filler or glaze will be applied, and no color added to transparent finishes and wax.

For the home craftsman who does not own spray equipment, the newer synthetic resin finishes should provide a very fine finish.

How To Decorate

There are times when a craftsman wants to add a special touch to his finished product. The ideas listed below range from applying a gold-leafed leather edge to wood burning for novelty effects and lettering.

Gold Leaf on Leather. Many small pieces of traditional furniture, particularly tabletops, are covered with leather whose edges are embossed with designs in gold leaf. The device for embossing is portable and heats an embossed wheel. Gold leaf from a reel is played over the hot wheel and with considerable force is pressed into the leather.

The amateur should spend a substantial amount of time practicing before attempting this process on a project. The corners on square and rectangular pieces of leather cause the most trouble.

The operator should carefully read the instructions that come with the device.

Marquetry and Inlay Work. Often two pieces of contrasting woods are fastened together and the design is laid out on the top piece. A very fine fret saw or jeweler's saw is used to cut the two pieces after a small hole is drilled in one corner for the insertion of the blade. After the sawing, the dark and light pieces are interchanged.

Inlays of different designs can be purchased with the contrasting pieces of different colored woods assembled and glued to a piece of paper. These inlays are usually inserted into a veneered surface. A fine, sharp line is scribed around the inlay on the veneer surface. The veneer is removed within the scribed line with a sharp chisel. Glue is applied to the face (not to the papered side) of the inlay and placed in the recess with the paper side up. A wood pad is placed over the inlay and clamped or covered with a heavy weight until the glue is dry. The weight or clamp is removed and the paper and inlay are sanded down until they are flush with the surface.

Carvings. Carvings are used to enhance the surface of small projects. A simple, but attractive carving on such things as letter opener handles and small jewel boxes can be done with one chisel—the V-shaped veining tool.

Machine carving of recessed letters on outdoor signs and door plates may be done speedily and efficiently with a V-shaped or round-point router bit in a power electric router.

Wood Burning. Wood burning works best on light colored woods. A burning tool has an electric heating element in the handle. It is used a great deal for novelty effects and lettering.

Decals. Decals in many shapes and sizes are available. Decals are applied after some basic finishes have been applied to the project. Instruction for applying decals should be carefully followed.

HOW TO APPLY FURNITURE HARDWARE

Catches, hinges, rollers, glides, etc., are all included in the general term, hardware. The following pages describe each and instruct the home craftsman in their proper application.

Casters

Casters are made of wood, rubber, glass, metal and other suitable materials.

Socket Casters. Socket casters require holes in furniture legs. The socket is driven into a 3/8 in. hole and grips the neck (top) of the caster shank. Teeth on the socket are driven into the wood.

Ball Casters. The rolling member is an offset ball. Ball casters are usually of the socket type. This easy riding caster comes in sizes up to two inches in diameter.

Plate Casters. Plate casters are fastened to the furniture with four screws. They can be safely used on heavy furniture including pianos. They are available in sizes up to four inches in diameter for the wheels with a 1 5/8 in. tread and plate size 3 3/4 in. by 4 5/8 in.

Rubber Cushion Glides

The rubber cushion glide has a nail-like projection and is driven in with a hammer. No metal-to-metal contact is made between the base of the caster and the furniture leg. Sizes are 15/16 in. and 1 1/4 in.

Steel Glides

Steel glides are equipped with three prongs which are driven into the wood with a hammer. Steel glides are used on lighter pieces of furniture such as chairs, tables, chests, and foot stools.

Catches

Catches are both decorative and useful. They are used on cabinets, doors, furniture pieces, chests, tool boxes, trunks, etc.

Elbow Catches. The elbow is a spring-loaded catch used frequently on cupboard doors to hold the two doors. They are attached flush on the back of the doors with screws.

Friction Catches. The *ball-friction catch* is sometimes called the bullet catch. The ball is fitted into a spring-loaded socket that looks like a bullet. When the door is closed the ball fits into a stamped brass recess that holds the door closed. They are available in sizes of 1/4 in., 5/16 in. and 3/8 in. Holes must be bored into which the ball and socket are driven. The stamped brass receptacle is fastened with a small brass screw or escutcheon pin. The ball and socket are fitted into the edge of the door.

The *wedge-friction catch* is made of tempered spring steel. One part is wedge shaped and the other part has two grippers that hold the wedge when closed. Four small screws hold the two parts. The gripper part is fastened to the lower part of a shelf and the wedge to the door.

Cupboard Catch. The cupboard catch is a surface catch attached to the outside of doors and door jambs. It is of two parts; one part is spring-loaded and the other part is a receptacle into which the latch fits. The knob/latch is fastened onto the door with four screws. The receptacle requires only two.

Magnetic Catch. There are two types of magnetic catches. The *knob-side catch* is used on the knob side of the door. The magnet is enclosed in a metal casing with a lip on either side. Each lip has an elongated screw hole for easy adjustment. The other part of the catch is a simple flat piece of steel with a countersunk screw hole and two smaller holes for escutcheon pins. Ovalhead brass screws are used on both parts.

The magnetic part is installed on a shelf and the plate on the inside of the door.

The catch has up to ten pounds holding power.

The *magnetic hinge* is not really a catch but it acts as both hinge and a catch. This cabinet-type hinge, for flush or lipped doors, has a strong magnet installed near the hinge pin. The magnetic hinge is a much more efficient type as it pulls the door in an arc of approximately 30 degrees while the knob-side magnetic door catch does not operate until the door is nearly closed.

Box Catch. The box catch is a surface catch used on chests, tool boxes and trunks. One part of the catch has a spring-loaded rectangular or oval-shaped loop which fits over a knob or rectangular keyhole receptacle on the other part. Three ovalhead screws hold one part and two screws hold the other.

Dull Black Wrought Iron Catch. This is a simple surface catch that looks like the letter "H" when the latch is in place. The latch is attached to the right vertical member and is free swinging around a rivet-like pin. A small, round knob is in the center of the latch. The left vertical member has a receptacle into which the latch enters when the door is closed. Each vertical member is three inches long and two special screws which imitate handmade nails are used to install each member to the project.

Dull black wrought iron hardware is used extensively on Early American and Colonial furniture.

Hinges

Hinges are found on most of the same places as catches. The variety of hinges is extensive, each serving a particular need. If it is necessary for a hinge to be placed on the outside of a finished piece, decorative varieties are available.

Butt Hinges. There are two types of butt hinges. The *loose pin hinge* is used only in a vertical position. It is easy to, inadvertently, install this hinge upside down which allows the pin to fall out.

The *stationary pin hinge* is used on all types of doors.

How To Install Butt Hinges. Mark the position of hinges in relation to the top and bottom face of the door. Extend the mark across the edge of the door with a try square and chisel-edge, hard lead pencil.

Place the door into the position it will assume when hung, and mark the position on the door frame or jamb where the stationary part of the hinge will be located. Extend these lines across the edge of the jamb or frame with a try square and pencil.

Set a marking gauge for the thickness of the hinge and scribe a line between the hinge marks on the face of the door.

Measure the distance of one leaf from the edge to the pin and set the marking gauge. Scribe lines on the edge of the door between these hinge marks.

Secure the door in a vise or clamp in an upright position and chisel a gain for the hinge.

Lay the hinge in the gain and with a scratch awl, mark the screw holes.

Drill pilot holes for screws and attach the hinge with flat-head screws.

Hold the door in its final position and mark screw holes for the stationary part of the hinge.

Drill screw holes and attach the door to the frame or jamb with flat-head screws. It will be much easier if the hinge is of the loose pin type.

Surface Hinges. Surface hinges are attached to the outside of a door and door frame. Semi-surface or half surface hinges expose only one-half of the hinge. It is best to attach the hinge with only one screw in each leaf until the hinge is adjusted so that the door swings freely.

Regular Chest Hinge. The regular chest hinge has one straight leaf and one L-shaped leaf for attaching lids to chests.

Combination Chest Hinge. This is a very fine hinge for any chest-like container. This patented hinge is not only a hinge but it also holds the lid in an upright position. There is a left and right hinge for each chest.

To install the hinge determine which is the back of chest.

Clamp the hinge to the back inside corner so that the top of the hinge aligns with the top edge of the back and end of the chest. A piece of scrap wood laid across the corner will help in aligning the hinge.

Mark the screw holes with a pencil. Unclamp the hinge and drill pilot holes for the screws.

Attach the hinge with screws.

Line up the chest lid in a closed position. Hold the back edge down and raise the front edge far enough to mark the screw holes on the other part of the hinge. You may need some help with this operation.

Drill one hole for each hinge and attach the hinge to the top. Try the lid for correct position. If no further adjustments have to be made, drill the other holes and drive the screws in.

Continuous Hinge. The continuous hinge is similar to the piano hinge. It is 48 in. long but with care can be cut into shorter lengths. Available in bright brass plate or bright nickel plate, the hinges are 1 1/16 in. wide.

Invisible Hinge. The invisible hinge has a four-leaf hinge mechanism attached to two 1/2 in. diameter posts which are set into bored holes. When the door or lid is closed the hinge is invisible. Four small screws hold the posts in position.

Drop Leaf Table Hinge. This patented hinge permits the leaf to butt closely to the table top in the up position, and butts closely to the underside of the top when in the down position.

Rule Joint Hinge. A common hinge used on commercial drop leaf tables, the top and the leaf are shaped with matched cove and convex blades either with a shaper or a power router.

Regular Hasp

The regular hasp or *box hasp* is made up of two parts. The upper part, which is attached to the top or lid, is hinged in the middle. The movable part of the hinge has a slot cut in it which fits over a half-round staple attached to the lower part. When closed a padlock may be attached to the lower part.

Safety Hasp

The safety hasp is similar to the regular hasp except all screws are covered when the chest or box is locked. The staple has some freedom of movement to compensate for shrinkage and swelling.

Mending Plates

Mending plates are used for repair and reinforcement. The four common mending plates are: flat plate, flat corner, bent corner or angle and "T" plates.

Knobs

Knobs are made of wood, metal, glass, porcelain, plastic and other materials.

Knobs are usually shaped in squares, round and balls.

Chapter 3

Designing, Constructing, Distressing, and Finishing Early American Projects

DESIGNING, CONSTRUCTING, DISTRESSING
AND FINISHING EARLY AMERICAN PROJECTS

Early American projects require some skills and decisions that even the experienced woodworker may never have encountered. Decisions start as early as the proper selection of a project for the craftsman's particular abilities, facilities, and supply of appropriate tools.

The last decisions made by the weekend woodworker involve the proper methods for finishing his carefully constructed project.

This chapter will help the woodworker with the important decisions necessary to complete a beautifully designed wood project. Appropriate instructions are given for selection, design, construction, and finishes for all the Early American projects listed in this book.

GENERAL CONSTRUCTION PROCEDURE

The following pages instruct the home craftsman in general construction procedures ranging from designing patterns for curved portions of Early American furniture, through gluing up stock, to sizing and construction of accurate joints.

How To Select a Project

If this is your first weekend project, it might be advisable to select a project of simple design involving a minimum of operations.

If you have had considerable woodworking experience, you might try your hand at designing your own project following the principles set forth in Chapter 2, "How To Design Early American Pine Projects."

How To Develop Full-Size Patterns for Curved Portions

Mark off 1/2 in. or 1 in. squares on heavy paper. Place a pencil dot on the pattern wherever a curve crosses a marked-off square. It will be necessary to estimate the distance if the curve does not fall on the intersections of the lines that make the square. Continue until all points are established on the pattern.

With a well-sharpened piece of chalk, connect all points. This process will indicate which points are not exactly where they should be. The chalk marks can be removed with ease if it is thought desirable to alter the design. Another advantage of chalk is that free flowing curves are easier to make with chalk than with a pencil. After a satisfactory pattern is established with the chalk, draw in the design with a soft black drawing pencil or with a black felt tip pen.

If the pattern is symmetrical on both sides of the centerline, it is necessary to develop only half of the pattern. Do this on a folded piece of paper with the centerline on the fold. After the pattern is cut in the folded position, the pattern then opens into a full-size pattern. See Fig. 3-1.

Rough Cut Stock

Saw out all pieces "in the rough." This means that some excess is allowed for working to exact size by planing, sanding or by using other tools. Generally, *rip* (cutting with the grain) *sawing* is done before *crosscut* (cutting across the grain) *sawing*. By using the *fine cut*, a combination of blades or planer blades on a motorized universal saw or radial saw, stock can be cut to finished size. Very little sanding will be necessary.

Gluing Up Stock

Sometimes it is necessary to glue up stock to provide boards of sufficient width. At other times it may be necessary to cut wide boards into narrow pieces and then glue to eliminate or prevent warping. The most important guiding principle is to *line up the annular rings on adjacent pieces so they face in opposite directions*. See Fig. 3-2.

After arranging and fitting adjoining boards, mark them so they may be assembled and glued correctly.

Bar clamps are used for clamping. Alternate clamps from one side to the other, making sure that the wood is in contact with the bar of the clamp. See Fig. 3-3.

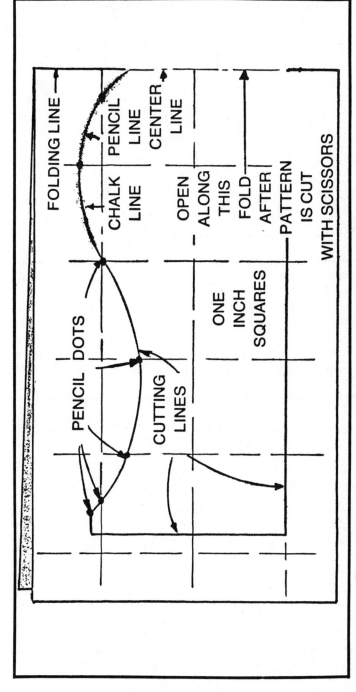

Fig. 3-1. A demonstration of the development of a symmetrically curved pattern. Scale: full size.

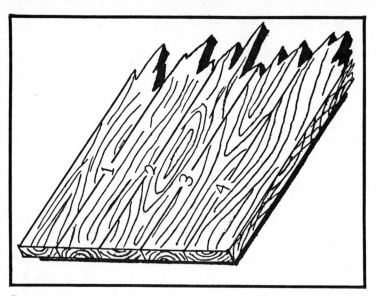

Fig. 3-2. Gluing up stock. Note the line of the annular rings of adjacent pieces.

Occasionally it is possible to purchase pine in widths up to 28 inches. In that event, the craftsman may not want to cut the board for gluing. It will be necessary, however, to relieve internal stress so the board will not warp after the project is assembled. This is accomplished by cutting *saw kerfs* in the board, with the grain, about

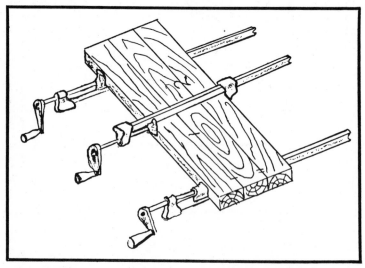

Fig. 3-3. Proper clamping procedures when gluing up stock.

two-thirds through the board. *Wedges* are glued and inserted in the ends to cover the saw kerfs. When the glue is dry, the excess is cut off and the ends sanded flush. Figure 3-4 offers a demonstration of saw kerfs and wedges.

Cut to Size and Make the Necessary Joints

The three most common joints in making Early American Pine Projects:

1. The *dado joint* is a simple and strong joint made *across* the grain. A dado joint is demonstrated in the grain. See Fig. 3-5.
2. The *groove joint* is similar to the dado joint except that it runs *with* the grain as in Fig. 3-6.
3. The *rabbet joint* is usually a *corner* joint. See Fig. 3-7.

The most efficient way to cut these joints is with a motorized circular saw (or radial saw) with the accompanying dado heads and blades. Other tools used are hand and motorized routers, power planes, and hand-rabbet planes.

Cut Curved Pieces

Outside curves may be cut with a hand coping saw, motorized jigsaw, band saw or saber saw.

The band saw is, by far, the fastest, easiest and most accurate method of cutting outside curves. However, it does have certain limitations. For instance, in cutting small radius curves it is neces-

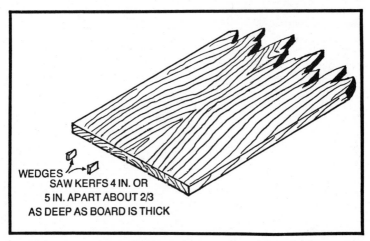

WEDGES
SAW KERFS 4 IN. OR
5 IN. APART ABOUT 2/3
AS DEEP AS BOARD IS THICK

Fig. 3-4. To prevent wide boards from warping, saw kerfs are cut and wedges inserted.

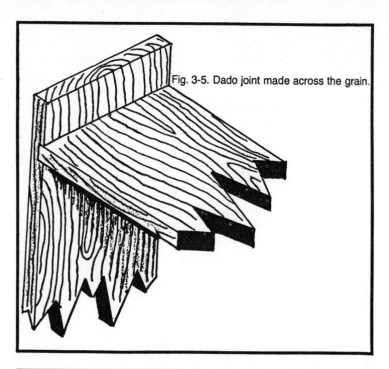

Fig. 3-5. Dado joint made across the grain.

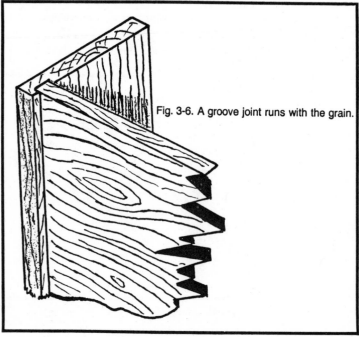

Fig. 3-6. A groove joint runs with the grain.

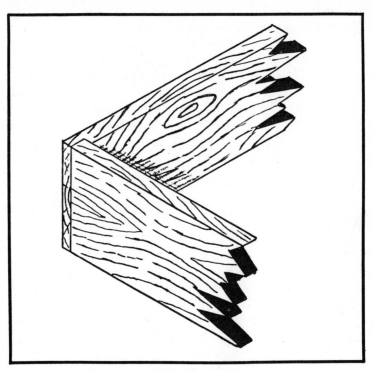

Fig. 3-7. The rabbet joint is usually a corner joint.

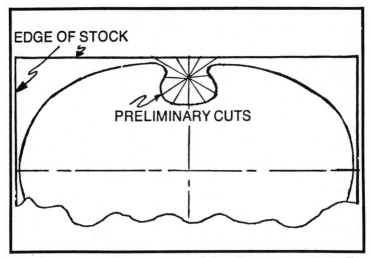

EDGE OF STOCK

PRELIMINARY CUTS

Fig. 3-8. Preliminary cuts are a necessity before the use of a band saw. The drawing above represents the curves needed to make the hearthstool of Chapter 4. Scale: one-quarter actual size. Note: Of course, these procedures follow for any curved piece.

sary to make preliminary cuts to prevent the blade from binding. Figure 3-8 describes these preliminary cuts.

Inside curves may be cut with a coping saw, motorized jigsaw, compass saw, keyhole saw or motorized saber saw.

All inside curves are started by drilling or boring one or more holes in which to insert the blade of the saw. When using the coping saw or motorized jigsaw, the blade must be detached from the saw, inserted in the hole, and reattached to the saw. See Fig. 3-9 relative to the cutting of inside curves with a keyhole or compass saw.

Glue and Assemble

All of the Early American Pine Projects in this package can be glued and assembled with white glue (e.g. Elmer's) and brads, nails or small screws.

If it is necessary to nail close to the end or edge of the stock, it is best that holes be drilled by using the same size brad as a drill bit in a hand drill or portable motorized hand drill.

Of course, brads, nails and screws should be avoided if at all possible. See Fig. 3-10 for drilling holes for brads and nails.

Fig. 3-9. Using a keyhole or compass saw to cut inside curves.

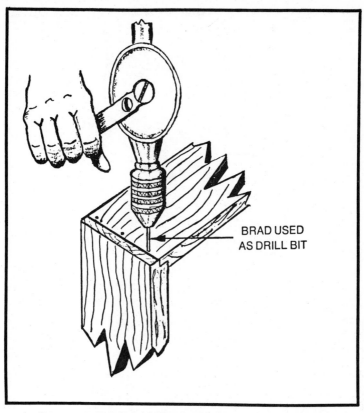

Fig. 3-10. Drilling holes for brads and nails using a hand drill.

HOW TO TURN RECESSED KNOBS IN SPICE DRAWER FRONTS

Although the directions given below deal specifically with knobs for a spice cabinet, they may apply to any construction where recessed knobs are required.

Determine Size of Knob and Width of Recessed Portion

A convenient size for spice drawer fronts is 1/2 in. ×2 3/4 in. ×4 in. For this size drawer, the knob diameter should be 3/4 in. across and the diameter of the recessed portion approximately 2 in. See Fig. 3-11 for the knob size.

Lay out a Cross Section of the Drawer Front Through Center of Drawer

The depth of the recess should be 5/16 in. See Section A—A' in Fig. 3-12.

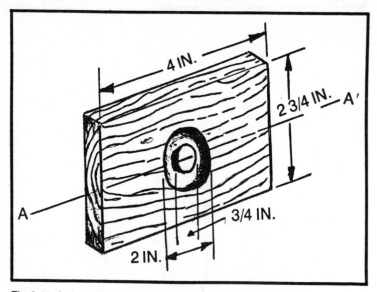

Fig. 3-11. A sketch of the sizing of recessed knobs of the spice-drawer cabinet discussed in Chapter 4. Scale: approximately one-half actual size.

Grind Special Chisel From Old Flat Mill File

Make certain that the clearance is in the underside of the chisel and that the width of the point is not over three-quarters as wide as the recessed portion. Figure 3-13 shows this special chisel.

Make Faceplate Jig for Turning

Turn a 6 in. diameter piece of stock on the faceplate about 1 in. thick. Lay out and cut on a band saw or jigsaw the special chuck or fig to hold spice drawer front. Fasten this with countersunk flat-head screws to the 1 in. turned piece. Be sure the recessed chuck is centered. Insert two small sharpened brads in the bottom of the recess to keep the drawer front from shifting in the chuck. See Fig. 3-14.

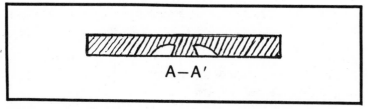

A—A'

Fig. 3-12. A cross section of the drawer front for the spice cabinet referenced in Fig. 3-11. Scale: approximately one-half actual size.

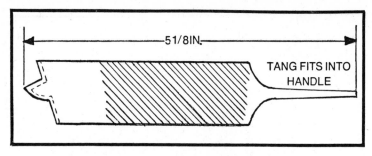

Fig. 3-13. A special chisel for the spice cabinet drawers.

Make Marking Tool

The tool shown in Fig. 3-15 will mark a recess 2 in. in diameter and a knob 3/4 in. in diameter. The spurs are made by driving small brads into the handle and sharpening the heads to a point with file.

Mark Drawer Front Recess

Place the drawer-front blank in the recess in the faceplate jig. Strike firmly with your fist or a soft mallet so that the sharp brads will penetrate into the blank. In this position, the blank will not fly out of the lathe or shift around in the jig, and the exact center will be maintained.

Turn on the lathe and place the tool rest about 1/2 in. from the blank. With the piece turning, the exact center will be easily observed. Place the marking tool on the tool rest with the center pin about 1/8 in. from the turning blank. The two other pins will then be to the *left* of center.

Push the marking tool toward the blank until the center pin penetrates the center of the blank and the other two pins scribe circles on the blank. These circles define the recessed portion.

Cut Recessed Portion

With the lathe still running, insert the special chisel into the space on the blank between the two scribed circles and move the chisel slowly back and forth until the scribed circles are reached. See Fig. 3-16.

Sand and Remove

Sand the recess with coarse sandpaper (garnet #1 or similar) and finish with #2-0 or #3-0.

Remove the drawer front from the faceplate jig by using the cut out portions for finger insertion and easy pull out.

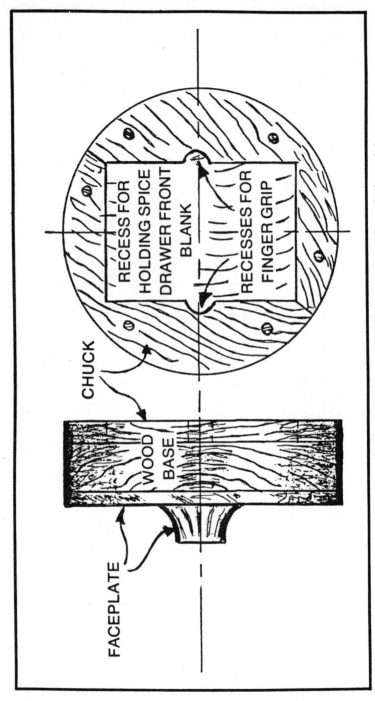

RECESS FOR HOLDING SPICE DRAWER FRONT BLANK

RECESSES FOR FINGER GRIP

CHUCK

WOOD BASE

FACEPLATE

Fig. 3-14. A faceplate jig for turning recessed knobs. Scale: approximately one-half actual size.

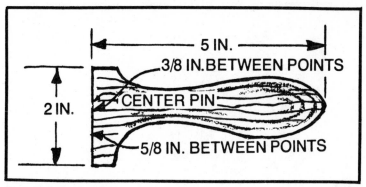

Fig. 3-15. A marking tool to locate the recess diameter and knob diameter. Scale: one-half actual size.

At least two dozen spice-drawer fronts can be recessed in one hour.

STEP-BY-STEP PROCEDURE

The following uses the same example, a spice cabinet, to instruct the woodworker on proper wood turning procedures for constructing recessed knobs. However, the following step-by-step guide is detailed and illustrated to aid the craftsman in a thorough understanding of this specialized skill.

Turn Base for Chuck or Jig

Cut a circular blank of wood. It should be a little thicker and larger than 1 in. thick and 6 in. diameter. Fasten the base securely to the faceplate with flat-head screws. Turn the base to the required size (1 in. × 6 in. diameter). Check with a straightedge to make sure that the surfaces are perfectly flat—particularly the surface away from the faceplate. See Fig. 3-20.

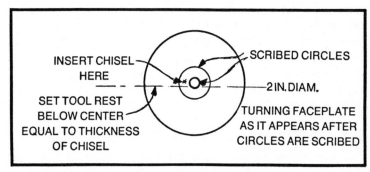

Fig. 3-16. Cutting the recessed portion.

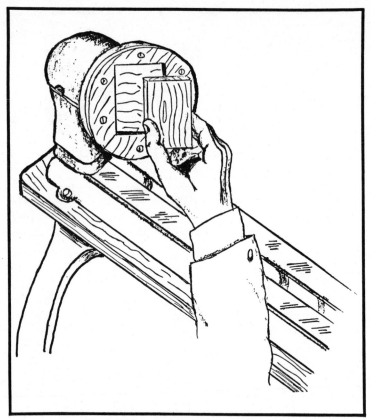

Fig. 3-17. Inserting the blank into the chuck.

Make and Fasten Chuck (or Jig) to Base

Cut two semicircles of 1/2 in. stock about 6 1/4 in. in diameter. Along the radius, cut out one-half of a rectangle (2 3/4 in. ×4 in.) in each semicircular segment. At the same time, cut recesses for finger grips. Before fastening the chuck (or jig) to the base, drive two small brads into the base in the location where the drawer-front blank will come in contact with it. Leave the brad extending about 1/8 in. Sharpen brad heads to a sharp point with a file. Fasten the chuck segments to the base with flat-head screws. Do not glue. Later it might be necessary to replace the segments. Check the chuck rectangle to see if it is properly centered. See Fig. 3-21.

Insert Blank Drawer Front Into Chuck (or Jig)

With the lathe turned off, insert a 1/2 in. thick blank drawer front into the chuck. **Caution:** Never attempt to insert a drawer blank when the lathe is running. Drive the blank onto the sharpened brad points until the blank is flush with the chuck. Use your fist or wooden or rubber mallet for this purpose. See Fig. 3-17 for a demonstration of inserting the blank.

Mark Lines for Recessed Knob

With the marking tool of Fig. 3-15, scribe the lines for the recessed knob while the lathe is running. Be sure to take a close look at Figure 3-18 which illustrates the marking process.

Turn Recessed Knob with Special Chisel

Study Fig. 3-19 carefully to judge turning the recessed knob with the special chisel. The chisel was described earlier and shown in Fig. 3-13.

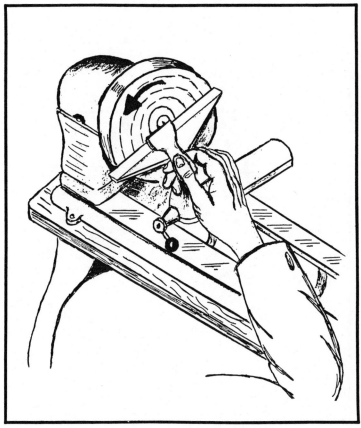

Fig. 3-18. Marking lines for the recessed knobs.

Fig. 3-19. Turning the recessed knob with a special chisel.

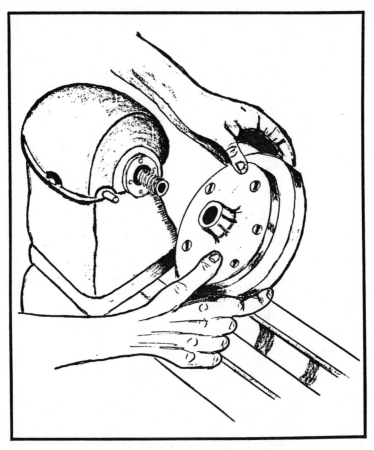

Fig. 3-20. Turning the base for the chuck or jig.

Sand Recessed Knob and Remove From Chuck

Sand the recessed portion with a folded piece of sandpaper. Sand first with coarse paper (#1) and follow with #2-0 or #3-0. The lathe must be turned off before the drawer front is removed from the chuck. See Fig. 3-22.

HOW TO PREPARE EARLY AMERICAN PROJECTS FOR FINISHING

Several steps must precede the actual application of finishing materials to any wood project. The following suggestions prepare the surface sufficiently to receive a fine finish.

Remove Excess Glue

After the project has been assembled and all glue is thoroughly dry, use a *sharp chisel* to remove any excess glue.

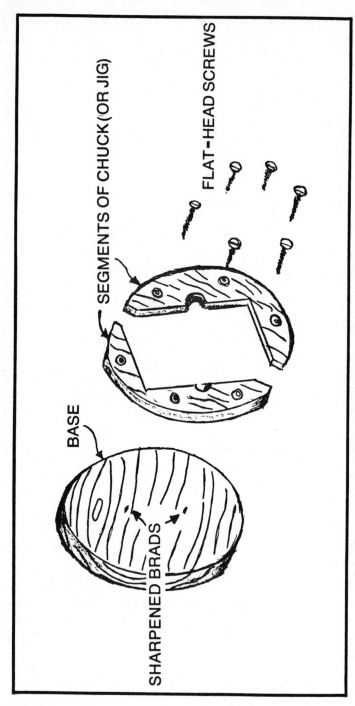

Fig. 3-21. Making a faceplate jig for turning. This is an exploded view of the base, chuck segments, and screws.

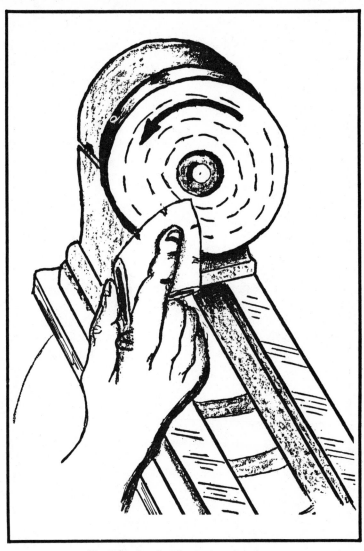

Fig. 3-22. Sanding the recessed portions.

Check Rolled Edges

Quite often pine projects have rolled edges to simulate wear and age. Another reason is that sharp edges and corners will roll very soon anyway due to the softness of the wood. By rolling the edges first, they are then protected when the finish is applied. This rolling can be done by using a *wood rasp* followed by coarse sandpaper 1 1/2–40, then by 1/2–60, and then to 2/0–100.

Sand

Sand only with the grain. Use 2/0–100 sandpaper, preferably garnet.

Glue Sizing

Mix one part (by volume) of animal glue with nine to thirteen parts (by volume) of warm water not over 140°F.

Apply the glue sizing to the entire project with a sponge, roller, rag, or other method. Dampen only, do not flood the surface. Wipe up any excess moisture that stands in pools. Let the project dry in a warm room overnight.

Applying hot water to a wood surface swells the defects above the surface of the wood. These defects are eliminated with subsequent sanding.

Finish Sand

Sand the entire project with 6/0–220 sandpaper. This sanding will remove the minute, stiff wood fibers that have raised and will prepare the wood for the finishing process. Dust off with a brush or air hose any dust left as the result of the sanding process. Cover the project with paper, plastic or cloth until the finishing process is started.

ABRASIVES

Abrasives were discussed in some detail in Chapter 2. The succeeding pages explain quality abrasives even further and detail their proper use and appropriate application to pine projects.

There are two large categories of abrasives, natural and manufactured.

Natural abrasives are *flint, garnet* and *emery*. *Flint sandpaper* is cream in color, and is of poor quality and durability. *Garnet sandpaper* is red in color. It is of good qulaity and long lasting. Garnet sandpaper is the best for the homecraftsman. *Emery paper* and *cloth* are grayish black. They are used almost exclusively on metal.

Manufactured abrasives are aluminum oxide and silicone carbide. Both are high quality and can be used on metal and wood finishes.

Paper Backing of Abrasives

Paper backing varies from 40 lb paper to 130 lb paper. The lighter weights are used for hand sanding. The heavier weights are

118

used on rolls, belts, sanding discs, and other sanding machines and devices. Only the coarser grits are used with the heavier backs.

Cloth Backing of Abrasives

Cloth backing is used for machine sanding operations where flexibility is essential (e.g. belt sanding of moldings).

Type	Old System	New System
Very Coarse	2	36
	1 1/2	40
	1	50
Coarse	1/2	60
	0	80
	2/0	100
	3/0	120
	4/0	150
Fine	5/0	180
	6/0	220
	7/0	240
	8/0	280
Very Fine	9/0	320
	10/0	400

Grit Size

The numbers in the new system indicate the number of holes per square inch of screen used to sort the grains of abrasives into individual sizes. In the new system the larger the number the finer the sandpaper. In the old system the grain size became smaller as the number of 0's increased.

Things To Remember When Using Sandpaper

1. Never use sandpaper as a substitute for cutting tools.
2. Never sand a joint or surface to be glued.
3. Never sand at right angles to the grain of the wood.
4. Be sure that all cutting and machining operations are done before sanding is started.
5. Use sandpaper with a sanding block on all flat surfaces.
6. Be sure to sand out all pencil marks.
7. Use fingers or palm of the hand on irregular surfaces.
8. In general, use coarser sandpaper on hardwoods than on softwoods.

9. Start sanding with coarse and end up sanding with fine sandpaper.
10. Tear sheet sandpaper over a sharp corner or over the cutting edge of a worn out hand saw.

HOW TO "DISTRESS"
EARLY AMERICAN PINE PROJECTS

"Distressing" is the process of imparting aging or worn characteristics to wood artificially. Glazing contributes to this process by emphasizing the natural accumulation of dust in corners and recesses. Distressing is accomplished by different methods, a few of which are described below.

Rolled (Worn) Edges

The edges and corners of pine projects will naturally become worn, particularly if the piece is handled to any great extent, because of the soft nature of the wood. This is simulated by rounding over the edge where the hand would normally come in contact with the piece.

In order to accomplish this simulation, roll the edge with a rasp, coarse file, coarse sandpaper, or cylindrical power sander in a lathe or drill press. Follow up with succeeding grades of fine sandpaper until no sanding marks are discernible.

Worm Holes

Punch small holes with an ice pick and scratch artificial worm holes not more than 3/8 in. long. Sand with fine sandpaper to remove raised fibers. **Note:** This process can easily be overdone. It is best to be on the conservative side. Do not follow a definite or symmetrical pattern.

Bruises, Nicks and Dents

Perhaps the best device for accomplishing this process is a lash made of several short lengths of chain with a few pieces of different shaped metal (ball bearings, nuts, bolts, screws, scrap metal, etc.) welded to the end of some of the pieces of chain. This chain will cause bruises and dents and the pieces of metal will cause deeper nicks. Due to the fact that the chains fall haphazardly, a stereotyped pattern will be prevented.
Note: Again, do not carry this to the extreme.

Fly Specks

Place a small amount of thick, dark brown or black enamel, lacquer, or paint in a shallow dish or can cover. Pick up a small amount of this paint on the bristles or a stiff bristled tooth brush. Hold the brush near the project and rub a piece of sheet metal over the bristles. Small specks of paint will be deposited on the project. **Note:** Experiment on scrap stock until the desired pattern is óbtained. Apply specks before the last finish coat.

Imitation Knots

Very realistic knots may be burned into pine with a burning pencil.

HOW TO FINISH EARLY AMERICAN PINE PROJECTS

The following suggestions for finishing products are especially suitable for Early American pine pieces. They supply the final touch to the furniture to make each piece a beautiful addition to any room.

Stain

Apply a very thin coat of *walnut stain* from a spray can. The stain should discolor the wood only slightly. With time, pine will naturally turn to a rich orange-red or an orange-brown. Allow the stain to dry for at least two hours.

Seal

Spray on one coat of *cacquer sealer* or "Deft." Apply just enough to cover, otherwise runs will develop. *Sand* with 4/0–150 sandpaper. Apply a *second coat* of the sealer. (Each coat should dry at least two hours.) *Sand* again with the same grit sandpaper. All turnings, carvings, recesses and nonflat surfaces should be rubbed with 000 steel wool.

Glaze

Mix *burnt umber* (colors ground in oil) with *turpentine* or *mineral spirits* until it's about the consistency of coffee cream. Estimate the amount needed for the project. Apply the mixed glaze with a rather stiff brush to the entire exterior portion of the project. *Immediately* wipe off the glaze with rag. Do not apply very much pressure when wiping off the glaze. If a darker effect is desired leave the glaze on longer before wiping. **Note:** Do not attempt to remove the glaze around knobs, corners, carvings, and all recessed parts.

Blend

This is the most important and the most difficult operation in finishing Early American projects. Using a *soft brush* (*badger* or *fitch*), blend the heavy accumulation of glaze *away from* the recesses, knobs, carvings, etc. The shading should be *gradual* from dark to light. There should be no pronounced demarcation between the two. It would be wise to practice on scrap stock beforehand.

Finish

Apply one spray coat of lacquer sealer or "Deft." Allow this to dry three hours. *Sand* with 6/0–220 sandpaper and steel wool (000). Apply at least *three coats* of spray lacquer. Allow at least four hours between the first and second coats and overnight on the last coat. *Sand* each coat with 9/0–320 sandpaper or steel wool.

Wax

Apply *two coats* of *paste wax* and buff. If the glaze did not come out satisfactorily, a dark brown shoe polish can be applied to the darker portions before the finish coat of clear wax is applied. **Note:** Shellac and varnish (or polyurethane) may be substituted for the lacquer, sealer/lacquer system. All coats but the last may be brushed on. Brushing is apt to smear the glaze on the last coat. The shellac/varnish system usually takes much more time for drying between coats.

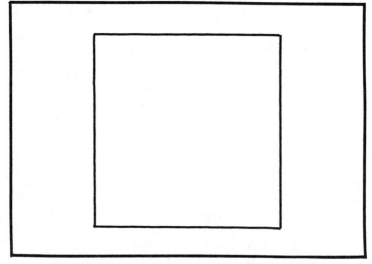

Fig. 3-23. The square is not a desirable rectangular shape.

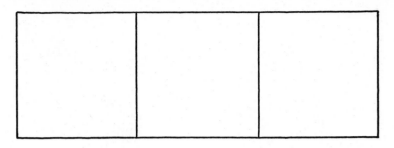

Fig. 3-24. Multiple squares are not pleasing to the eye and should be avoided when designing furniture.

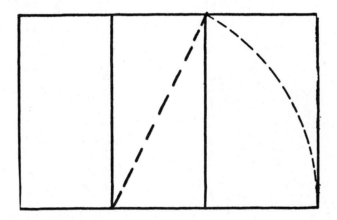

Fig. 3-25. The divine section or golden mean rectangle is the most satisfying of all the rectangular forms.

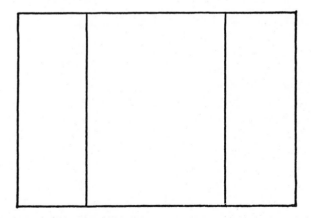

Fig. 3-26. Dividing a rectangle into odd sections.

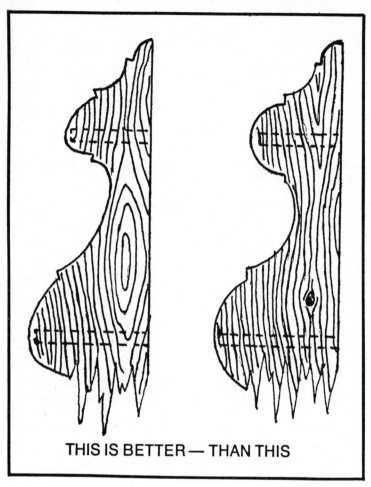

THIS IS BETTER — THAN THIS

Fig. 3-27. Changing radii for curves.

HOW TO DESIGN EARLY AMERICAN PINE FURNITURE

When a craftsman has mastered techniques described in this book and has constructed several pieces from Chapters 4 and 5, he may feel motivated to create his own designs. The remainder of this chapter is devoted to designing instruction to enable the home woodworker to create specialized products to suit his particular needs.

The Mirror Method for Symmetrical Designs

Almost all Early American projects are symmetrical in design—the two sides are identical. Due to their nature, all turned

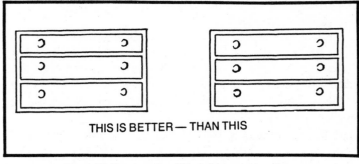

THIS IS BETTER — THAN THIS

Fig. 3-28. Drawers should be of progressive sizes.

projects (lamp bases, ashtrays, candle sticks, salt and pepper shakers and mills) will automatically be symmetrical. But even here the mirror method has its advantages.

The purpose of the mirror is to experiment visually on the relationship between the width, length and configuration of the object before commitment to the final design.

First, draw the outline of one side of the object on tracing paper.

Second, place the mirror upright (at right angles to the paper) beside the drawing on its vertical axis.

Third, move the mirror toward and away from the temporary, vertical center line until the right proportion is derived.

Fourth, when the right position has been established, draw a vertical line along the lower edge of the mirror extending the line

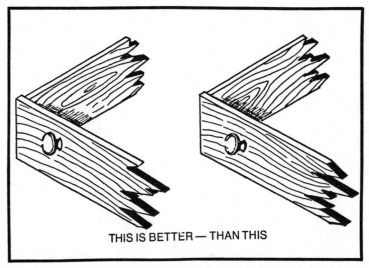

THIS IS BETTER — THAN THIS

Fig. 3-29. Drawer knobs are more balanced when slightly above the center.

125

through the ends of the drawing. This line will then be the permanent center line of the project.

Fifth, on this new center line fold the drawing over so that the original half is on the inside.

Sixth, on the reverse side of the original half drawing, trace the outline. The pencil graphite will be transferred to the inside, opposite the original half. When the paper is opened the drawing will be complete and symmetrical.

Some Miscellaneous Rules Relating to Traditional Design

The *square* is the least desirable rectangular shape. See Fig. 3-23.

Multiple squares, likewise, are not the most pleasing to the eye as shown in Fig. 3-24.

The most satisfying of all rectangular forms is called the *divine section* or the *golden mean rectangle*. The ratio of length to width is 1 to 1.618. It can be drawn geometrically by bisecting the square, then drawing a diagonal of half the square, and using the diagonal as a radius to swing an arc that will strike the base of the square extended. From this point complete the rectangle. See Fig. 3-25 for a divine section.

When dividing a rectangle into parts by using *vertical lines*, it is better to divide the *rectangle* into odd rather than an even number of

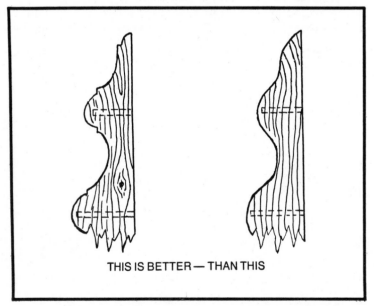

THIS IS BETTER — THAN THIS

Fig. 3-30. Abrupt curves are best separated by a break.

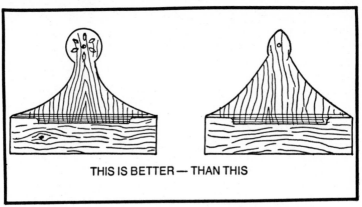

THIS IS BETTER — THAN THIS

Fig. 3-31. Curves should be parallel to the axis.

parts. The center section should usually be larger than the end sections. See Fig. 3-26.

Curves are more pleasing if the *radius* is ever changing rather than being a portion of a circle as in Fig. 3-27.

In dividing a *rectangle* by *horizontal lines* (shelves, chest of drawers, etc.) it is more desirable if the drawers or distance between shelves are progressively larger toward the bottom or base. See Fig. 3-28.

Drawer knobs or *handles* look more balanced if they are slightly above the center of the drawer as in Fig. 3-29.

Curves moving abruptly from one direction to another are best separated by a break. See Fig. 3-30.

Curves should end up parallel or at right angles to the axis of the project. See Fig. 3-31.

Chapter 4
Early American and Other
Traditional Projects

EARLY AMERICAN AND
OTHER TRADITIONAL PROJECTS

Although the projects listed in this chapter were specifically styled for Early American settings, they have found their way into many homes featuring other traditional decor. Specialty items to be placed on tables or hung on walls are included in this chapter, as well as furniture suitable for any room in the house.

Each project includes an introduction, a list of materials (in table form), step-by-step directions for accurate project completion, and figure references including scale drawings.

ASHTRAY

The ashtray shown in Fig. 4-1 and 4-2, although of Early American design, will fit into almost any decor. It is not only attractive because of its simplicity, but is practical as well.

Material:

One piece of 2 in. thick white pine at least 6 1/2 in. square.

Procedure:

1. *Mark cutting circle* by swinging a 6 1/2 in. circle on the stock with a compass. Make sure that the center mark is clearly defined.
2. *Saw* just *outside* the circle with a band saw or other curve-cutting tool (turning saw, saber saw, jigsaw, etc.).

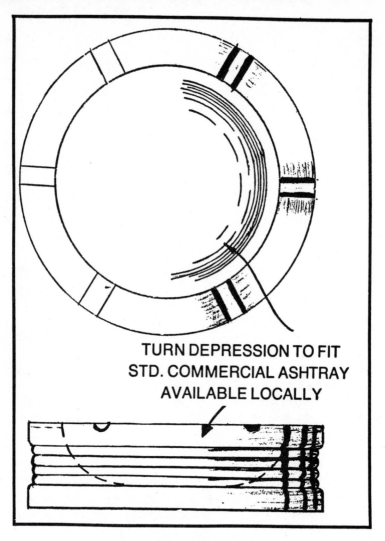

**TURN DEPRESSION TO FIT
STD. COMMERCIAL ASHTRAY
AVAILABLE LOCALLY**

Fig. 4-1. Early American ashtray.

3. *Attach faceplate to stock.* Make certain the center mark is aligned with the center hole of the faceplate. Attach faceplate to stock with short flat head bright (FHB) screws.
4. *Turn stock* to 1 3/4 in. thick by 6 3/8 in. diameter. Check the flatness of the face of the stock with a straightedge.
5. *Turn the ashtray depression.* The tool rest should be positioned at right angles to the bed of the lathe and about 1/4 in. from face of the stock. The tool rest should be

Fig. 4-2. Ashtray showing details of craftsmanship.

below the centerline of the face equal to the thickness of the turning tool.

Using the round-nose lathe tool turn the stock to the desired depth. Check from time to time to ascertain if proper progress is being made by comparing to a standard ashtray. **Warning:** When testing the size be sure the lathe is turned off.

6. *Mark grooves on the perimeter.* Turn the tool rest parallel with the lathe bed and about 1/4 in. from the perimeter and slightly below center. On a piece of scrap lumber about 1/8 in. thick and 3/4 in. wide mark the groove spacings with a sharp pencil. Hold the marking stick about 1/8 in. from the slow turning stock and with the sharp pencil mark groove spacings on the rotating stock. Small Vs cut with a sharp knife on the edge of the marking stick where the groove marks are located will help control the pencil point. *Never* use a scale, rule or other measuring tool close to or against rotating stock. The measuring tool can be damaged or broken.

7. To turn grooves on the perimeter adjust the lathe to regular speed. Then cut the grooves with a sharp point of a

skew lathe tool. Finally, round over the beads with a diamond point lathe tool.

8. Use folded sandpaper to *sand the beads*. The end grain will cause a problem. Be sure to use coarse sandpaper until the rough portions are smooth.

BEDSIDE STAND

The solid and sturdy piece of furniture sketched in Fig. 4-3 is attractive in any traditional setting. The top will probably be used for a lamp and a clock, the second shelf may be suitable for a telephone, and the lower portion reserved for general utility space. Another shelf may be constructed behind the doors if needed.

Materials:

Table 4-1 lists materials needed for construction of the beside stand.

Table 4-1.

Quantity	Description	Thick	Width	Length	Wood
1	Back	1/2	9 1/4	27	White pine
2	Sides	3/4	11 1/4	30	White pine
1	Top shelf	3/4	10 3/4	14	White pine
1	Second shelf	3/4	10 3/4	15	White pine
1	Bottom shelf	3/4	10 3/4	15	White pine
1	Bottom rail	3/4	4	18	White pine
1	Door stop	5/8	1	1	Maple or birch
2	Doors	3/4	6	15	White pine
1	Door support	3/4	2 1/2	15	
2	Turned knobs		3/4 diam.	1	
4	2 Inch ''H'' hinges				

Note: Measurements in inches

Procedure:

1. *Construction of the sides* begins by making patterns of heavy paper for the curved portion. Mark appropriate designs on the sides. Cut dadoes for the shelves. Be sure to allow for the angle. (Butt joints may be used if tools are limited.) Cut rabbets for back. Then cut curved designs on band saw or other curve-cutting tool.

2. *Cut the three shelves.* Allow for the angle already designated on the sides.

3. *Assemble the three shelves and two sides.* Use only glue if parts are dadoed. If butt joints are used, use sunken finish-

134

ing nails, screws, or dowels. Use glue for additional reinforcement.

4. *Cut back* to fit sides.
5. *Lay out, mark, and cut bottom rail* on band saw.
6. *Install bottom rail.*
7. *Cut two door* to fit the front.
8. *Cut and fit two door supports* and install
9. *Attach the doors* to the supports with hinges.
10. *Attach knobs.*

BOOKCASE

A fairly simple, but attractive bookcase, that does not follow all of the characteristics of true Early American design appears in Fig. 4-4. The design does two things quite effectively: it conserves lumber and cuts down on the number of operations. This is a particularly sturdy piece of furniture, especially if the craftsman has dado blades and head to use on his power circular saw.

Materials:

Appropriate materials are listed in Table 4-2.

Table 4-2.

Quantity	Description	Thick	Width	Length	Wood
2	Sides	3/4	9 1/2	43 3/4	White pine
3	Shelves (If shelves are dadoed add 1/2" to length of shelves)	3/4	8	15 3/4	White pine
1	Bottom shelf	3/4	9	15 3/4	White pine
1	Back	1/2	15 3/4	45 1/4	White pine

Note: Measurements in inches

Procedure:

1. To *construct the sides,* make patterns for curved protions. *Cut rabbets* if the back is to be recessed into the sides. *Cut* 1/4 in. deep *dadoes,* if dado joints are to be used. *Mark curved portions* from patterns. *Cut curved portions* on bandsaw or other curve-cutting tool (turning saw, saber saw, jibsaw, etc.).
2. *Cut stock for the four shelves.* Keep in mind that the bottom shelf is 1 in. wider than the other three. Be sure to add 1/2

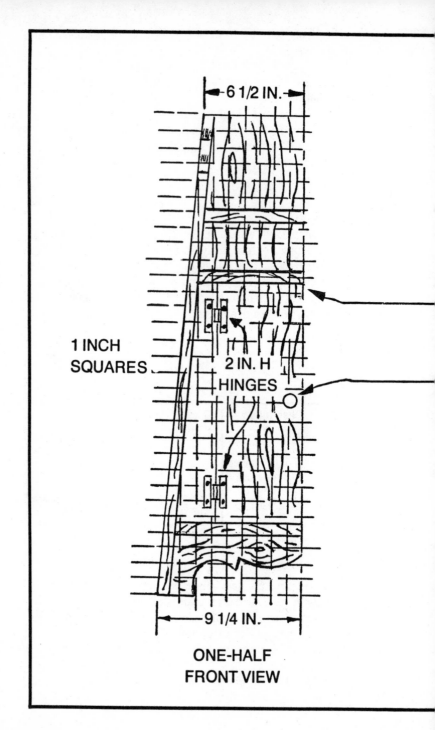

6 1/2 IN.

1 INCH
SQUARES

2 IN. H
HINGES

9 1/4 IN.

ONE-HALF
FRONT VIEW

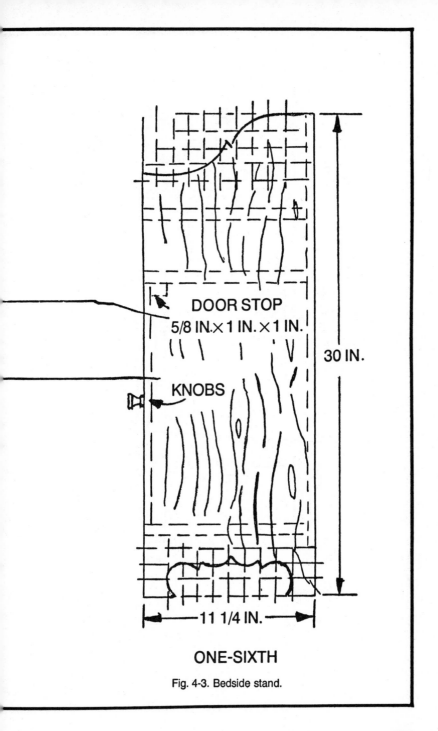

DOOR STOP
5/8 IN. × 1 IN. × 1 IN.

KNOBS

30 IN.

← 11 1/4 IN. →

ONE-SIXTH

Fig. 4-3. Bedside stand.

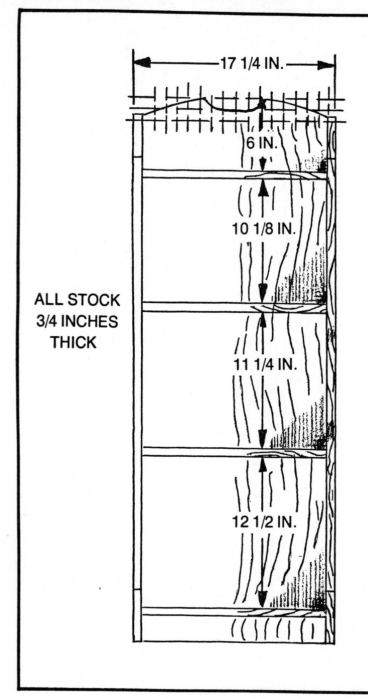

17 1/4 IN.

6 IN.

10 1/8 IN.

11 1/4 IN.

12 1/2 IN.

ALL STOCK
3/4 INCHES
THICK

1 INCH
SQUARES

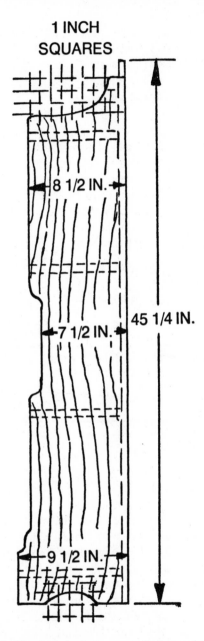

8 1/2 IN.

7 1/2 IN.

45 1/4 IN.

9 1/2 IN.

Fig. 4-4. This sturdy bookcase saves lumber and time.

in. to the length of the shelves if they are to be dadoed in the sides.

3. *Cut 1/2 in. stock for back.* Add 1/2 in. to width if the back is to be rabbeted 1/4 in. into the sides.

4. *Assemble and glue* if project is dadoed and rabbeted. If butt joints are used, use sunken finishing nails, screws, or dowels in addition to glue.

BOOKENDS

This weekend project would be attractive, as well as useful, on any desk or table. In fact, it would be appropriate on any flat surface where books are needed for ready reference.

It is desirable that felt be glued to the bottom of the expansion runners and inner faces of the bookends. These surfaces should be protected with masking tape and heavy paper while the finishing is being done. Figure 4-5 serves as reference for the procedure below.

Materials:

Table 4-3 lists all necessary materials.

Table 4-3.

Quantity	Description	Thick	Width	Length	Wood
2	Ends	2 1/4	7 1/2		White pine
2	Runners	3/4	2	12	White pine
1	Runner	3/4	2 7/8	12	White pine
6	FHB screws No. 7-1 1/2				

(If bookends are used regularly, on a day-to-day basis, it is recommended that runners be made of maple or birch)

Note: Measurements in inches

Procedure:

1. *Cut the ends* to measure 2 1/4 in. × 7 1/2 in. × 7 in. Plane the inside face on each blank until they are smooth and flat. *Mark taper* on edge of each piece 1 in. to 2 1/8 in. *Cut taper* or angle on a band saw. *Make the pattern* for the face. *Mark the curved portion* on the face.

   Note: Due to the angle, the pattern must be placed on the blank so that the rounded portion extends to the top of the blank. Let the bottom fall where it may, but the edge of the pattern must be parallel with the bottom of the stock. *Cut ends* on a band saw or other curve-cutting tool. *Cut out* *recesses* for runners with the band saw or circular saw with dado head. The center hole in the decorative rosette is drilled with a 1/8 in. bit about 1/2 in. deep and counter-sunk. The eight carvings are done with a "V" carving chisel.

2. *Cut* the *runner* with a circular saw. *Sand rubbing surfaces* very smooth. Allow about 1/32 in. between the runners for expansion, contraction of wood and the added finishing material.

3, *Assemble* with the necessary screws (FHB No. 7-1 1/2 in.) Do not glue. It might be necessary to alter or replace runners.

4. If bookends are to be used regularly, an extra coat of *final finish* should be added. Rubbing with pumice stone or rotten stone before waxing will add to the lustre.

5. After the project is completed, *coat* the contacting or rubbing surfaces of the runners with paraffin.

CANDLE HURRICANE LAMP

This is the same basic design used for the ashtray shown in Figs. 4-1 and 4-2. This distinctive Early American accessory, depicted in Figs. 4-5 and 4-7, in addition to being decorative, has a practical aspect in the event that the electricity is shut off for a time. During the Christmas holidays it can add to the Yuletide atmosphere if a bright red candle is used.

Material:

Table 4-4 lists materials necessary for the hurricane lamp.

Table 4-4.

Quantity	Description	Thick	Width	Length	Wood
1	Base	1 3/4	4 1/4	4 1/4	White pine
1	Handle	3/8	2 1/4	2 1/2	White pine
1	6 1/2-inch Standard lamp chimney				

Note: Measurements in inches

Procedure:

1. *Purchase the chimney* before starting the project. It might be necessary to use a chimney of different dimensions than the one shown in Fig. 4-6, in which case the rest of the lamp would have to be altered accordingly.

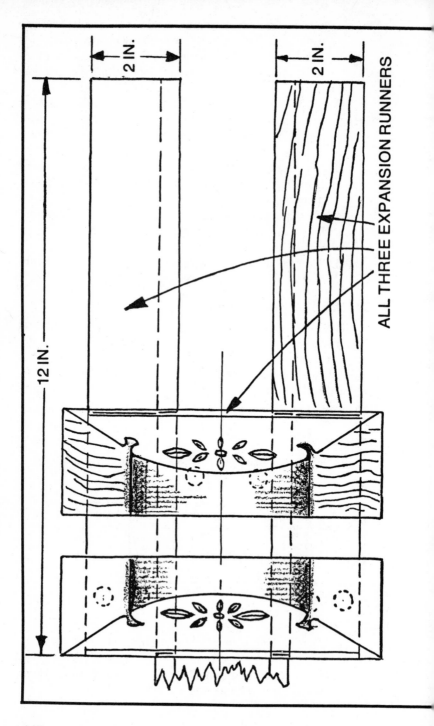

2 IN.

2 IN.

12 IN.

ALL THREE EXPANSION RUNNERS

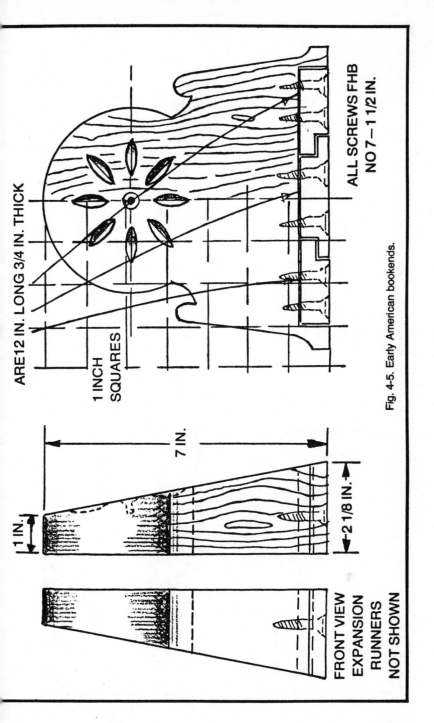

ARE 12 IN. LONG 3/4 IN. THICK

1 INCH SQUARES

ALL SCREWS FHB NO 7 – 1 1/2 IN.

7 IN.

1 IN.

2 1/8 IN.

FRONT VIEW EXPANSION RUNNERS NOT SHOWN

Fig. 4-5. Early American bookends.

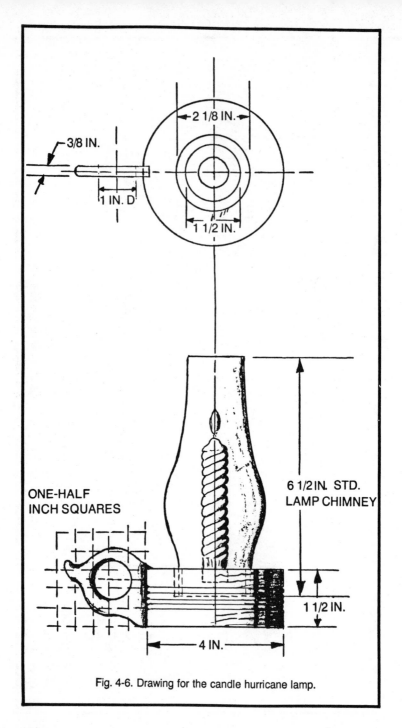

3/8 IN.

2 1/8 IN.

1 IN. D

1 1/2 IN.

ONE-HALF
INCH SQUARES

6 1/2 IN. STD.
LAMP CHIMNEY

1 1/2 IN.

4 IN.

Fig. 4-6. Drawing for the candle hurricane lamp.

2. *Start with the base and plane* one face of the stock until it is smooth and flat. Switch a 4 1/8 in. circle on this flat side. Be sure the center of circle is clearly identified. *Attach the faceplate to the stock. Align the center mark on* the stock with the hole of the faceplate. Attach the faceplate to the stock with short FHB screws. *Turn stock* to 1 1/2 in. thick by 4 in. diameter. Check the face of the turning with a straightedge for flatness. *Turn the recess* for the chimney using a parting or square nose chisel. At the same time, cut the candle recess. The size will be determined by the candles available. The tool rest should be positioned at right angles to the lathe bed and about 1/4 in. from the face of the stock. The tool rest should be below the centerline of the face equal to thickness of the turning tool. A marking stick or dividers may be used to advantage to mark the size of the circle. *Mark and turn grooves and beads.* Turn the tool rest parallel with lathe bed and about 1/4 in. from the perimeter and slightly below center. On a piece of scrap lumber about 1/8 in. thick by 3/4 in. wide mark the groove spacings with a sharp pencil. Hold the marking stick about 1/8 in. from the slow turning stock and with a sharp pencil mark a groove spacing on the rotating stock. Small "Vs", cut with a sharp knife on the edge of marking stick where the groove marks are located, will help control the pencil point. *Never* use a scale, rule or other measuring tools close to or against rotating stock. The measuring tool can be easily damaged or broken. In turning the grooves, first adjust the lathe to regular speed; second, cut the grooves with the sharp point of a skew lathe tool; third, round over the beads with a diamond piont lathe tool. *Sand and remove the base from the faceplate.* Use folded sandpaper for sanding the beads. Be careful not to flatten the tops of beads. Use coarse sandpaper to smooth all end grain before using finer sandpaper. *Cut* a 1/4 in. dado slot for handle

3. To *construct the handle, bore* a 1 in. hole in rough 3/8 in. stock. *Make a pattern* for the handle on heavy paper. Be sure to locate the position of the 1 in. hole. *Mark* the curved portion on stock with the 1 in. hole in proper position. *Roll* all edges of the handle except the part that fits into base. This may be accomplished by using long strips of coarse sandpaper with the handle held in a vise.

Fig. 4-7. A candle holder with an Early American flavor.

After the edges are rolled, use fine sandpaper to finish the surface.

4. *Assemble* the hurricane candle lamp by attaching the handle to the base with glue.

CANDLE BOX PLANTER

This present-day adaptation of an Early American candle box is evidence that our American heritage is still alive. The clean, crisp lines of this beautiful accessory is typical of many Early American pieces. Almost anyone, from an adolescent to senior citizen, who has a coping saw and a few other household tools can make the exquisite wall ornament sketched in Fig. 4-8.

Materials:

Table 4-5 lists materials for the candle box planter.

Table 4-5.

Quantity	Description	Thick	Width	Length	Wood
2	Sides	3/8	4	5 3/8	White pine
1	Front	3/8	2 1/4	9 3/4	White pine
1	Back	3/8	9 3/4	8 1/2	White pine

Note: Whenever the length is indicated as shorter than the width, it simply indicates which way the grain runs in the wood. See drawing for further clarificaiton.
Note: Measurements in inches

Procedure:

1. *Make the pattern* for all curved parts.
2. *Cut* (saw) all parts to squared dimensions (see materials list).
3. *Cut* the 1/8 in. ×3/8 in. *rabbets* on the two sides.
4. *Cut the curved portions* with a band saw, jigsaw, saber saw or coping saw. A coping saw works well on this thin stock.
5. *Assemble* with glue and small brads. Don't forget to drill a hole in back either before or after assembly.

CANNONBALL LAMP

The charming lamp of Fig. 4-9 will add elegance to any traditional setting. The craftsman should be especially selective in choosing a shade for this lamp that will enhance rather than detract from the overall effect. When finished, this valuable lamp will greatly outweigh the short time it takes for completion. And just think what a conversation piece it will be for your friends and neighbors—and you.

Materials:

The cannonball lamp requires the materials listed in Table 4-6.

Procedure:

1. It will probably be necessary to glue up stock for before *turning.* After glue is dry, *bore* a 3/8 in. hole lengthwise

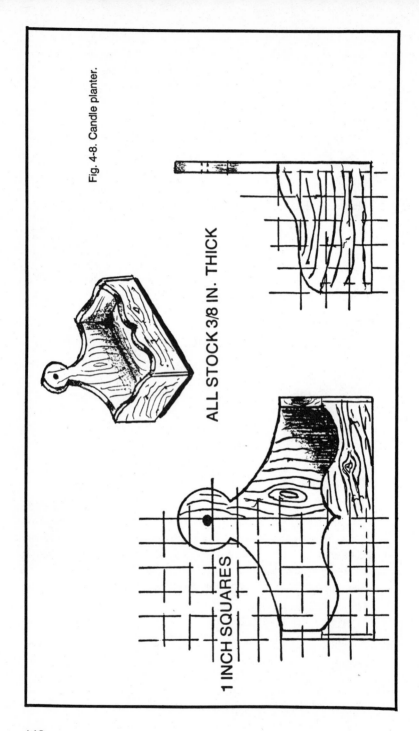

Fig. 4-8. Candle planter.

ALL STOCK 3/8 IN. THICK

1 INCH SQUARES

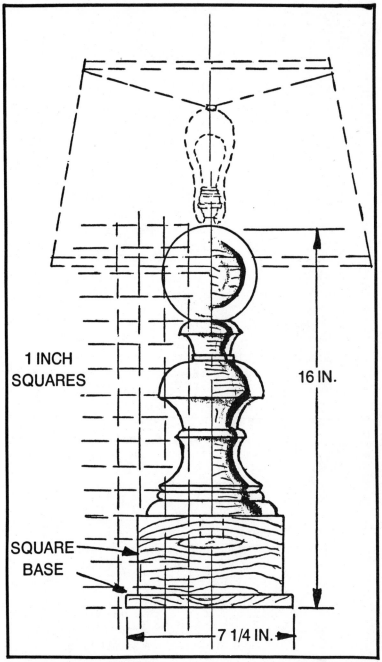

1 INCH
SQUARES

16 IN.

SQUARE
BASE

7 1/4 IN.

Fig. 4-9. An Early American cannonball lamp. The drawing is representative of one-quarter the actual size.

Table 4-6.

Quantity	Description	Thick	Width	Length	Wood
1	Base	3 1/2	6	6	White pine
1	Sub base	1/2	7 1/2	7 1/2	White pine
1	Turning Continuous thread pipe for cord 1/8-inch pipe (3/8 inch outside diameter)	5 1/2	5 1/2	13	White pine

Note: Measurements in inches

through the stock for the continuous thread pipe for the cord. This pipe fits into the base of the light socket. *Drive* a short plug into the end that is placed against the driving-spur center of the lathe. The other open end will ride against a cone-shaped tail center. *Mark* and *cut* a pattern from cardboard or thin wood. Turn a column 12 in. long with round-nose, skew, diamond point, or other appropriate lathe tools. Sand being careful not to flatten beads and sharp edges.

2. *Cut the base* to size. Sand the four sides and top. Do not sand bottom as it will be glued to sub base. *Bore* 1 in. diameter hole, 1 in. deep in top center of base to receive dowel on turning. *Bore* 3/8 in. for cord pipe down through base but not the sub base. *Bore* 3/8 in. hole from one side of square until it meets the 3/8 in. hole. This hole is for the lamp cord. The hold should be about 3/4 in. from the bottom of base. **Note:** The continuous thread pipe only extends 4 in. or 5 in. down from the top of the turned column.

3. *Cut the sub base* to size. Sand all sides and edges except for the portion that will be glued to the base.

4. For proper *assembly*, follow these steps carefully. With a 1/4 in. diameter rod poke out the plug in the upper end of the turning. *Insert* four or five inches of thread pipe in the top of the turning. Allow about 1/2 in. to extend out of the top to attach to the lamp socket. Thread cord into the base and up through the turning. *String* a brass inlet bushing onto the cord and thread into the hole near the bottom of base. *Assemble* and glue turning, base and sub base. During the finishing operation cover the brass inlet bushing, a few inches of cord, and the exposed thread pipe with paper and masking tape. After finishing is done, *screw* on the lamp

socket, add a harp for the shade, and select an appropriate finial to screw on the top of the harp. *Attach* a rubber plug to the end of about 6 feet of cord.

CHAIR TABLE

Although this piece of furniture is not too comfortable as a chair or bench, it can be made so by adding cushions. The chair table is ideal for a cottage or vacation cabin because of its space-saving attributes. As demonstrated by Fig. 4-10, it is a combination table, chair or bench, and a storage compartment.

Materials:

Materials necessary to complete the chair table are listed in Table 4-7.

Table 4-7.

Quantity	Description	Thick	Width	Length	Wood
1	Top	3/4	36	48	White pine
2	Top supports	1 1/8	4 1/2	36	White pine
2	Ends	1	12	24	White pine
1	Seat top	3/4	14	31	White pine
1	Seat bottom	3/4	11 1/4	31	White pine
1	Seat front	3/4	9	31	White pine
1	Seat back	3/4	8 1/4	31	White pine
1	1/2-inch Dowel			4	Birch
1	1/2-inch Dowel (Each dowel is inserted into a turned handle.)			39	Birch
3	3-inch Brass hinges				

Note: Measurements in inches

Procedure:

1. To *construct the top*, begin by gluing and clamping up stock. After glue is thoroughly dry, *cut* to size. If top has a tendency to warp, cut saw kerfs on the underside.
2. *Square up stock* and *cut* to dimensions to make the top supports. Make *patterns* for curved portions. *Mark* curved portions with the patterns. *Cut* curved portions with a bandsaw. *Bore holes for 1/2 in. dowels.*
3. *Assemble top and top supports.* *Bore* four holes one-half way through the top on each side to align with center of top supports. The holes should be slightly larger than the top (slotted) diameter of the screw and consistent with one of

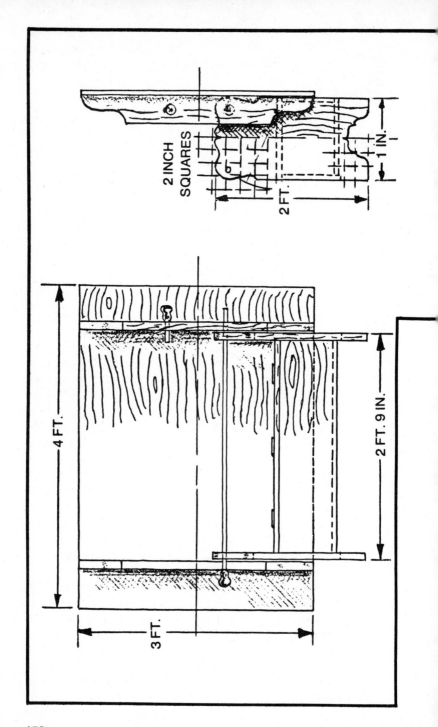

2 INCH SQUARES

1 IN.

2 FT.

4 FT.

2 FT. 9 IN.

3 FT.

152

Fig. 4-10. A scaled drawing of the space-saving chair table.

the dowel sizes. *Drill holes* through the rest of the table top in the eight holes just bored. The holes should be slightly larger than the shank of the FHB No. 9-2 1/2 in. screws used. *Center* the top supports under the holes just drilled in to the top. Mark the holes on the supports with an awl. Drill pilot holes in the supports slightly smaller in diameter than the threaded portion of the screw. *Assemble* using glue and the screws mentioned above. Be sure screws are driven securely. *Cut eight dowels 1 in. long of the appropriate diameter. Place glue on the ends of the dowels and drive them into the holes covering the screw heads (slotted part). After glue is dry, cut off the surplus end of the dowels close to the top. Sand dowels even with the top.*

4. *Construction of the table ends* begins by squaring up stock to dimensions. *Make a pattern* for the curved portions. *Mark* the design on stock. If dadoes and rabbets are used, they should be cut at this stage. *Cut curve portion* with a curve-cutting saw (a bandsaw is best). **Caution:** Do not bore the front hole on right end piece (facing drawing) at this time.

5. *Square up stock* to dimensions to make the *seat top*. *Cut recesses* for hinges. Roll the front edge with a plane or wood rasp and sandpaper.

6. *Square up stock* to dimensions for seat bottom front and back.
7. *Assemble the seat portion.* If dadoes and rabbets are not used, assemble with screws, dowels or nails. Glue and clamp.
8. *Assemble the seat and top.* After glue is dry, place top on seat in such a position that the long 1/2 in. dowel will enter the two rear holes. With the tabletop down, and the short dowel removed, bore the 1/2 in. hole in the right end piece using the hole in the top support as a guide.

CHEST

It would probably be more appropriate to construct the graceful, modified Chippendale piece drawn in Fig. 4-11 of cherry, mahogany, walnut, chestnut, or butternut; but white pine will do quite well unless the piece is to receive hard usage. One of the advantages of white pine is that any bruises, nicks or worn spots simply add to the overall effect of time-worn elegance.

Material:

Table 4-8 lists materials needed to complete the modified Chippendale chest.

Procedure:

1. *Construction of the chest top* begins by gluing up and clamping stock. After glue is dry, *cut* the top to dimensions. Use a router or shaper to *cut the molded edge* on ends and front. If router or shaper is not available, saw an edge kerf around the three sides and round over the edge with a plane and sandpaper block.
2. Glue up and clamp stock to *make the sides.* After glue is dry, *cut the sides* to dimensions given in Fig. 4-11.
3. *Cut the bottom rails* to dimensions. *Miter* the four corners 45 degrees. *Make patterns* and mark curved portions. *Cut spline recesses* on mitered faces. *Make splines* to fit spline recesses of hardwood or veneer stock. **Note:** Splines must be cut with grain of wood at right angles to the length of spline. *Assemble bottom rails* by placing glue on splines and mitered portions. Clamp from front to back and end to end. Set aside to dry.
4. *Cut front and back bearer rails and runners* (12 pieces) to dimensions. *Assemble* each set (4 pieces) with 1/4 in.

Table 4-8.

Quantity	Description	Thick	Width	Length	Wood
1	Top	1	17 1/2	26	White pine
2	Sides	3/4	15 1/4	25 1/4	White pine
2	Bottom end rails	3/4	4	16 1/2	White pine
2	Front and back bottom rails	3/4	4	25	White pine
1	Top drawer front	3/4	6 1/2	21 1/2	White pine
1	Middle drawer front	3/4	7 1/4	21 1/2	White pine
1	Bottom drawer	3/4	8 1/2	21 1/2	White pine
2	Top drawer sides	1/2	6	15	White pine
2	Middle drawer sides	1/2	6 3/4	15	White pine
2	Bottom drawer sides	1/2	8	15	White pine
1	Top drawer back	3/4	6	20 1/4	White pine
1	Middle drawer back	3/4	6 3/4	20 1/4	White pine
1	Bottom drawer back	3/4	8	20 1/4	White pine
3	Drawer bottoms	1 4	14 3/4	20 1/4	Masonite or hardboard or plywood
6	Front and back bearer rails	3/4	3	21	Birch
6	Side runners	3/4	2 1/2	10	Birch
1	Back dust cover	1/4	24	26	Plywood
2	Front-side member drawer stops	3/4	1 1/2	25 1/4	White pine
1	Top member drawer stop	3/4	1 1/2	21	White pine
6	Drawer guides	5/8	3/4	15 1/4	Birch
	59 linear inches cove molding				
6	Chippendale pulls, brass, 1765 design, 4 7/8-inch x 3 1/2 inch plate, 3 1/2 inch, or 3 3/4-inch post holes				

Note: Measurements in inches

dowels. See Fig. 4-11, rails and runners. *Attach* 1/2 in. ×1 in. ×15 1/2 in. strips to the side pieces with glue and brads so drawer bearer rails and runners will rest on the strips in the proper position. On the top (outside edge) of the runners, *drill angling holes* (three in each runner) that will allow all FHB No. 6-1 1/2 in. screws to enter side pieces. The holes should be deeply countersunk. **Note:** At the same time drill and deeply countersink holes in *one set* of

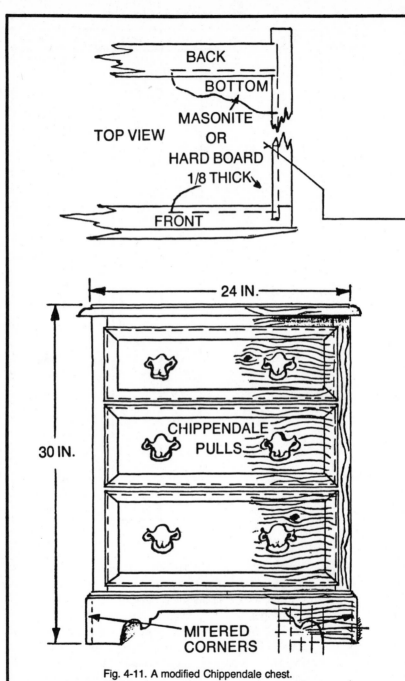

TOP VIEW

BACK

BOTTOM

MASONITE
OR
HARD BOARD
1/8 THICK

FRONT

24 IN.

30 IN.

CHIPPENDALE
PULLS

MITERED
CORNERS

Fig. 4-11. A modified Chippendale chest.

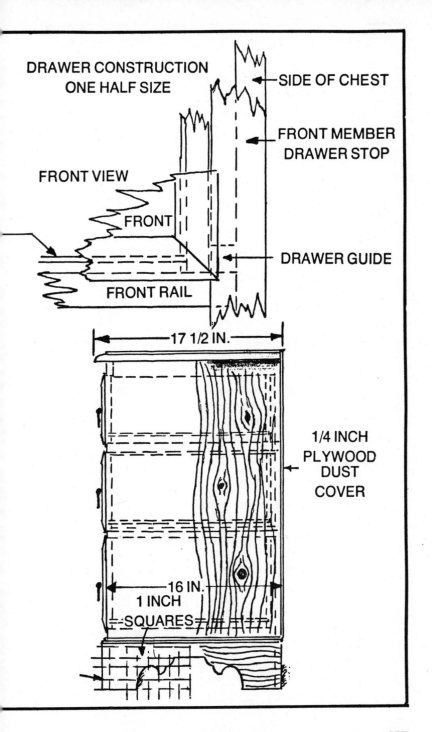

DRAWER CONSTRUCTION
ONE HALF SIZE

SIDE OF CHEST

FRONT MEMBER
DRAWER STOP

FRONT VIEW

FRONT

DRAWER GUIDE

FRONT RAIL

17 1/2 IN.

1/4 INCH
PLYWOOD
DUST
COVER

16 IN.
1 INCH
SQUARES

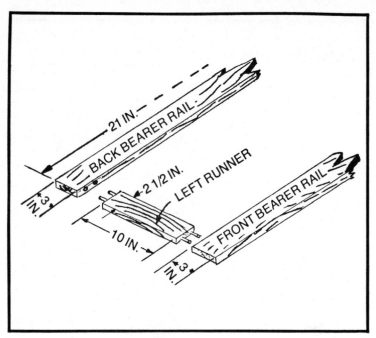

Fig. 4-11. cont.

rails and runners to be used on the top of assembly. These holes will be used to attach the top with FHB No. 5-1 in. screws. *Attach* the rails and runners, with FHB No. 6-1 1/2 in. screws, to the side panels.

5. Use FHB No. 5-1 in. screws through bearer rails and runner previously described to *attach the top to sides, rails* and *runners.*

6. *Fasten 1/4 in. plywood dust cover* on the back of the assembly with small nails and glue. This will greatly increase the stability and squareness of the assembly.

7. *Set the assembly* on the previously assembled *bottom rails.* The assembly should extend over the bottom rails about 1/4 in on the front and two sides. *Make 4 blocks* (2 for each end) 3/4 in. ×2 in. ×3 1/2 in. Cut a rabbet in each block so that portions of the block will be flush with the bottom rails and side pieces. Fasten the blocks to the side pieces and bottom rails with flat head screws.

8. It is now possible to proceed with *drawer construction.* Compensation for errors in measurement can also be accomplished.

9. *Cut stock to dimensions for the three drawer fronts. Measure* the drawer opening and cut the necessary grooves and rabbets accordingly. (A dado head and blades work best.) *Check drawer fronts* with drawer openings. *Cut the dadoes* in each end of the drawer fronts into which the tongue on the drawer sides will be inserted. *Set the saw blade* at the required angle *to cut the bevel.* First test on scrap stock. The bevel should be an inch wide and the edges of the drawer about 3/16 in. thick. Refer to Fig. 4-11. *Cut bevels* on all drawer fronts.

10. *Cut drawer sides to appropriate dimensions.* Be sure to include stock for tongue. *Cut* the necessary *rabbets* approximately 3/8 in. square. Side pieces must align with the recessed end of drawer and the tongue must fit into the drawer front dadoes. In the other end of drawer sides *cut* a 3/4 in. *dado* across the side pieces about 5/16 in. from the end. The dado is the same depth as the tongue is thick (1/8 in. to 3/16 in.) These dadoes will be the retainers for the 3/4 in. thick drawer backs.

11. *Cut drawer backs* to appropriate dimensions. Test the size by inserting into the dadoes in the side pieces.

12. *To construct drawer bottom grooves,* cut a 1/4 in. wide groove, about 5/16 in. deep, about 5/16 in. to 3/8 in. up from the bottom edge on all drawer pieces. *Do not change setting* of saw or dado blades until all twelve drawer parts have been slotted. This is the appropriate time to cut the drawer bottom to fit the grooves. One-quarter inch plywood, hardboard, or masonite should be used.

13. Test all parts before *gluing and clamping the drawers.* Glue and clamp the three drawers.

14. *Complete assembly of the drawers.* Test each drawer by pushing gently near either end of the drawer front. If the drawer binds, proper adjustments must be made. *Attach the necessary pulls* (Chippendale) to drawer fronts. It is best to make a pattern of cardboard or thin wood with the postholes properly located. This will speed up the installation of drawer pulls substantially. After the chest is *finished with the necessary coats of finishing materials*, rub paraffin on drawer runners, drawer guides, and the lower part of drawer sides.

CHEVAL MIRROR

This piece of furniture drawn in Fig. 4-12 would probably be classified as Early Twentieth Century rather than Early American, although it would easily fit in with the latter. Full-length mirrors of this type are rapidly becoming popular again. The simple construction depicted here should present few, if any, problems for the serious craftsman.

Material:

The materials listed in Table 4-9 are all that is necessary to complete a beautiful Cheval mirror.

Table 4-9.

Quantity	Description	Thick	Width	Length	Wood
1	Mirror frame, top	2	6	24	White pine
2	Mirror frame, sides	2	2	57	White pine
1	Mirror frame, bottom	2	2	24	White pine
2	Mirror supports	2	2	49 1/2	White pine
1	Bottom stretcher	2	2 1/2	24 1/2	White pine
2	Feet	2	4 1/4	14	White pine
4	Lag screws 3/8 inch x 3 1/2 inch				
2	Wooden washers	1/2	1 3/4-inch D		

Note: Measurements in inches

Procedure:

1. *Cut stock* to squared dimensions *for the top of the mirror frame.* **Note:** Stock will probably have to be cut special at the lumberyard. Two-inch commercial lumber is only 1 1/2 in. thick. Not a very satisfactory second choice is to glue up your own stock. *Make a pattern* and mark curved portion. **Caution:** Do not cut through mortise and tenons or 1/2 in. ×1/2 in. rabbets until all four parts of mirror are completed up to these two operations.
2. Cut 2 in. stock to the required dimensions for the bottom of the mirror frame.
3. *Construct the sides of the mirror frame* by sawing 2 in. stock to the required dimensions. Now saw or dado all through mortise and tenons as well as the 1/2 in. ×1/2 in. rabbets. It is best to cut mortises first (1 in. wide) and then cut tenons to fit mortise. **Caution:** Do not change dado or saw setting until all cuts are completed.
4. *Cut mirror supports* to squared dimensions (see Table 4-9). *Make a pattern* and mark the curved portion at the top. *Cut 1 in. mortises* in the opposite ends. *Drill holes* for lag screws.

5. *Saw bottom stretcher* to required squared dimensions.
6. *Saw or cut feet* to required squared dimensions. *Cut* the 1/2 in. ×2 in. dadoes on both sides. *Make a pattern* and mark curved portion. *Bore or drill holes* for lag screws.
7. *Assemble mirror frame* with glue. Clamp and set aside. Assemble supports, stretcher and feet. *Glue feet* to side supports. When dry, bore holes for lag screws. *Bore pilot holes* in stretcher for lag screws. Glue, assemble, clamp, and set aside.
8. *Total assembly* begins by setting the frame between the supports. Use Jorgenson adjustable hand clamps to hold frame in place. Place blocks of wood between stretcher and mirror frame bottom to help hold the frame in position (gap should be approximately 1 1/2 inches). Using the holes in the supports as guides, bore pilot holes in the frame for lag screws. Insert lag screws through the supports, wooden washers, and into frame. Before starting to *apply finish*, disassemble frame from supports. At this time the lag screws for the mirror frame should be provided with a ring so that the frame can be loosened or tightened in position without having to use a wrench.
9. Reassemble all parts after finish has been applied.

MAGAZINE RACK

This handy little gadget will fit into most any setting, be it traditional, modern or contemporary. The design roughly follows the shape of a Chippendale ladder-back chair. This project is a real test of curve-cutting ability. The magazine rack is pictured in Fig. 4-13.

Material:

Materials for the magazine rack are listed in Table 4-10.

Procedure:

1. *Make patterns* for all curved parts.
2. *Cut the bottom* to required squared dimensions. *Roll all edges* with a plane and sandpaper. *Drill and countersink holes* from the top face in each corner. Flat-head bright screws will be used later to hold feet in place.

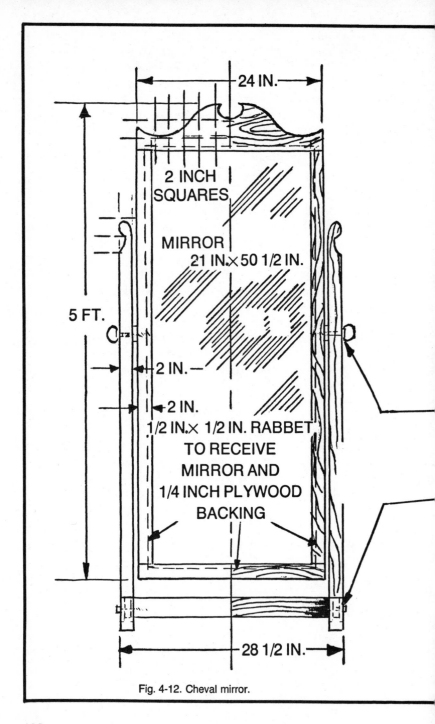

24 IN.

2 INCH
SQUARES

MIRROR
21 IN. × 50 1/2 IN.

5 FT.

2 IN.

2 IN.
1/2 IN. × 1/2 IN. RABBET
TO RECEIVE
MIRROR AND
1/4 INCH PLYWOOD
BACKING

28 1/2 IN.

Fig. 4-12. Cheval mirror.

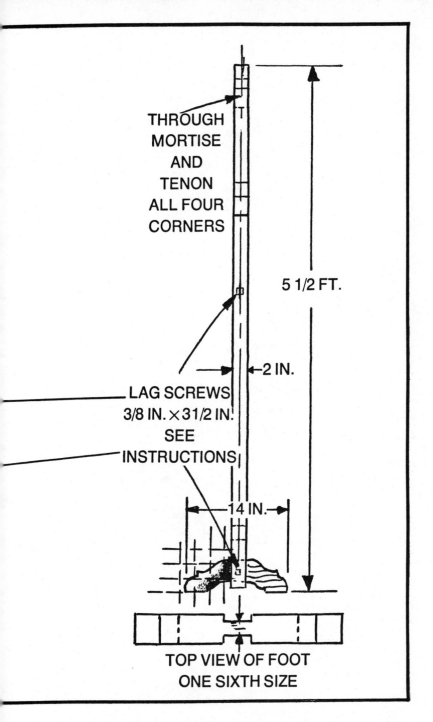

THROUGH
MORTISE
AND
TENON
ALL FOUR
CORNERS

5 1/2 FT.

←2 IN.

LAG SCREWS
3/8 IN. × 31/2 IN.
SEE
INSTRUCTIONS

14 IN.

TOP VIEW OF FOOT
ONE SIXTH SIZE

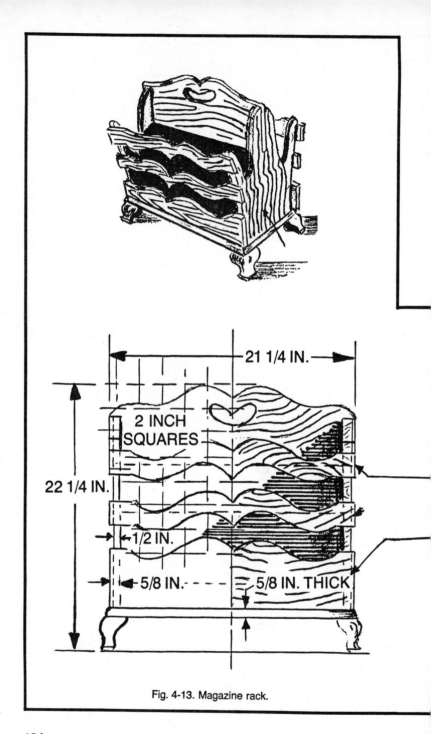

Fig. 4-13. Magazine rack.

Dimensions shown in figure:
- 21 1/4 IN.
- 22 1/4 IN.
- 2 INCH SQUARES
- 1/2 IN.
- 5/8 IN.
- 5/8 IN. THICK

3. *Mark outside curves and handle hole* with appropriate pattern to create the center handle. *Cut outside curves* with band saw, saber saw, jigsaw, or coping saw. *Cut handle hole* with coping saw or jigsaw after drilling holes in each end of the portion to be removed (not too close to the marked line) large enough to allow saw blade to pass through.
4. *Cut bottom center piece* to squared dimensions.
5. *Cut ends* to squared dimensions (see Table 4-9). *Make a pattern* and mark the curved portions. *Cut* with any curve-cutting tool. *Cut slots* where handle will fit.
6. *Cut lower side pieces* to squared dimensions. *Mark curves* with a pattern. Saw curves with any curve-cutting tool.
7. The four upper side (Cupid's Bow) pieces should be cut to squared dimensions. Mark the curves with a pattern. Saw with any curve-cutting tool.

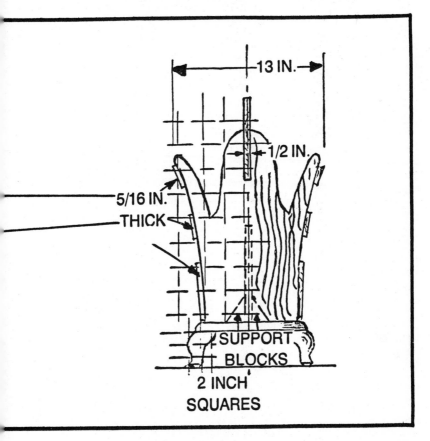

Table 4-10.

Quantity	Description	Thick	Width	Length	Wood
2	Ends	1/2	13	16	White pine
1	Center handle	1/2	7	21 1/4	White pine
1	Bottom center piece	1/2	8	20	White pine
2	Lower side pieces	5/16	5	21 1/4	White pine
4	Upper side pieces	5/16	4	21 1/4	White pine
4	Feet	3	3	3	White pine
1	Bottom	5/8	9	21 3/4	White pine

Note: Measurements in inches

8. *Cut the feet to squared dimensions. Mark the curves* with a pattern on *one* face. *Saw curves.* The band saw is the only practical tool here. Hint: Save all waste pieces. These waste pieces are fastened onto the feet with brads. Locate brads in a position so they will not be hit on subsequent cuts. On this reconstructed cube, *mark the foot outline* on a second side (at a right angle to the first face cut). *Saw the curves* just marked. *Remove the brads* from the waste pieces. The legs are now completed.

9. *Begin the assembly. Fasten the feet* onto the bottom with glue and FHB No. 6-1 1/2 in. screws. Line up the bottom center piece and fasten with brads from the underside of the bottom. Glue triangular support blocks on each side. See Fig. 4-13. Glue and brad the ends to the bottom center piece and bottom. Glue and insert the center handle. After glue is dry, fasten on the side pieces with glue and brads.

COBBLER BENCH

This modified version of a shoemaker's bench, almost extinct in today's world, has become an attractive and useful table in many modern homes. The top can be used as a cocktail table, coffee table, or a repository for books and magazines, and the drawer and compartments can be used for pencils, pens, stamps, paper clips. Figure 4-14 is a scale drawing of a cobbler bench.

Material:

Table 4-11 contains a listing of materials needed for a cobbler bench.

Table 4-11.

Quantity	Description	Thick	Width	Length	Wood
1	Top	1 1/2	12	30	White pine
4	Legs	1 1/2	1 1/2	10 1/2	White pine
2	Sides	3/4	5 1/2	16	White pine
2	End piece and compartment piece	3/4	4	12	White pine
1	Shallow compartment piece	3/4	1 1/4	9	White pine
1	Shallow compartment piece	3/4	1 1/4	4 1/2	White pine
1	Shallow compartment piece	3/4	1 1/4	4	White pine
2	Leg supports	1 1/2	3	10	White pine
1	Drawer front	3/4	2 1/2	7 1/2	White pine
2	Drawer sides	1/2	2 1/2	6	White pine
1	Drawer back	1/2	2 1/2	7	White pine
2	Drawer guides	1	1 1/2	6	White pine
2	Drawer guides	1	1 1/2	6	White pine
1	Drawer bottom—cut to fit after grooves are cut				1/4 Plywood or Masonite
2	Drawer runners	1/2	1/2	6	White pine
	3/8-inch Dowel—approximately 15 linear inches				
14	FHB No.9—2 1/4 inch				
1	Drawer knob				

Note: Measurements in inches

Procedure:

1. *Make heavy paper or cardboard patterns* of all curved parts.
2. *Cut the top* to the squared dimensions designated in Table 4-10. *Mark the curved portion* with the appropriate pattern. Cut the curved portion with bandsaw.
3. *Cut sides* to the squared dimensions. *Mark the curved portion* with a pattern. *Cut the curved portion* on a bandsaw.
4. *Cut the 1 1/2-in. square stock for the legs* about 1 in. longer than called for to allow for angle cut. *Set both cross cut fence* and *saw blade* at the same angle (about 10 degrees). This will produce the necessary compound angle. *Cut to length* (10 1/2 in.) with the same saw settings.
5. *Cut the leg supports* to the required dimensions. The support at the rounded end of the table will also have to be rounded to conform to the contour of the table top.
6. Cut the end piece and compartment pieces to the required squared dimensions of Table 4-10.
7. Cut drawer parts, runners and guides to the required squared dimensions. Cut the bottom to fit the grooves in the drawer.

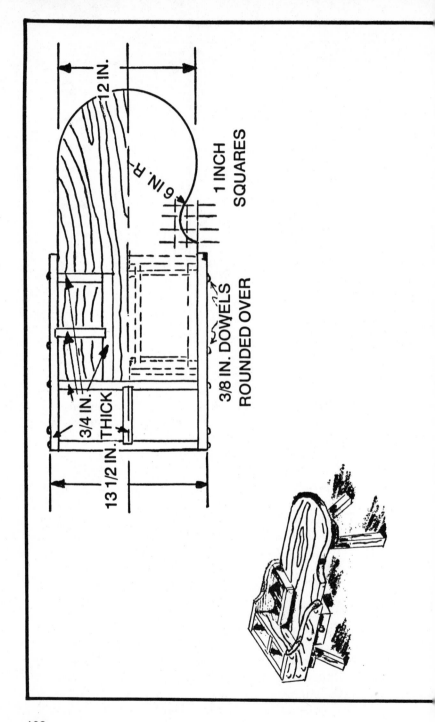

12 IN.

6 IN. R.

1 INCH
SQUARES

3/8 IN. DOWELS
ROUNDED OVER

3/4 IN. THICK

13 1/2 IN.

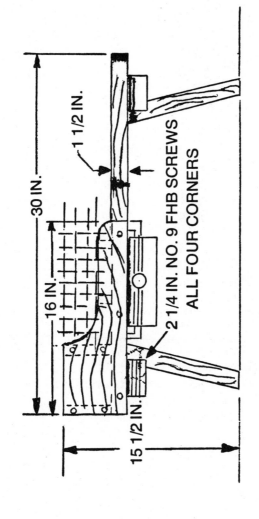

30 IN.

1 1/2 IN.

16 IN.

2 1/4 IN. NO. 9 FHB SCREWS
ALL FOUR CORNERS

15 1/2 IN.

Fig. 4-14. Drawing of a cobbler's bench.

8. *Cut dadoes* in the one side piece and compartment pieces before beginning assembly. *Assemble end, side* and *compartment pieces* with glue and dowels. Attach this subassembly to the top with glue and dowels. *Assemble the drawer. Attach the drawer runner* to the drawer side. *Attach drawer guides* to the underside of the top with glue and screws. *Attach leg supports* to the underside of the table with glue and screws. *Cut* the necessary *rabbets* on the legs. *Attach the legs* to leg supports with glue and screws.
9. Apply the finish. Keep the drawer separate from the bench until finishing operation is completed.

COMMODE

The commode pictured in detail in Fig. 4-15 is still a highly useful piece of furniture. Originally, it was used as a combination washstand and a depository for the chamber pot. The present-day commode can be used to advantage in nearly every room in the house for any number of decorative purposes.

Materials:

The materials listed in Table 4-12 are needed to complete the beautiful commode.

Procedure:

1. *Glue* and *clamp stock* (oversize 1/2 in. both width and length) *for the top of the commode.* Cut to size after glue is dry. Mold front and two ends with router or shaper. If neither is available, saw a kerf around the three edges and finish with a plane and sandpaper.
2. *Construct the sides* by first gluing up stock and clamping. Make it 1/2 in. oversize, width and length. Cut the stock to the correct dimensions.
3. *Cut rails* to the squared dimensions of Table 4-12. *Make patterns* of the curved portions on heavy paper or cardboard. *Mark the curves* on the stock with the patterns. *Cut the curves* with a band saw or other curve-cutting tool. *Cut 45-degree angle* miters on the ends of the four pieces. *Cut saw kerf* in the face of all mitered angles. Cut them to 1/2 in. to 3/4 in. deep. *Make splines* to fit kerfs. **Caution:** Make sure that the splines are made of cross-grain hardwood. *Glue* and *clamp* the four lower rails; check for squareness. Put them aside to dry.

Table 4-12.

Quantity	Description	Thick	Width	Length	Wood
1	Top	3/4	18 3/4	35 1/2	White pine
2	Sides	3/4	18	27	White pine
2	Front and back lower rails	1 1/2	3	36	White pine
2	End lower rails	1 1/2	3	20	White pine
4	Top and bottom door rails	3/4	1 1/2	12 1/2	White pine
2	Door stiles for knobs	3/4	1 1/2	21	White pine
2	Door stiles for hinges	3/4	1 1/2	21	White pine
2	Door panels	1/2	12 1/2	16	White pine
1	Bottom	3/4	18	32 1/4	White pine
1	Door divider strip	3/4	1	21	White pine
1	Front bearer rail (drawer)	3/4	3	32 1/4	White pine
1	Back bearer rail (drawer)	3/4	2 3/4	32 1/4	White pine
2	End runners (drawer)	3/4	2 1/2	12 1/4	White pine
1	Drawer front	3/4	4	32 1/4	White pine
2	Drawer sides	3/4	4	16	White pine
1	Drawer back	1/2	4	30	White pine
1	Drawer bottom	1/4	14	30	White pine
1	Strip between top and top of drawer	3/4	1 1/2	32 1/4	White pine
2	Drawer guides	Approximately 3/4 (Fashion to fit the space available)	3/4	18	Maple or birch
1	Dust cover	1/4	29	33 3/4	Masonite, hardboard or plywood
4	Dull black wrought iron knobs				
4	Narrow cabinet hinges (steel)		1 9/16	2	
2	1/4-inch Door friction catches				

Note: Measurements in inches

4. *Glue* and *clamp stock* for the *bottom section*. Cut to dimensions after glue is dry.
5. *Cut* all four parts for the *drawer rails* and *runners* to size. Assemble and install them at the same time as bottom is attached to sides. (See procedure in Fig. 4-11.)
6. *Attach top* by using short dowels or screws at an angle from the inside.
7. Install the door divider strip.
8. Attach the dust cover.
9. *Cut* all *eight stiles* and rails a little oversize *for the doors*. (Door should be trimmed to fit door openings.) Cut a

171

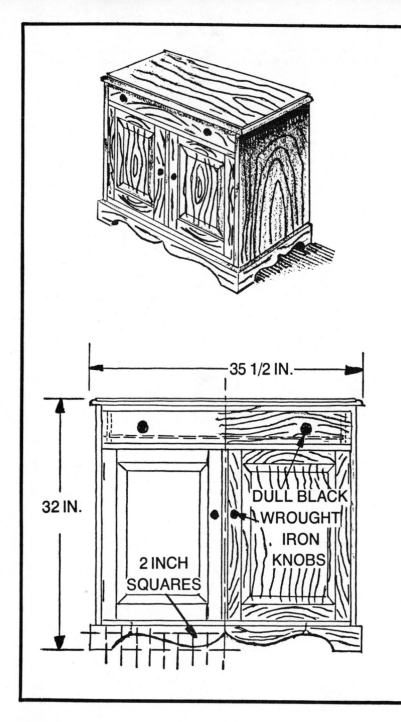

35 1/2 IN.

32 IN.

DULL BLACK
WROUGHT
IRON
KNOBS

2 INCH
SQUARES

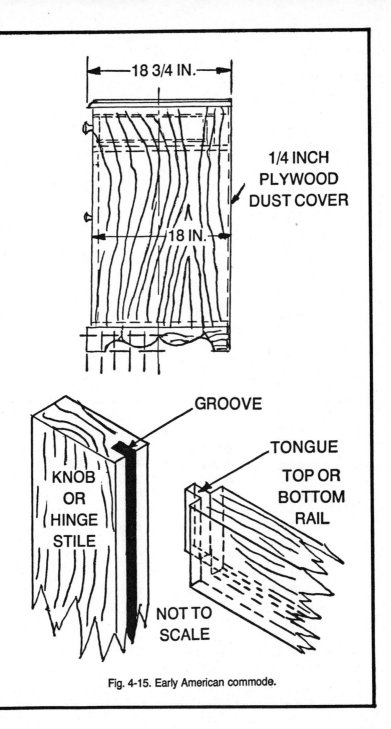

18 3/4 IN.

1/4 INCH PLYWOOD DUST COVER

18 IN.

GROOVE

KNOB OR HINGE STILE

TONGUE

TOP OR BOTTOM RAIL

NOT TO SCALE

Fig. 4-15. Early American commode.

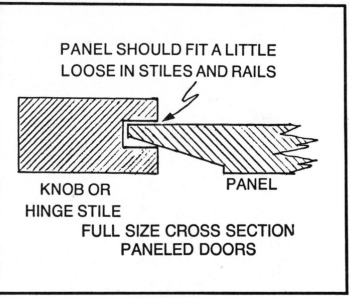

PANEL SHOULD FIT A LITTLE
LOOSE IN STILES AND RAILS

KNOB OR
HINGE STILE

PANEL

FULL SIZE CROSS SECTION
PANELED DOORS

Fig. 4-15. cont.

1/4 in. groove 1/4 in. to 3/8 in. deep in the center of one edge of all stiles and rails. This groove has a dual purpose: first, it contains the door panels and second, it provides space for the tongues on the upper and lower levels. See Fig. 4-15.

10. *Glue* and *clamp stock* for the *panels. Saw stock* to dimensions. *Make a saw kerf* around the four sides of each face, about 1 in. wide. (See Fig. 1-15.) *Set saw at the required angle* and saw a bevel. The edge that fits into the groove should be between 1/8 in. and 5/32 in. thick. **Note:** Check continually with stiles and rails for correct size. Keep in mind that the panel should fit a little loosely to allow for the expansion and contraction of the wood.

11. *Assemble* the doors. *Apply glue* only to the tongue of the top and the bottom rail. Clamp and set aside. **Caution:** Under no circumstances apply glue to panel edges or to the grooves that hold the panel. When the glue is dry, fit the doors to the door openings. Remember, the doors will be slightly oversize. Plane off an equal amount from all four sides. *Do not* remove excess from only *one* rail or stile. *Attach hardware.* Cut hinge gains (recesses) and attach the hinges to the doors. Attach the hinges to the sides of the cabinet. Attach the knobs to the door slightly above center.

12. *Cut the stock* to the dimension of the drawer opening *for the drawer front* allowing about 1/16 in. (undersize) for the necessary clearance. *Cut* the necessary groove and rabbets.
13. Cut drawer sides to dimension. Allow extra length if tongue-dado or rabbet construction is used. (Butt construction is the simplest, but is a much weaker joint.) On the other end of the drawer sides *cut* a 1/2 in. dado across side pieces and about 5/16 in. from the end. Cut the dado 1/4 in. deep. The dadoes will be retainers for the drawer back.
14. *Cut drawer back* to dimensions. Test for size by inserting into the dadoes in the side pieces.
15. *Construct drawer bottom grooves* by cutting 1/4 in. wide groove, from 5/16 in. to 3/8 in. deep, up from the bottom edge about 3/8 in. on all four pieces of drawer. Do not change setting of saw or dado blades until all four parts of drawer have been slotted.
16. *Cut drawer bottom* to size. *Test with the grooves* recently cut.
17. *Begin drawer assembly* by testing all parts before gluing and clamping. *Glue* and *clamp. Test drawer* by pushing gently near each end of drawer after drawer runners have been temporarily tacked in place. New runners might have to be made or more wood planed from existing runners. Attach knobs.
18. *Set cabinet* on lower base rails. Attach the base to the cabinet with FHB screws through the thinnest (or narrowest) part of the base on the curved portion (See Fig. 4-15).

COMPOTE

It takes little imagination to envisage the shapely and symmetrical gem in wood pictured in Fig. 4-16 in the center of a table or breakfront filled with fruit and nuts. Butt joints are used in the square container to eliminate the troublesome problem of figuring how to set the compound angles on the circular saw to cut mitered joints on the corner. Even the beginning craftsman would have trouble going wrong on this truly weekend project.

Material:

Materials for the functional compote are given in Table 4-13.

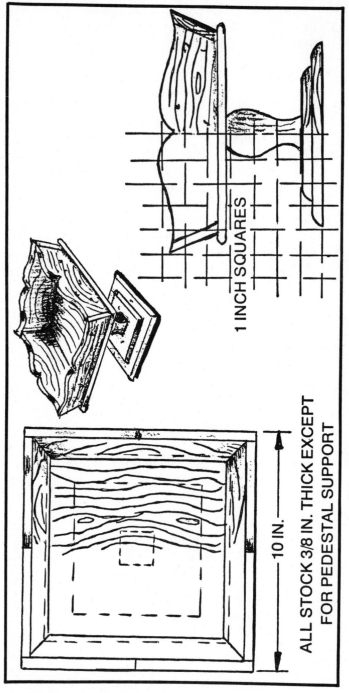

1 INCH SQUARES

ALL STOCK 3/8 IN. THICK EXCEPT
FOR PEDESTAL SUPPORT

10 IN.

Fig. 4-16. Decorative compote scaled to one-quarter actual size.

Table 4-13.

Quantity	Description	Thick	Width	Length	Wood
1	Pedestal	2	2	3 1/4	White pine
1	Small base	3/8	5 1/2	5 1/2	White pine
1	Large base	3/8	7 3/4	7 3/4	White pine
1	Container bottom	3/8	9	9	White pine
2	Container side pieces	3/8	2 3/4	9 1/4	White pine
2	Container side pieces	3/8	2 3/4	10	White pine

Note: Measurements in inches

Procedure:

1. Make the patterns for the pedestal and container parts of heavy paper.
2. *Cut stock* to squared dimension *for the pedestal.* See Table 4-13. *Mark a curved design* on one side of the block with the pattern. Cut with a band saw or other curve-cutting tool. **Note:** Save waste stock. Attach to pedestal cut so far with brads. Draw a curved design on second side of this reconstructed block (right angles to first side). Check to make sure brads will not be lined with saw cut. Make the *second series of cuts* with a bandsaw.
3. *Cut* to squared dimensions for the *small base* (the one directly below pedestal) and the *large base. Roll edges* with a plane, a wood rasp and sandpaper.
4. *Cut the container bottom* to squared dimensions. *Roll edges* to a complete semicircle with a plane, a wood rasp, and sandpaper.
5. *Cut container sides* to squared dimensions of Table 4-13. *Mark curved portions* with patterns. **Note:** Check to make sure that the pattern for the two sides is longer (about 3/4 in.) than the pattern for the two other sides. *Saw* with a curve-cutting tool. A coping saw also works well on this thin stock.
6. To begin *assembly, glue small base* to large base. **Note:** Do not sand where glue is to be applied. *Attach the base* to the pedestal with a FHB No. 6-1 1/2 in. screw and glue. *Fasten* the four side pieces together with glue and brads. *Attach the bottom* to the container side pieces with glue and brads. In the center of the container bottom, *drill a shank hole* for a FHB No. 6-1 1/2 in. screw. Countersink about

halfway through the container bottom. *Center the shank hole* just drilled over the pedestal. Mark for a pilot hole and drill. *Drive in the screw* which will hold the assembly together after glue has been placed on the end of the pedestal. *Cover the countersunk screw* with Plastic Wood or some similar substance. When dry, sand flush with container bottom before applying finish.

CORNER CABINET

When your friends and relatives, particularly the older ones, see the elegant piece pictured in Fig. 4-17 in the corner of your dining room, a twinge of nostalgic memory will take them years backward to Thanksgiving and Christmas festivities at Grandmother and Grandfather's house at the old homestead.

Materials:

Table 4-14 lists materials needed to construct a corner cabinet.

Table 4-14.

Quantity	Description	Thick	Width	Length	Wood
2	Corner posts	3/4	4	78 3/4	White pine
1	Top	3/4	13	44	White pine
6	Shelves (including bottom)	3/4	10 1/2	40	White pine
2	Front members with scrolled part	3/4	4	74	White pine
1	Top-front scrolled member	3/4	3 1/2	28	White pine
2	Slanting back pieces	3/4	13	78 3/4	White pine
1	Back piece	3/4	25	78 3/4	White pine
1	Bottom rail	3/4	4 3/4	36	White pine
4	Top and bottom door rails	3/4	2 1/2	10 1/2	White pine
3	Door stiles	3/4	3	24	White pine
2	Door panels	5/8	10 1/2	18 1/2	White pine

Note: Measurements in inches

Procedure:

1. *Cut the top* to squared dimensions. Glue up stock beforehand if necessary. *Cut* to the correct width. Lay out

178

and cut the end. Keep in mind that all angles are 45 degrees in reference to the front and back.

2. *Cut the corner posts* slightly larger than the squared dimensions designated in Table 4-14. *Set the saw* at 22 1/2 degrees or 67 1/2 degrees and saw first edge. *Mark* 4 in. and make the second cut at 0 degrees or 90 degrees (right angle). *Cut the recesses* for splines.

3. *Saw three back pieces* to proper dimensions. **Note:** The larger back piece has 45 degrees on each edge. The two smaller pieces have 45 degrees on one edge only as referenced in Fig. 4-17. *Cut slots* for the splines on the two smaller pieces.

4. *Cut the bottom rail* to slightly longer than the squared dimension. *Make a pattern* for the curved portion. *Cut the necessary miter* (22 1/2 degrees or 67 1/2 degrees) close to one end of the rail. *Measure and cut the miter* on the other end. *Mark the curved portion* and *cut* on band saw.

5. *Nail* together temporarily the corner posts, three back pieces, bottom front rail and top with long brads. Leave the brads extending from the surface long enough to be extracted by a claw hammer if necessary. *Measure carefully* for shelf size. Any previous errors can now be remedied.

6. *Cut the six shelves* consistent to measurements just taken. *Nail temporary cleats* (about 1/2 in. ×1 in.) to the three back pieces for the shelves to rest on. *Place glue* on shelf edges (one at a time) and set them in place. Nail brads (about 1 1/2 in.) through the back pieces into the shelves. **Note:** Take particular care in measuring and marking line on the back portion where the brads go. *Sink the heads* of the brads about 1/16 in. with a nail set. It will not be necessary to nail brads into corner posts. When glue is dry, remove temporary cleats.

7. *Cut the two pieces* for the *front members* with scrolled edges to the squared dimension including the stock for the angle. See Fig. 4-17. *Cut saw kerfs* for splines. *Make a pattern* and mark the curves (scrolled) portion. *Saw the curved portion* with a band saw. *Attach these members* to the subassemlby. Use glue on the spline and mitered corner. Place glue on the front of the shelves that these members cover. Nail brads through the members into the shelves. Sink brads with a nail set and fill in over the heads with Plastic Wood or some other similar material.

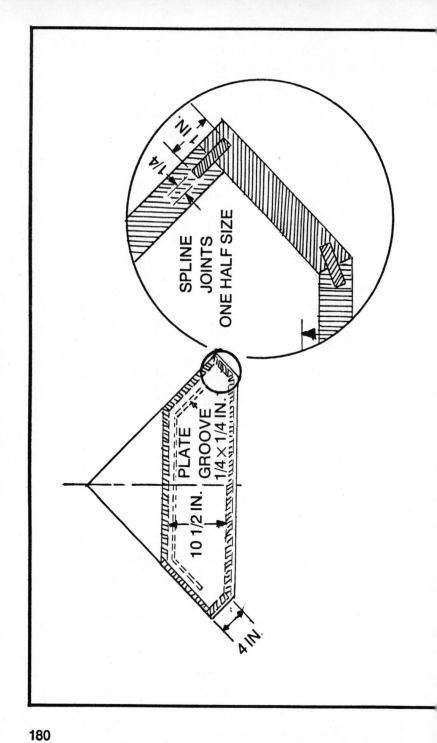

SPLINE JOINTS
ONE HALF SIZE

1/4"

1/2"

PLATE
GROOVE
1/4 × 1/4 IN.

10 1/2 IN.

4 IN.

180

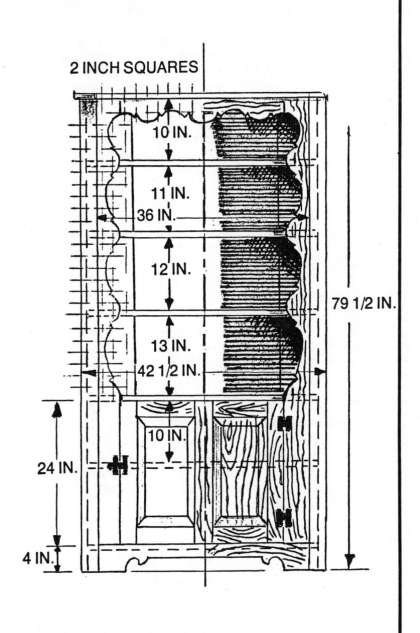

2 INCH SQUARES

10 IN.

11 IN.
36 IN.

12 IN.

13 IN.
42 1/2 IN.

10 IN.

24 IN.

4 IN.

79 1/2 IN.

Fig. 4-17. Corner cabinet. The circular insert shows the spline joints.

8. The length of the *top front scrolled member* is now accurately determined. Any previous errors can be corrected when the gap is measured. *Cut this member* to dimension. *Make a pattern* for the scrolled portion. *Cut miters* and spline slots. Mark the curved portion with the pattern and cut on a band saw. *Attach* this to the subassembly with glue on miters and splines. Put glue on the straight top edge and nail brads from the top into this piece.

9. *Cut the three stiles* and *four rails* at little oversize. The *door* will be trimmed to fit the door opening. *Cut a 1/4 in. groove* 1/4 in. to 3/8 in. deep in the center of one edge of all stiles and rails. This groove has a dual purpose. First, it contains the door panels, and second, it provides space for the tongues on the upper and lower rails. See Fig. 4-17.

10. Clamp and glue up stock if necessary to *construct the panels*. *Saw stock* to dimensions. *Make a saw kerf* around the four sides of each face, about 1 in. wide. See Fig. 4-17. *Set the saw* at the required angle and saw a bevel. The edge that fits into the groove should be between 1/8 in. and 5/32 in. thick. **Note:** Check continually with stiles and rails for correct size. Keep in mind that the panel should fit a little loosely to allow for the expansion and contraction of the wood.

11. To assemble door, apply glue only to the tongue of the top and bottom rail. Clamp and set aside. **Caution:** Under no circumstances apply glue to panel edges or to the grooves that hold panel. When glue is dry, *fit the door to the door opening*. Remember the door will be slightly oversize. Plane off an equal amount from all four sides until door fits. Do *not* remove excess from only *one* rail or stile.

12. *Attach hardware.* Two 3 in. "H" dull black wrought iron hinges and one 3 in. "H" dull black wrought iron catch are designated in the drawing.

CORNER SHELVES

This quaint but distinctive Early American project (Fig. 4-18) is a wonderful place for knick-kancks, miniatures, Hummel's, and small ceramic pieces. It can be a wonderful addition to any boy's or girl's room. This easy project requires a minimum of tools.

Material:

Materials needed to create a corner shelf are listed in Table 4-15.

Table 4-15.

Quantity	Description	Thick	Width	Length	Wood
1	Shelf support	1/2	12 1/2	30	White pine
1	Shelf support	1/2	13	30	White pine
1	Shelf (quarter circle)	5/8	4	Radius	White pine
1	Shelf (quarter circle)	5/8	5 1/2	Radius	White pine
1	Shelf (quarter circle)	5/8	6 1/2	Radius	White pine
1	Shelf (quarter circle)	5/8	8 1/2	Radius	White pine
1	Shelf (quarter circle)	5/8	11 1/4	Radius	White pine

Note: Measurements in inches

Procedure:

1. *Make* a 12 1/2 in. wide *pattern* for the curved portion.
2. *Glue up stock* and clamp. Make stock about 14 in. wide and 45 in. long. By overlapping the two curved portions at the small end, a saving of 15 in. of stock can be made.
3. When glue is dry, *mark on the curved portion* with the pattern. Allow an additional 1/2 in. width to the pattern on one piece as shown in Fig. 4-18.
4. *Cut curved* or scrolled edges with a curve-cutting tool.
5. *Make a heavy paper pattern* of each of the five shelves. A framing square and pencil compass are the only tools necessary. Cut out with shears.
6. *Arrange patterns* on the stock for the greatest conservation of lumber.
7. *Mark patterns.* It will probably be necessary to trace the squared corners and use the pencil compass on the wood.
8. *Cut the shelves* with any curve-cutting tool.
9. *Establish squared lines* to line up with the bottom of the shelves. Lines are on face side.
10. *Establish squared, center-of-shelf lines* on the backs. These lines are for nailing brads through the backs into the shelves.
11. *Butt the shelf* supports together. One piece is held in the vice. Make sure the 13 in. wide support overlaps the 12 1/2 in. wide support. The exposed faces of shelf supports should both be 12 1/2 in. wide when shelves and supports

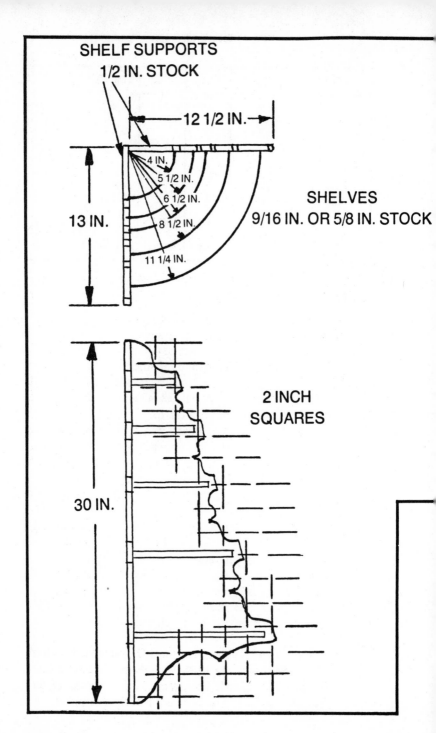

SHELF SUPPORTS
1/2 IN. STOCK

12 1/2 IN.

4 IN.
5 1/2 IN.
6 1/2 IN.
8 1/2 IN.
11 1/4 IN.

13 IN.

SHELVES
9/16 IN. OR 5/8 IN. STOCK

2 INCH
SQUARES

30 IN.

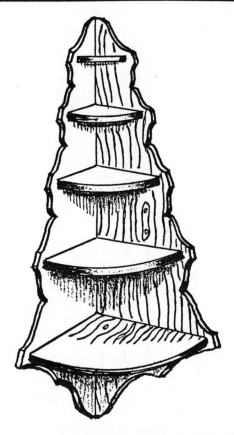

Fig. 4-18. Corner shelves are ideal for knick-knacks and collections.

are assembled. (An error in this operation will end with one face 13 in. wide and the other 12 in. wide.)

12. *Glue* and *brad* the two supports together.
13. *Line up the shelves* with the pencil marks.
14. *Glue and brad shelves* to the supports, one at a time.

CRANBERRY-PICKER PLANTER

This modified version of a cranberry picker pictured in Fig. 4-19 and 4-20 is an instant conversation piece. The container part should be lined with heavy aluminum foil before earth is placed in the container.

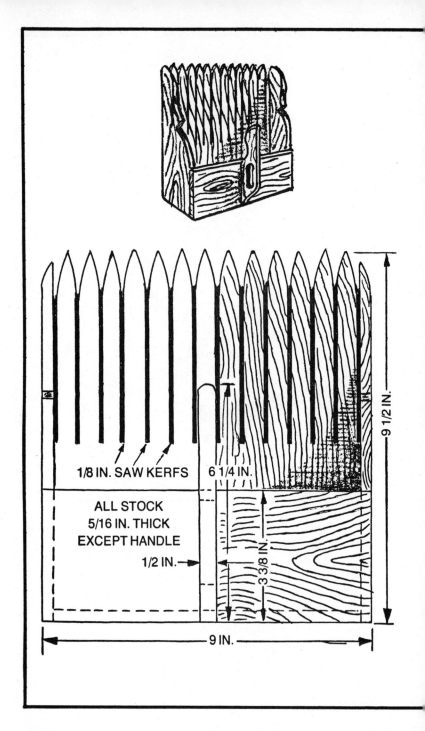

1/8 IN. SAW KERFS

ALL STOCK
5/16 IN. THICK
EXCEPT HANDLE

1/2 IN.

6 1/4 IN.

3 3/8 IN.

9 1/2 IN.

9 IN.

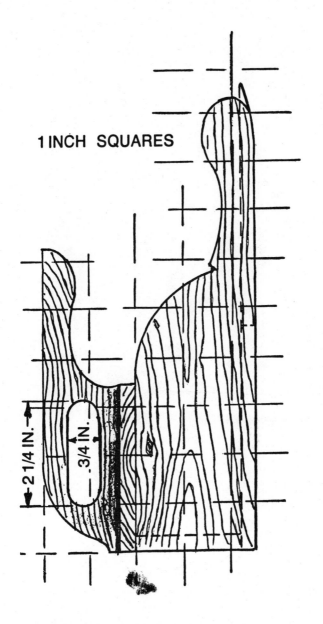

1 INCH SQUARES

2 1/4 IN.

3/4 IN.

Fig. 4-19. Cranberry-picker planter.

Fig. 4-20. Cranberry-picker planter in its final form.

Material:

Table 4-16 lists materials needed to complete the cranberry-picker planter.

Procedure:

1. *Make patterns* for all the curved parts.
2. *Cut the front* to the specified dimensions.
3. *Cut a handle* to the squared dimensions. *Mark the curved portions* with the patterns. *Cut outside* curves with curve-cutting tool. After boring holes for insertion of the blade, *cut inside curves* with coping or jigsaw. Attach the handle

Table 4-16.

Quantity	Description	Thick	Width	Length	Wood
1	Back	5/16	8 3/8	9 1/2	White pine
2	Ends	5/16	2 5/8	9 1/4	White pine
1	Front	5/16	3 3/8	9	White pine
1	Handle	1/2	1 5/8	6 1/4	White pine
1	Bottom	5/16	2 1/4	8 3/8	White pine

Note: Measurements in inches

   to front with glue and brads or glue and FHB No. 3 1/2 in.
   screws.

4. *Cut the sides* to squared dimensions. *Mark curves* with a
   pattern. *Cut curved parts* with a curve-cutting tool. The top
   of the sides should be sanded to an edge as demonstrated in
   Fig. 4-19.
5. *Cut the bottom* to the dimensions given in Table 4-16.
6. *Glue and assemble* with brads the handle, the two ends and
   the bottom.
7. *Accurately measure* and cut the back to squared dimensions
   to fit the subassembly just completed. Any errors will thus
   be corrected. *Lay out and cut* the 14 saw kerfs to a length of
   5 inches. *Lay out or mark* patterns outlining the curved
   points. Cut curved points with a curve-cutting tool. Plane
   or sand points on the back until they form a point. Insert
   back into subassembly and *fasten* with glue and brads.

CUP SHELVES

   Little cups, big cups, middle-size cups—Fig. 4-21 demonstrates a wonderful way to display your special cups and heirloom treasures. The special grooves will provide a place for saucers
as well. This classic design will fit well in almost any decorating
scheme.

Material:

   Necessary materials to construct the cup shelves drawn in Fig.
4-21 are given in Table 4-17.

Procedure:

1. *Cut the sides* to dimensions listed in Table 4-17.
2. *Cut the top* and bottom to proper dimensions. Roll the
   edges with a plane and sandpaper.

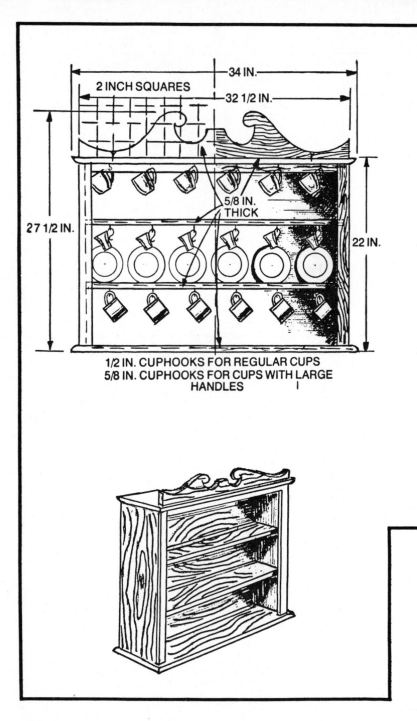

34 IN.

2 INCH SQUARES

32 1/2 IN.

5/8 IN.
THICK

27 1/2 IN.

22 IN.

1/2 IN. CUPHOOKS FOR REGULAR CUPS
5/8 IN. CUPHOOKS FOR CUPS WITH LARGE
HANDLES

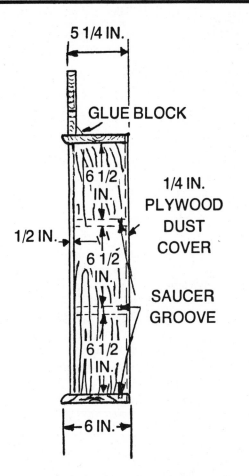

5 1/4 IN.

GLUE BLOCK

6 1/2 IN.

1/2 IN.

6 1/2 IN.

6 1/2 IN.

1/4 IN. PLYWOOD DUST COVER

SAUCER GROOVE

6 IN.

Fig. 4-21. Cup shelves are ideal for displaying any China pieces.

3. *Cut front-side rails* to the dimensions given.
4. *Cut the top rail* to designated dimensions.
5. *Cut dadoes* into the sides if dado construction is to be used.
6. *Assemble top*, bottom, and sides with glue and long brads or FHB No. 6-1 1/2 in. screws.
7. *Accurately measure* the opening for the shelves. If previous errors have occured, they can now be corrected.
8. *Cut shelves* to fit and install them with glue and brads.
9. *Attach the front-side rails* to the side with glue and brads.

Table 4-17.

Quantity	Description	Thick	Width	Length	Wood
2	Top and bottom	5/8	5 3/4	34	White pine
2	Sides	5/8	4 3/8	20 3/4	White pine
2	Front-side rails	5/8	1 1/2	20 3/4	White pine
2	Shelves (Add 1/2 inch to length if dadoes are used.)	5/8	4 3/8	31 1/4	White pine
1	Ornamental curved top	5/8	5 1/4	32 1/2	White pine
1	Top rail	5/8	1	28 1/2	White pine
4	Glue blocks	1	1	4	White pine
1	Dust cover	1/4	22	32 1/2	1/4-inch Plywood

Note: Measurements in inches

10. *Attach the top rail* with glue and brads. Drive 1 1/2 in. brads into the top rail through the top of the structure.
11. *Cut the curved top* to squared dimension. *Make a pattern* for the curved portion and mark on the stock with the pattern. *Cut the curved portion* with a curving-cutting tool. *Attach the curved top* to assembly with FHB No. 6-1 in. screws and glue. *Cut* the four right-triangle cross-section blocks. These are used for gluing and to reinforce the curved top. See Fig. 4-21.

Note: Rubbed-glue blocks are used extensively in carpentry to reinforce existing construction. Only glue (preferably hot animal glue) is used as the attaching force. No brads or other fasteners are

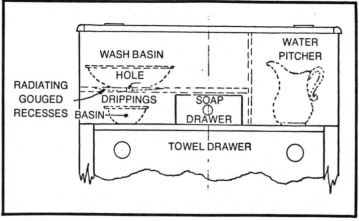

Fig. 4-22. A demonstration of the original use for the dry-sink chest.

used. Glue is spread on the two faces at right angles to each other. The block is rubbed vigorously back and forth (about 1 in. strokes) until it becomes difficult to continue rubbing. At this stage, the block is held in place for at least 30 seconds.

DRY SINK CHEST

The design demonstrated in Fig. 4-22 through Fig. 4-25 is a faithful reproduction of an authentic antique that has been in the author's family for more than a century and a half.

The only liberty taken with the original construction and design, was to remove the loose-fitting square-cut nails and replace them with flat head screws covered with short pieces of dowels. Strict adherence to the original is maintained in spite of the fact that some construction practices would not conform to present-day techniques.

The original dry sink was used as a washing stand and was quite often located in the bedroom.

On the left side of the compartment above the large drawer an elevated platform of wood extended over the small top drawer. A hole of about 1 in. diameter was bored in the center of the platform. Radiating from this hole were a number of gouged recesses made increasingly deeper as the recesses approached the hole. A wash basin was located on top of the platform and a much smaller basin was placed under the hole. Drippings followed the recesses down to the hole and into the smaller basin.

On the right side of the compartment a large pitcher of water was placed. The small top drawer was a depository for soap. The two large lower drawers were containers for wash cloths and hand towels.

The top was hinged and was only in the up position while a person was washing.

Currently, the platform has been removed and the upper compartment used for storage.

Material:

All materials necessary to construct the versatile dry-sink chest pictured in Fig. 4-25 are listed in Table 4-18.

Procedure:

1. *Cut the top* to dimensions required as given in Table 4-18.
2. *Cut two battens* to the proper dimensions.
3. *Cut a hinge strip* to dimensions given.

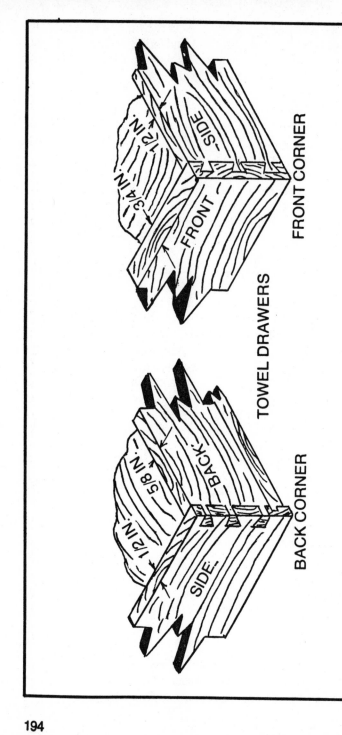

TOWEL DRAWERS

FRONT CORNER

BACK CORNER

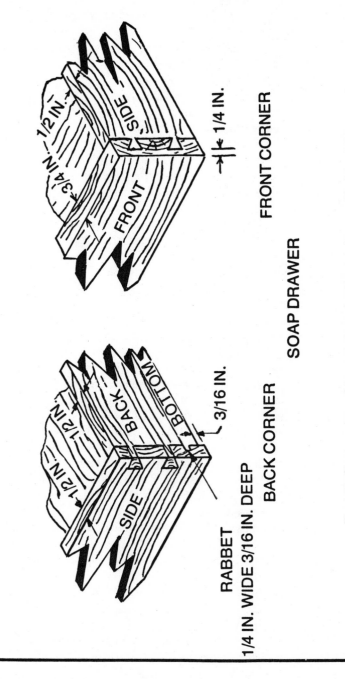

1/2 IN.

3/4 IN.

1/2 IN.

SIDE

FRONT

1/4 IN.

FRONT CORNER

1/2 IN.

1/2 IN.

BACK

BOTTOM

SIDE

3/16 IN.

BACK CORNER

RABBET
1/4 IN. WIDE 3/16 IN. DEEP

SOAP DRAWER

Fig. 4-23. Close-up views of the soap drawers and towel drawers with dovetail joints.

195

4. *Attach the battens* to ends of the top with glue and brads or with glue and dowels.
5. *Cut hinge gains* in the top and attach two 3/4 in. ×2 1/2 in. brass hinges.
6. *Attach the top* and hinges to the hinge strip with screws.
7. *Make patterns* for the curved portions.
8. *Glue and clamp* stock for the two ends.
9. *Cut ends* to required squared dimensions.
10. *Cut rabbets* to receive back.
11. *Mark* curved portions with a pattern.
12. *Cut curved portions* with a bandsaw or other curve-cutting tool.
13. *Glue* and *clamp stock* for the upper front. Set aside to dry.
14. *Cut the upper front* to the required dimension.
15. *Cut* a rectangular space for the soap drawer.
16. *Cut the front base rail* to the squared dimensions.
17. *Mark* the curved portion with the appropriate pattern and cut with a curve-cutting tool.
18. *Cut the front-side rails* to the required size.
19. *Glue* and *clamp* stock for the solid-top drawer bearer. Be sure to cut a 3/4 in. ×1 7/8 in. notch for the front-side rails.
20. *Cut drawer bearers* and runners for the two large drawers. Be sure to cut a notch for the front-side rails. Now drawer fronts can be carefully measured and errors in previous construction can be corrected. *Cut the three drawer fronts* to a size consistent with drawer openings. *Cut the drawer sides* for the soap drawer to measure 1/2 in. ×3 3/4 in. ×13 5/8 in. of white pine. *Cut a drawer back* for the soap drawer of white pine to measure 1/2 in. ×2 15/16 in. ×9 in. *Cut a drawer bottom* of solid wood (white pine) with the grain running the short way of the bottom (side to side rather than front to back) to measure 5/8 in. ×13 7/16 in. ×8 3/8 in. *Cut dovetail joints* in the front, back, and sides. See Fig. 4-23 for the dovetail joints of the dry-sink drawers. *Cut the drawer sides* for the top large drawer to measure 1/2 in. ×6 1/2 in. ×13 5/8 in. of white pine.
21. *Assemble* drawer bearers and runners with glue and dowels. See Fig. 4-24.
22. *Attach* upper front to ends with screws, dowels, and glue.

> **Note:** Bore a hole halfway through the member. Use a bit of a dowel size which is *larger* than the *head* of the FHB No. 6-1 1/2 in. screws used. Then drill a hole slightly *larger* the the *shank* of screw through

the rest of the member. Drill a *pilot* hole in the second member slightly *smaller* than the spiral part of the screw.

Attach all drawer bearers to the ends with glue and brads or glue and dowels. *Attach the front-side rails* to the ends with glue, screws, and dowels. *Cut and attach* (temporarily) the drawer runners for all three drawers.

Cut the 1/8 in. × 1 in. × 6 in. drawer stops. Glue and brad 3/4 in. back of the drawer bearer front edge. Use one stop for the soap drawer and two for each large drawer—one at each end.

23. In preparation for constructing the doors, cut the drawer back for the large top drawer to measure 5/8 in. × 5 11/16 in. × 31 in. of white pine. Cut the drawer bottom for the

Table 4-18.

Quantity	Description	Thick	Width	Length	Wood
1	Top	3/4	15 1/8	33 1/4	White pine
2	Battens (to reinforce ends of top)	3/4	1	15 1/8	White pine
1	Hinge strip	3/4	1 1/2	35 1/4	White pine
1	Upper front	3/4	12 7/8	34 3/4	White pine
2	Ends	3/4	16	33 3/4	White pine
2	Front-side rails (adjacent to lower drawer fronts)	3/4	1 7/8	21	White pine
1	Front base rail	3/4	4 1/2	31	White pine
1	Top drawer bearer (solid wood between top towel drawer and soap drawer)	3/4	15 3/4	33 1/4	White pine
2	Front bearer rails (under towel drawers)	3/4	3	33 1/4	White pine
4	Side runners (under towel drawers)	3/4	2 1/2	10	White pine
2	Back bearer rails	3/4	2 3/4	33 1/4	White pine
1	Back				White pine

(Solid pieces, 1/4-inch thick, 34-inch long, of miscellaneous widths to cover back. Pieces are set into 1/4-inch × 3/4-inch rabbets in end pieces)

Note: Measurements in inches

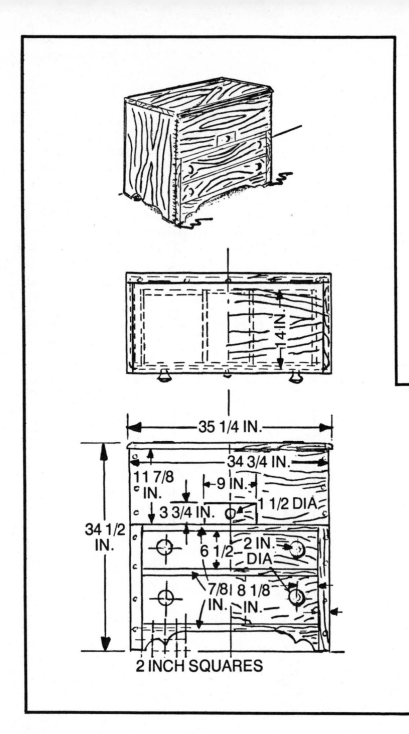

35 1/4 IN.

34 3/4 IN.

11 7/8 IN.

9 IN.

1 1/2 DIA

3 3/4 IN.

34 1/2 IN.

6 1/2

2 IN. DIA

7/8 IN.

8 1/8 IN.

2 INCH SQUARES

14 IN.

large top drawer to measure 5/8 in. ×13 7/16 in. ×30 5/8 in. of white pine. Cut the drawer sides for the large bottom drawer of white pine to measure 1/2 in. ×8 1/8 in. ×13 5/8 in. Cut the drawer back for the large bottom drawer to measure 5/8 in. ×7 5/16 in. ×31 in. of white pine. Cut the drawer bottom for the large bottom drawer of white pine to measure 5/8 in. ×13 7/16 in. ×30 5/8 in. With a 1/4 in. wide dado head, cut a groove 3/16 in. deep around all 12 drawer parts. It is set 9/16 in. from the bottom edge. **Caution:** Do not change setting of dado until all cuts are made. Cut 3/16 in. ×3/8 in. rabbets on the sides of *all* drawer bottoms with a dado head. See Fig. 4-22. *Cut dovetails* on the drawer parts for the two large drawers as in Fig. 4-23. To *assemble drawers,* glue and clamp all four corners at the same time. The bottom should be in place. **Caution:** Under no circumstances glue in the bottom of drawer or nail through the bottom into the back of drawer. The solid bottom *must* have a chance to expand and contract with variations in humidity. Test drawers in the cabinet. Adjustments might have to be made in order to prevent binding.

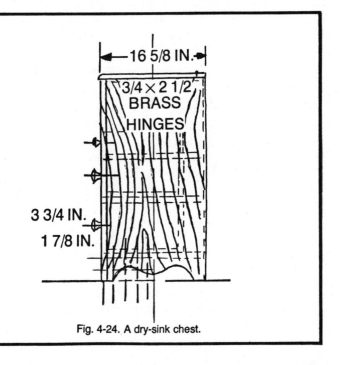

Fig. 4-24. A dry-sink chest.

Fig. 4-25. An Early American dry-sink chest is utilitarian as well as beautiful.

24. *To complete* the dry sink, *attach the back* to the cabinet with glue and brads. *Attach* the top and hinge strip to the cabinet. Check again for proper drawer fit. After the *finish* is applied, rub paraffin on all drawer guides, drawer runners, and lower sides of drawers.

ETAGERE

The etagere sketched in Fig. 4-26 has been made much easier to construct by using standard commercial birch dowel rods instead of lathe turnings. The dual practicality of a display area for knickknacks and a storage cabinet will appeal not only to the craftsperson but to every other member of the family. Not only can this project be used to display ceramics, miniatures, Hummels and trophies, but it can be used as a partial room divider.

Material:

Table 4-19 lists materials needed to complete an etagere.

Procedure:

1. *Make heavy paper patterns* of the curved portions on the base rails.

Table 4-19.

Quantity	Description	Thick	Width	Length	Wood
1	Top shelf	5/8	10	18	White pine
2	Shelves	1/2	10	18	White pine
1	Shelf and cabinet top	1 1/8	13 1/2	22 1/2	White pine
2	Cabinet sides	3/4	9 1/2	18 1/4	White pine
4	Birch dowels		1 inch in diameter	36	
4	Shelf support brackets	5/8	2	3	White pine
2	Front and back base rails	1 1/8	3	19 1/2	White pine
2	End base rails	1 1/8	3	11 1/4	White pine
4	Top finial turnings	2	2	6	White pine
2	Short top shelf rails	3/4	2	8	White pine
2	Long top shelf rails	3/4	2	16	White pine
2	Vertical front rails (cabinet)	3/4	1 1/2	18 1/4	White pine
1	Horizontal rail over top of door	3/4	2	15	White pine
1	Cabinet bottom	3/4	9 1/2	16 1/2	White pine
2	Knob and hinge door stiles	3/4	2	17	White pine
2	Top and bottom door rails	3/4	2	12	White pine
1	Door panel	5/8	12	13 1/2	White pine
1	Cabinet back	3/4	16 1/2	18 1/4	White pine
1	3/4-inch diameter dull black wrought iron knob				
2	2-inch Brass hinges				

Note: Measurements in inches

2. *Cut the cabinet top shelf* to required dimensions.
3. *Bore* 1 in. holes 3/4 in. deep in each corner of the cabinet top shelf.
4. *Cut the cove mold* with a shaper or router on the underside of the cabinet top shelf.
5. *Turn* top finials on a lathe.
6. *Bore* 1 in. holes 1 in. deep in the center of the top finial opposite the turning as demonstrated in Fig. 4-26.
7. *Insert* the four dowels into the 3/4 in. deep holes in the cabinet shelf top.
8. *Temporarily place* the top finial pieces on the top end of the four dowels.

201

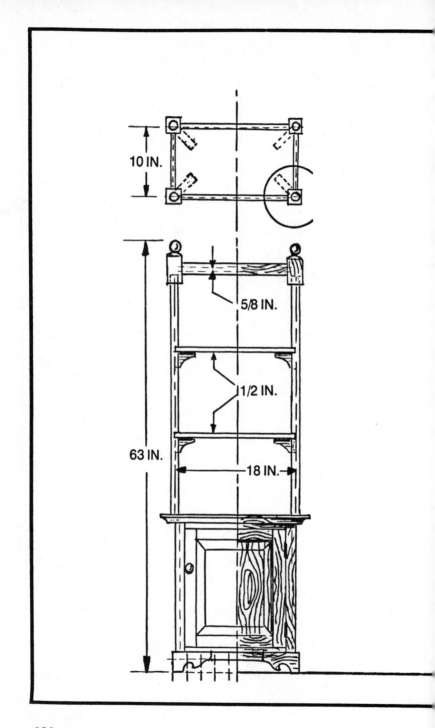

10 IN.

5/8 IN.

1/2 IN.

63 IN.

18 IN.

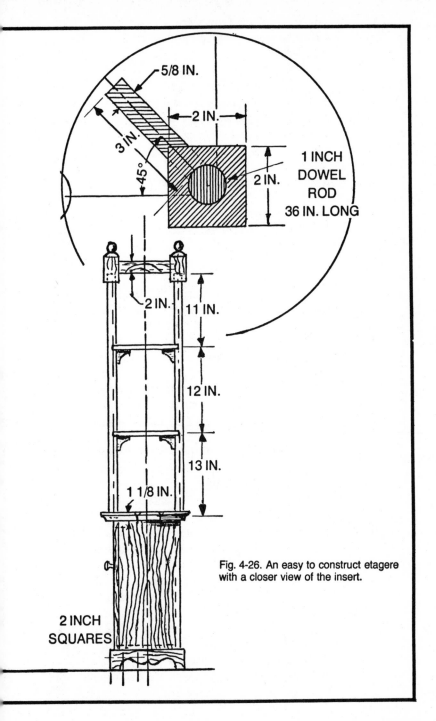

5/8 IN.

2 IN.

3 IN.

45°

1 INCH
DOWEL
ROD
36 IN. LONG

2 IN.

2 IN.

11 IN.

12 IN.

13 IN.

1 1/8 IN.

2 INCH
SQUARES

Fig. 4-26. An easy to construct etagere
with a closer view of the insert.

203

9. With scrap material, *cut four sticks* the exact dimensions of the distance between the four dowels at the surface of the cabinet top shelf.

10. *Place the sticks* (2 short and 2 long) just below the top finial pieces and clamp or wrap them tightly with heavy cord.

11. *Measure the short* and *long distances* between the top finial pieces. These distances will be the lengths of the short and long top rails.

12. *Cut grooves* 5/8 in. wide and 1/4 in. deep in all four top rails with a dado head.

13. *Measure* and *cut the top shelf* to squared dimension given in Table 4-19.

14. *Layout* and *drill* two holes for 1/4 in. dowels in the ends of the top shelf rails. Drill corresponding holes with the same spacing in the top turning finial pieces.

15. *Cut the 16 dowels* to the proper length and insert in the holes.

16. *Join together* the four top shelf rails, the top shelf, the top turning finial pieces with the dowels, but *do not* glue at this time.

17. *Measure,* and *cut* the 1/2 in. thick lower shelves to proper dimensions and *cut out* the curved sections that fit around the dowels.

18. *Cut the eight shelf support brackets* to the squared dimensions. *Turn* a 7/8 in. dowel about 4 in. long on the lathe. *Remove* this from the lathe and glue coarse sandpaper on the cylindrical surface. When glue is dry, put the turned piece and sandpaper back in the lathe. On the short dimension of shelf support brackets *sand* a curved recess in the bracket that will fit around the 1 in. dowel standards. *Make sure* the bracket points toward the center of the revolving sandpaper cylinder while sanding takes place.

19. *Attach the brackets* to the 1 in. dowels with glue and one long brad. *Drill a hole* in the bracket with the brad to be used, otherwise the bracket is apt to split. After glue is applied to the curved portion, the bracket is bradded onto the 1 in. dowels. If the 1 in. dowels are especially hard, it might be necessary to drill brad holes in them as well.

20. After glue on brackets is dry, *lay the two* 1/2 in. thick *shelves* on the top of the brackets. If the shelves fit satisfactorily, place glue on the curved corners and replace on the brackets. The tops of the brackets are also coated with

glue. Be sure to wipe off smeared glue from the 1-in. dowels, shelves, and the brackets.

21. *Assemble the cabinet sides*, back, bottom, vertical front rails, and horizontal rail with glue and brads.

22. *Cut base rails* to the squared dimensions. *Cut the ends* to a 45-degree miter. *Cut a saw kerf* in each miter face for the spline. *Cut splines. Glue the splines* and miter faces and clamp. Set them aside to dry. When glue is dry, *attach the base* to the assembled cabinet with glue and flat head screws through the narrow parts of the base.

23. To construct the door first *cut top* and *bottom rails*, knob stile and hinge stile. Rails and stiles should be slightly oversize in width to allow for trimming to fit the door opening. *Cut* a 1/4 in. to 3/8 in. deep groove in the center of one edge of the stiles and rails. The groove is 1/4 in. wide. *Cut rabbets* on the ends of the top and bottom rails so that a 1/4 in. wide tongue is formed. The length of the tongue should be the depth of the groove. *Cut a panel* to size. Make a saw kerf around the four sides of the face, about 1 in. wide. Set the saw at the required angle and saw a bevel. The edge that fits into the groove should be between 1/8 in. to 5/52 in. thick. The panel should fit a little loosely in the door. *Assemble* the four rails with glue. *Never* glue the panel. When glue is dry, *fit the door* to the opening. Never remove excess width or length of stock from one stile or rail only. Attach the 3/4 in. diameter dull black wrought iron knob and the two 2 in. brass hinges.

24. *Glue* and *clamp* the upper assembly parts which have previously not been glued.

25. When glue is dry on the upper assembly, *attach the cabinet assembly* to the upper assembly with 1 in. square blocks glued and screwed to the top ends of the side pieces on the inside of the cabinet. The upper assembly is attached to the cabinet assembly with glue and screws from the lower side of blocks extending into the cabinet top.

GALLERY SHELVES

The primary purpose of the project pictured in Fig. 4-27 is to introduce the craftsman to gallery construction practices. The lengths and widths of shelves can be changed to accommodate the desire of the craftsman.

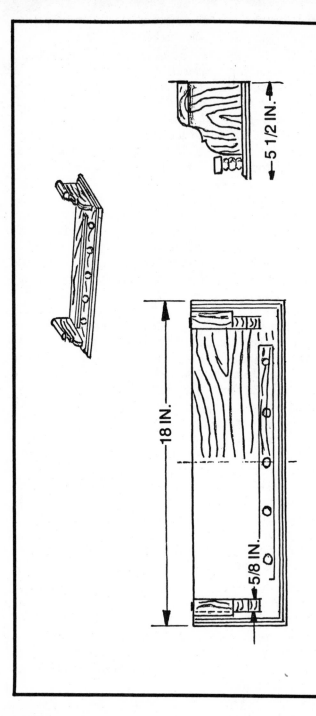

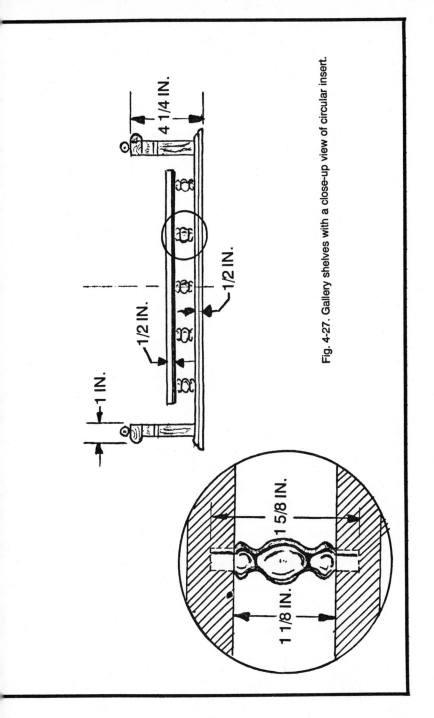

Fig. 4-27. Gallery shelves with a close-up view of circular insert.

4 1/4 IN.

1/2 IN.

1/2 IN.

1 IN.

1 5/8 IN.

1 1/8 IN.

Material:

Materials needed to complete gallery shelves are given in Table 4-20.

Table 4-20.

Quantity	Description	Thick	Width	Length	Wood
1	Base	1/2	5 1/2	18	White pine
1	Front rail	1/2	1	13	White pine
2	Ends	5/8	4	3 3/4	White pine
2	Half dowels on turnings		3/4-inch D	2 1/2	White pine
6	Gallery turnings	1/2	1/2	1 5/8	White pine
2	Metal hanger tabs				

Note: Measurements in inches

Procedure:

1. *Saw* the base to the required dimensions.
2. *Shape* the molded edges on the two ends and one side of the base with a router or shaper.
3. *Mark* a pattern for the curved portion of the ends.
4. *Cut* the ends to the appropriate squared dimensions.
5. *Mark* the curved portion with the pattern.
6. *Saw* the curved portion of the ends with a band saw or other curve-cutting tool.
7. *Turn* the half dowels and split them into two equal parts.
8. *Glue* the split turnings onto the ends.
9. *Cut off* the surplus of the split turnings with a band saw.
10. *Cut* the front rail to the required dimensions.
11. *Layout the centers* for gallery holes in the base and front rail at the same time.
12. With a 1/4 in. diameter bit, *drill holes* for the gallery spindles 1/4 in. deep into the base and front rail.
13. *Cut* 5 pieces about 5/8 in. square and about 2 1/4 in. long.
14. *Center* each piece in the lathe and cut a curved contour with a small round-nose lathe tool. *Turn* the 1/4 in. × 1/4 in. end dowels with a small square-nose lathe tool. (See the full size gallery spindle insert in Fig. 4-27.) *Sand* the spindles in the rotating lathe with narrow strips of sandpaper. Cut off excess stock with a parting tool or with the point of a skew-lathe chisel.
15. *Assemble* the gallery spindles, the base, and the front rail with glue.

16. *Attach* the end pieces to the base with glue and flathead countersunk screws (FHB No. 6-1 1/4 in.) from underneath the base.
17. *Attach* metal-hanger tabs.

GUN RACK

For the craftsman who has recently taken up hunting as a recreation, the gun rack sketched in Fig. 4-28 will be a useful "fill-in" until the craftsman-hunter has the time to build a gun cabinet.

Material:

Table 4-21 lists necessary material to complete a wall-mounted gun rack.

Table 4-21.

Quantity	Description	Thick	Width	Length	Wood
1	Upper back	3/4	7	28 1/2	White pine
1	Lower back	3/4	7	28 1/2	White pine
2	Sides	3/4	11	45	White pine
1	Butt rack	3/4	9	28 1/2	White pine
1	Butt rack front rail	3/4	3	28 1/2	White pine
5	Butt rack partition strips	1/2	3/4	9	White pine
1	Barrel rack	5/8	2 1/2	28 1/2	White pine

Note: Measurements in inches

Procedure:

1. *Mark patterns* for the curved portions of the sides, lower back, and barrel rack.
2. *Cut* the upper back to the squared dimensions.
3. *Place* the upper back stock on a large table or on the floor. With a trammel stick and points, or with a pencil-string-thumbtack, swing an arc of a circle along one edge of the stock. The radius of the circle should measure 60 in. **Note:** The point for swinging the circle must be on a center line which bisects the stock and the stock must be laid out at right angles to the center line.
4. *Cut* a curved line with a band saw.
5. On a piece of 3/4 in. stock 11 1/2-in. wide and 60 in. long, layout the sides with the appropriate patterns. (The nar-

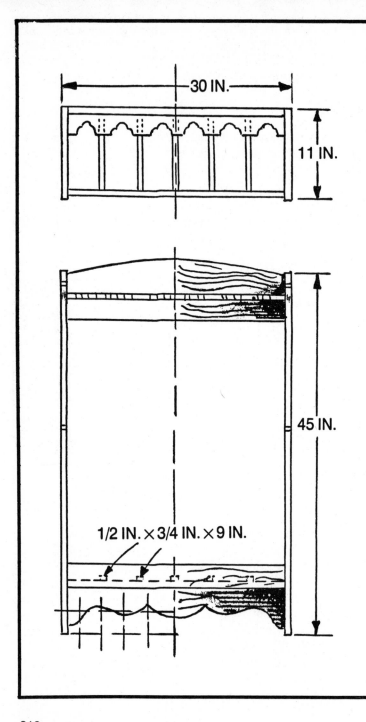

30 IN.

11 IN.

45 IN.

1/2 IN. × 3/4 IN. × 9 IN.

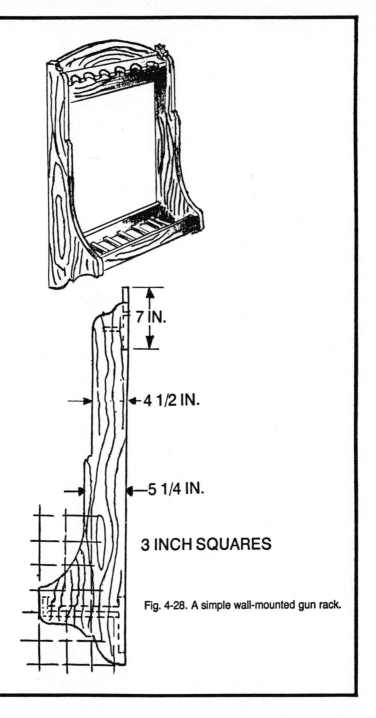

7 IN.

4 1/2 IN.

5 1/4 IN.

3 INCH SQUARES

Fig. 4-28. A simple wall-mounted gun rack.

rower parts *must* overlap. Otherwise, the two sides will take 90 in. of stock rather than 60 in.)

6. *Cut the two sides* on a bandsaw.
7. *Cut the lower back* to the squared dimension given in Table 4-20.
8. *Mark the curved portion* with the appropriate pattern.
9. *Cut the curved portion* of the lower back on a band saw.
10. *Cut the butt rack* to the required dimensions.
11. *Cut the butt rack partition strips* to the required dimensions.
12. *Attach the butt rack* partition *strips* to the butt rack with glue and brads.
13. *Cut the butt rack* front rail to the required dimensions.
14. *Cut the barrel rack* to the squared dimensions.
15. *Mark the barrel rack recesses* with the appropriate pattern.
16. *Cut the recesses* with a band saw or other curve-cutting tool
17. *Attach the sides* to the upper and lower backs with glue and finishing nails or glue and screws covered with short pieces of dowel. *Attach the barrel rack* to the upper rack with glue and finishing nails from the back and screws covered with dowels from the side. *Attach the butt rack* front rail to the butt rack with glue and long brads. *Attach* the butt rack assembly to the lower back with glue and finishing nails on the back and dowel covered screws on the sides.

GUN CABINET

The gun cabinet of Fig. 4-30 has several advantages over the gun rack. Guns and ammunition can be locked up. This is particularly important if there are children in the home. Another important advantage is that guns will be protected from damaging dust. In addition, the gun cabinet is an attractive and useful piece of furniture.

Material:

Table 4-22 designates all the materials you will need to create an attractive and serviceable gun cabinet.

Procedure:

1. *Make patterns* for the curved portions.
2. *Cut the top* to dimensions. *Cut rabbets* around the two ends and the front 13/16-in. deep and 1 1/4 in. wide. Cut 11/16 in. × 1 1/8 in. *cove molds* with mitered (45°) corners to fit in the rabbets. *Glue* and *attach* the cove molds with glue and small brads.

Table 4-22.

Quantity	Description	Thick	Width	Length	Wood
1	Top	1 3/8	13 1/2	29 1/2	White pine
1	Drawer cover	3/4	13	29	White pine
2	Front and back base rails	2	2 1/2	28	White pine
2	End base rails	2	2 1/2	13	White pine
2	Upper cabinet sides	3/4	12 1/4	52	White pine
1	Upper cabinet back	3/4	25 1/2	52	White pine
2	Drawer cabinet sides	3/4	6	12	White pine
1	Top ornamental rail	3/4	2 1/4	27	White pine
1	Barrel rack	1 1/2	3	25 1/2	White pine
1	Butt rack	1/2	10 3/4	25 1/2	Fir or birch plywood
2	Upper and lower door rails	3/4	2 1/2	25 1/2	White pine
2	Hinge and lock door stiles	3/4	2 1/2	52	White pine
1	Drawer front	3/4	6	25 1/2	White pine
2	Drawer sides	1/2	6	9 1/2	White pine or birch
1	Drawer bottom	1/4	8 7/8	24 1/4	Plywood, hardboard or masonite
1	Drawer back	1/2	6	24 1/4	White pine or birch
2	Drawer guides stops 3/16 x 1			10 3/4	Birch or maple
3	Glue blocks 1 x 1			4	White pine
3	Brass hinges 3/4 x 3				
2	Chippendale drawer pulls		3 5/8		

Note: Measurements in inches

3. *Cut the drawer cover* to size and roll the edges with a plane and sandpaper.
4. *Cut the base rails* to the squared dimensions. *Cut* 45-degree *miters* on the ends. *Cut saw kerfs* for the splines. *Cut the splines. Glue the splines* and mitered faces and clamp the four base rails together.
5. *Cut the upper cabinet sides* to actual dimensions.
6. *Cut the upper cabinet back* to size.
7. *Cut the drawer cabinet sides* to dimensions.
8. *Cut the top ornamental rail* to the squared dimensions given in Table 4-22.

Fig. 4-29. The gun rack, detailed in Fig. 4-28, is shown here in a natural Early American setting.

9. *Cut the barrel rack* to the squared dimensions. *Mark the curved portions* with a pattern. *Cut the barrel recesses* with a bandsaw.

10. *Cut the butt rack* to given dimension. *Mark the butt rack holes* with a pattern. *Cut out the butt rack holes* with a jigsaw, coping saw, or saber saw. *Bore holes* for inserting the blades of the saw before proceeding with the cutting.

11. *Assemble the top, sides and butt rack. Fasten the top to the sides* with glue and screws (FHB No. 8-2 in.). Screws should extend down through the top into the sides. *Attach the butt rack* to the sides and back with glue and 1 1/2 in. brads. Sink the heads of the brads with a nail set. Fill the holes with Plastic Wood or some similar material. *Attach the barrel rack* to the back with glue and FHB No. 7-1 1/2-in. screws. *Attach the top ornamental rail* to the top with glue and two FHB No. 7-1 1/2-in. screws down through the narrow sections of the curved portions into the top. *Reinforce the top ornamental rail* with rubbed glue blocks.

12. *Assemble the sides, back, drawer cover* and *base rails. Fasten the sides* to back with glue and 1 1/2 in. brads. *Fasten the base rails* to the sides and back with glue and FHB No. 7-1 1/2 in. screws. Be sure the screws are well countersunk because the upper cabinet assembly will be setting directly over the screw heads.

13. *Cut the lock stile, hinge stile* and *upper* and *lower door rails* slightly oversize in width. *Cut* two 1/4 in. wide *through the mortise* in the ends of the two stiles. (See Fig. 4-30). *Cut* two 1/4 in. *rabbets* on the ends of the upper and lower door rails. These rabbets will make a through tennon on the end of the rails *Cut* a 3/8 in. × 3/8 in. *rabbet on one edge* of the stiles and rails for a glass recess. *Cut hinge gains* on the hinge stile and attach hinges. *Install the wardrobe lock* on the lock stile. *Glue, assemble* and clamp the stiles and rails. When glue is dry, fit assembly to the door. *Do not install glass* in the door until all finishing is done, and *do not* install the door permanently to the upper cabinet until finishing is done.

14. *Measure the drawer front opening* carefully and cut the drawer front to fit. *Cut the drawer sides* to correct dimension and cut a rabbet for tongue and a dado for back. (Refer to Fig. 4-30, drawer construction.) *Cut the drawer back* to size. *Cut the bottom groove* on the front sides and back. *Put the drawer together* temporarily to measure for the bottom. *Cut the bottom* to the required dimension. *Glue, assemble*

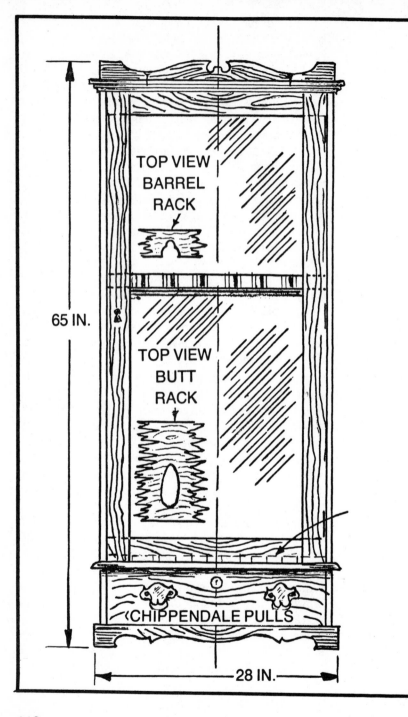

TOP VIEW
BARREL
RACK

TOP VIEW
BUTT
RACK

65 IN.

CHIPPENDALE PULLS

28 IN.

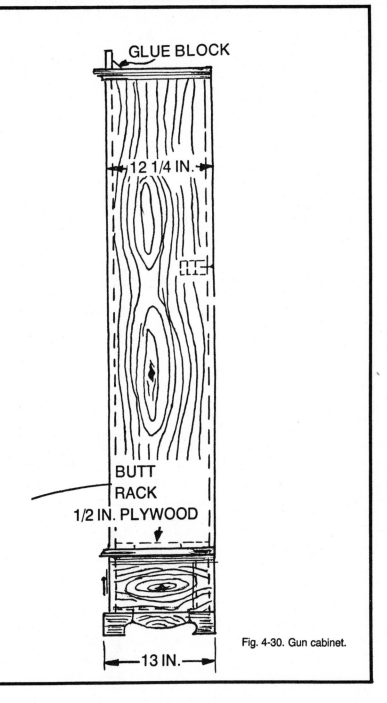

GLUE BLOCK

12 1/4 IN.

BUTT
RACK
1/2 IN. PLYWOOD

13 IN.

Fig. 4-30. Gun cabinet.

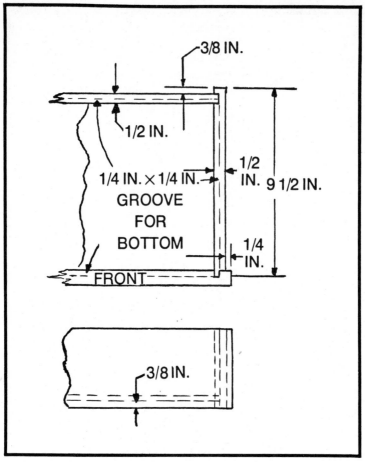

Fig. 4-30. cont.

and *clamp*. *Cut guide/stops* and *install* to the inside of the side pieces just above the base rails with brads. Do not glue until drawer fits satisfactorily. *Install Chippendale pulls* and the drawer lock to the drawer front.

15. *Set the upper cabinet* on the drawer cabinet. *Attach* the upper cabinet to the drawer cabinet with FHB No. 6-1 in. screws. *Do not glue*.

HEARTHSTOOL OR CRICKET

This cute little "jewel in wood" was originally used—and still may serve—to toast one's feet in front of an open fire.

The hearthstool of this distinctive design was sometimes called a "cricket" because many thought that it looked somewhat like the back of a cricket (Fig. 4-31). This is truly one weekend project that will fit into any traditional setting.

Material:

Materials needed to complete a hearthstool are listed in Table 4-23.

Table 4-23.

Quantity	Description	Thick	Width	Length	Wood
1	Top	1 3/8	10	16	White pine
4	Legs	1 1/4	1 1/4	5 3/4	White pine

Note: Measurements in inches

Procedure:

1. *Cut the top* to squared dimensions.
2. *Make a pattern* for the curved portion and mark it on the stock. *Do not cut* the curved portion until later.
3. From a piece of scrap, *cut a block of wood* 2 in. × 5 in. × 5 in.
4. *Bore a hole* 3/4 in. in diamter and at the proper angle through the center of the block. (See Fig. 4-31.) This block will be used as a guide or jig for boring all four holes.
5. *Layout the center* for holes on one face of the top stock.
6. *Center the boring guide* over one hole and clamp the guide to the stop stock. Be sure the angle of hole is correct.
7. Bore a 3/4 in. hole 3/4 in. deep in the top.
8. Remove the bit and move to the next hole. The guide must be turned 90° as progression is made from hole to hole.
9. After all four holes are drilled, *band saw* the curved portions laid out earlier and roll the edges with a wood rasp and sandpaper.
10. *Cut the stock for four legs* 1 3/8 in. × 1 3/8 in. × 7 in.
11. *Turn the four legs* to size with a round-nose and square-nose tools (See Fig. 4-31).
12. *Sand the lege* (while turning in the lathe) with strips of sandpaper.
13. *Cut off any excess* with the point of a skew or parting tool while lathe is turning.
14. Put *glue* on the dowel end of the legs and drive them into the holes in the top.
15. *Level the legs* so all four make contact with a flat surface at the same time.

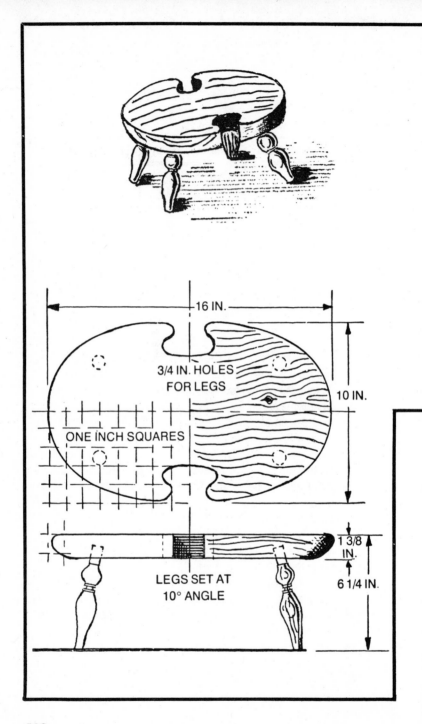

16 IN.

3/4 IN. HOLES
FOR LEGS

10 IN.

ONE INCH SQUARES

1 3/8 IN.

LEGS SET AT
10° ANGLE

6 1/4 IN.

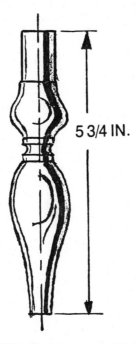

5 3/4 IN.

Fig. 4-31. A hearthstool or cricket bench.

JEWEL BOX

Why not store your jewelry in some organized fashion? A small chest lock added to the box shown in Fig. 4-32 would provide a little more security. Your rings, earrings, bracelets, charms, trinkets, necklaces, and other sundry items need not be constantly in one horrible mess that presents a problem akin to "looking for a needle in a hay stack." This is a truly one week-end project that presents few, if any problems.

Material:

Table 4-24 lists materials to complete the jewel box referenced in Fig. 4-32.

Procedure:

1. *Cut the top* and *bottom* to the required dimensions given in Table 4-24. You may cut these pieces together, as they are the same size.

Table 4-24.

Quantity	Description	Thick	Width	Length	Wood
1	Top	1/4	6	10	White pine
1	Bottom	1/4	6	10	White pine
2	Front and back (before sawing)	1/4	3	9	White pine
2	Ends (before sawing)	1/4	3	4 1/2	White pine
5	Lower compartment pieces	1/4	1 1/2	4 1/2	White pine
1	Lift-out tray bottom	1/4	3	8 1/4	White pine
2	Lift-out tray sides	1/4	3/4	8 1/4	White pine
7	Lift-out tray compartment pieces	1/4	3/4	2 3/8	White pine

Note: Measurements in inches

2. *Roll the edges* of the top and bottom with a plane and sandpaper.

3. *Cut the front, back* and *ends* at the same time.

4. *Glue* and *brad* the front, back and the two ends to form an open-faced box.

5. When the glue is dry, saw off a 1 in. wide section from the entire perimeter of box. (This 1 in. section will be a part of the top.) Be careful not to hit the brads with the saw blade.

   By assembling the box *before* cutting in sections, you eliminate the possibility of errors in matching the two sections.

6. *Attach the top* to the 1 in. section of the box with glue and small brads.

7. *Attach the bottom* to the bottom section of the box with glue and small brads.

8. *Attach the two small brass hinges* to the top section, then the other half of the hinges to the lower section. (Now remove the screws from one side of the hinge until the finish has been applied.)

9. *Measure the inside* of the box carefully, from side to side, and *cut* the *five lower compartment pieces* accordingly.

10. *Attach the compartment pieces* to the sides and bottom with glue and small brads.

11. *Cut the bottom* of the *lift-out tray* to dimensions given in Table 4-24. *Cut the sides* of the tray to dimensions. *Attach*

the bottom to the sides with glue and small brads. *Measure* the *inside* carefully, from side to side, and cut the seven compartment pieces accordingly. *Attach the compartment pieces* to the bottom and sides with glue and nails See Fig. 4-32.

12. *Set the heads* of the brads with a small nail set. Fill in the holes with Plastic Wood or some similar material. After finishing is completed, attach the top to the rest of the box with the half-hinges.

LOVE SEAT

The abbreviated sofa sketched in Fig. 4-33, will be a welcome "member" of any household (especially by the unmarried adults during their courting days). Care should be taken in the selection of the custom-made or homemade cushions to ensure that the fabric fits into the traditional setting.

Material:

Materials needed to construct a traditional love seat are given in Table 4-25.

Table 4-25.

Quantity	Description	Thick	Width	Length	Wood
2	End uprights	1	10	36	White pine
2	Arms	2	3	23	White pine
2	Front arm supports	1	7	21	White pine
2	End stretchers (arm support to end uprights)	1 1/2	3	21	White pine
1	Front stretcher (seat)	1	3 1/2	51	White pine
1	Back stretcher (seat)	1	4 1/2	48	White pine
1	Upper back stretcher (back)	1	3	48	White pine
1	Lower back stretcher (back)	1	3	48	White pine
6	Bottom slats (seat)	3/4	3	15	White pine
6	Back slats (back)	3/4	3	21	White pine

Note: Measurements in inches

Procedure:

1. *Make patterns* for all *curved parts*.

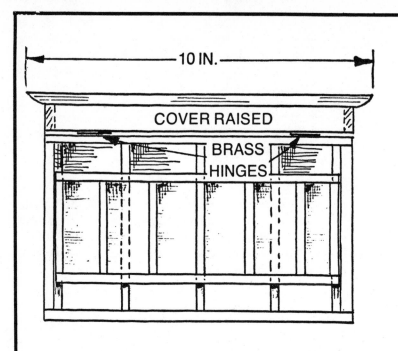

10 IN.

COVER RAISED

BRASS HINGES

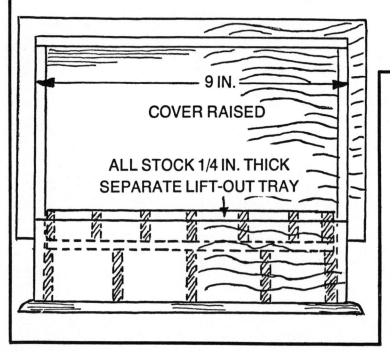

9 IN.

COVER RAISED

ALL STOCK 1/4 IN. THICK
SEPARATE LIFT-OUT TRAY

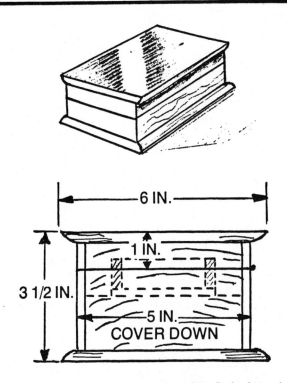

Fig. 4-32. Here is a jewel box pretty enough to display in any bedroom.

2. *Cut the end uprights* to squared dimensions. *Mark* the *curved* parts with the appropriate pattern. *Cut the curved portions* on a band saw. *Cut out recesses* for the back stretchers.

3. *Cut the arms* to the squared dimensions. *Mark the curved portions* on the *side* of the arm. Cut the curved parts with a band saw. *Mark the curved portions* on the *top* or *bottom* of the arm. *Cut the curved parts* with a band saw.

4. *Cut the front arm supports* to the squared dimensions. *Mark the curved portions* with the appropriate pattern. *Cut the curved parts* with a band saw. **Note:** Keep in mind that considerable stock can be saved by the overlapping of patterns.

    In this case, the "cutting to squared dimensions" can be disregarded.

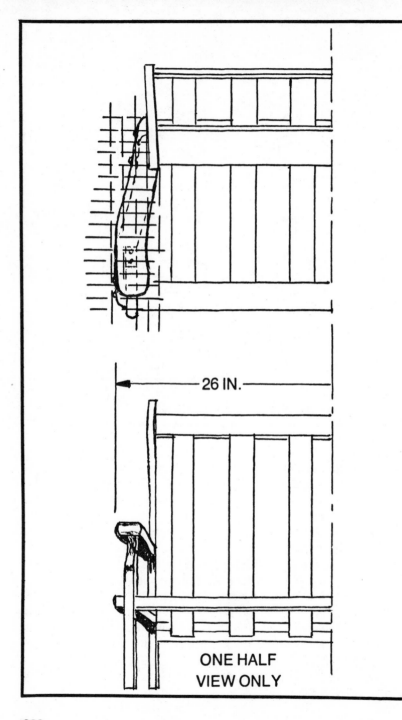

26 IN.

ONE HALF
VIEW ONLY

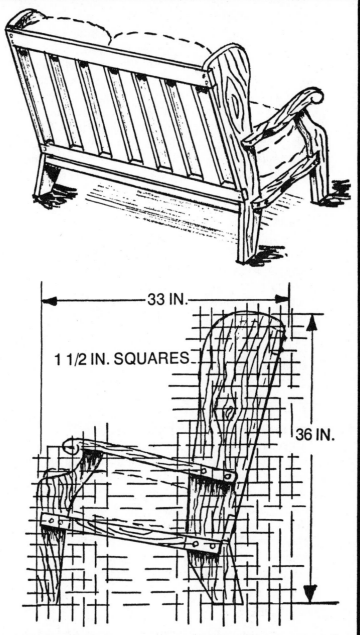

33 IN.

1 1/2 IN. SQUARES

36 IN.

Fig. 4-33. Demonstrated here is a love seat with graceful Early American styling. Scale: one-twelfth actual dimensions.

5. *Cut the end stretcher*—the member that reaches from the arm support to the end upright—to the squared dimensions. *Mark the curved part* with the appropriate pattern. *Cut* the *curve portion* with a band saw.

6. *Cut* all four *stretchers* at the same time. Although they vary somewhat in width, they do not vary in thickness.

7. *Cut* all 12 *slats* at the same time. Although they vary in length, they do not vary in thickness or width.

8. *Attach the slats* to the stretchers with 1/4 in. × 2 in. dowels. Use a doweling jig for greater accuracy and speed. *Drill holes* about 1 1/8 in. deep. *Apply glue* to the dowels and the end of the slats. Clamp them together and set the assembly aside.

9. *Bore two holes* 3/8 in. in diameter about 1/2 in. deep in the top of the arm directly over where the arm support is attached. *Drill a hole* through the rest of the arm (using the bottom of 3/8 in. hole as a guide). The hole should be approximately the size of the *shank* of a FHB No. 8-1 3/4 in. screw. Mark the holes on the top of the arm support with an awl. *Drill pilot* holes (slightly less in diameter than the spiral part of the FHB screw in the top of the arm support. *Attach* the arm to the arm support with glue and screws. The 3/8 in. hole over the top of the screw should be filled with a short length of 3/8 in. dowel. *Glue in dowel*. When glue is dry, *cut off the surplus* and sand the surface until smooth.

10. *Bore two holes* in the same fashion as above in the back of the arm. Also bore four holes in the end stretcher.

11. To complete the end assembly *drill pilot holes* and drive screws into the arm supports and the end uprights. Measure the screw length carefully as they may vary. *Cover all screw heads* with birch screw hole buttons No. 2 3/8 in. round head for 3/8 in. holes.

12. *Attach the back assembly* to the end uprights assembly with glue, and FHB No. 6-1 in. screws. Cover the screw heads with birch screw hole buttons. *Attach the seat assembly* to the uprights with 3/8 in. dowels and glue.

MAGAZINE HOLDER

This simply made, but attractive, accessory detailed in Fig. 4-34 will automatically find a place near the magazine reader's favorite chair.

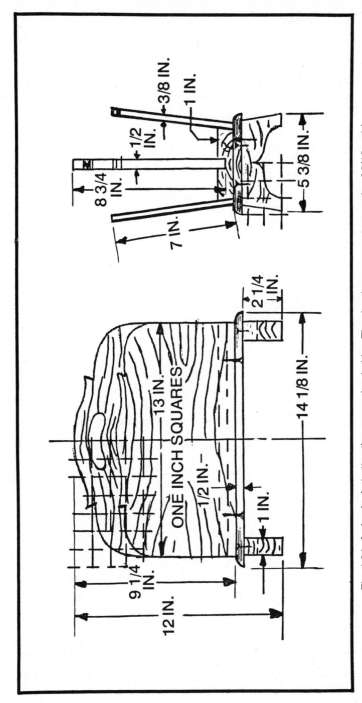

Fig. 4-34. A simple, but attractive, magazine holder. The drawing represents a scale of 3/16 = 1 in.

Material:

Table 4-26 lists materials to complete a magazine holder.

Table 4-26.

Quantity	Description	Thick	Width	Length	Wood
1	Center handle	1/2	9 1/4	13	White pine
1	Sides/center support	1	4	13	White pine
2	Sides	3/8	7	13	White pine
1	Base	1/2	5 1/2	14 1/8	White pine
2	Feet	1	2 1/4	5 3/8	White pine

Note: Measurements in inches

Procedure:

1. *Make patterns* for all curved parts.
2. *Cut the center handle* to the squared dimension given in Table 4-25. *Mark* the curved parts with an appropriate pattern. *Cut the outside curves* with a band saw or other curve-cutting tool. With a coping saw, jigsaw, or saber saw, cut *out* the *hand hole* after the holes have been bored for blade insertion.
3. *Cut the sides* to squared dimensions. *Mark the curved parts* with the appropriate pattern. *Cut the curved parts* with a band saw or other curve-cutting tools.
4. *Cut the base* to the required dimensions and roll the edges with a plane and sandpaper.
5. *Cut the feet* to squared dimensions. *Mark the curved parts* with an appropriate pattern. *Cut the feet* with a band saw.
6. *Attach the feet* to the base with glue and FHB No. 6-1 1/4 in. screws. Screws extend down through the base into the feet. *Cut the groove* for the center handle in sides/center support. *Insert the center handle* in the groove with glue applied to the bottom of the center handle. *Attach the sides* to the sides/center support with glue and small brads. *Attach the base* and the feet subassembly to the upper subassembly with glue and FHB No. 6-1 in. screws.

MILK STOOL

This one weekend, cute little gadget (Fig. 4-35) is wonderful for the kiddies while watching TV. To avoid arguments, the craftsman should make one for each child.

Material:

The only materials needed to create the milk stool of Fig. 4-35 are listed in Table 4-27.

Table 4-27.

Quantity	Description	Thick	Width	Length	Wood
1	Top	1 3/8	12	12	White pine
3	Legs	1 1/2	1 1/2	9 1/2	White pine or birch
3	Wedges	1/8	7/8	1 1/4	Birch

Note: Measurements in inches

Procedure:

1. *Cut the top* to squared dimensions. *Attach the stock* to the faceplate. *Turn the top* to dimensions and sand in the revolving lathe. (Make sure that the faceplate screw holes are on the underside of the top.) *Bore holes* of 7/8 in. diameter in the top with a guide or jig. (Refer to the procedure given for the hearthstool.)
2. *Cut the stock* for the three legs about 1 5/8 in. square and 11-in. long.
3. *Turn the legs* to dimensions. Make sure that the 1 1/2 in. dowel turned on the end is exactly 7/8 in. in diameter. *Remove excess stock* on the ends with the point of a skew or parting tool while the lathe is revolving. *Cut a saw kerf* with a band saw or bucksaw about 1 1/4 in. deep in the center of the dowel ends of the legs.
4. *Cut three wedges* 1/8 in. to 3/16 in. thick; 7/8 in. wide and 1 3/8 in. long. One end of the wedge will be a sharp edge.
5. *Apply glue* to the *dowel ends* of the legs and insert the legs into the holes in the top. *Immediately* put glue on the end of the wedges and drive them into the saw kerfs on the dowel end of the legs.
6. After glue is thoroughly dry, *cut off* the *excess* length of the wedges. *Sand* down the end of the dowel ends and wedges until they are perfectly flush with the surface of the top.

MINIATURE CHEST

The versatile chest of Fig. 4-36 can be used for anything from old love letters to colored slides, movie films, old coins, or stamps.

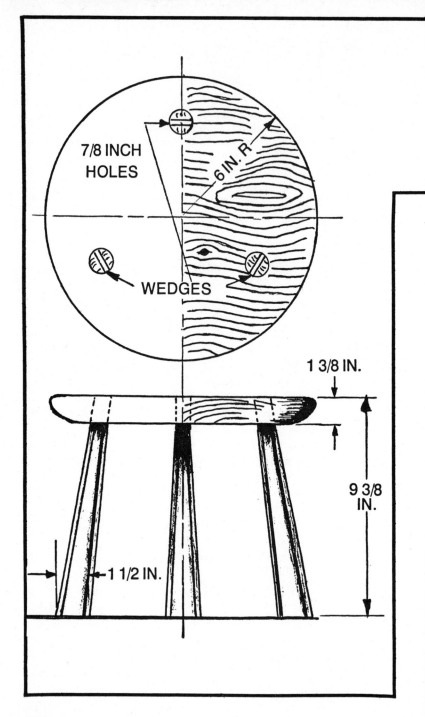

7/8 INCH HOLES

6 IN. R

WEDGES

1 3/8 IN.

9 3/8 IN.

1 1/2 IN.

Fig. 4-35. An old-fashioned milk stool.

Security may be improved somewhat by adding a small chest lock.

Material:

Table 4-28 lists materials needed to create a beautiful miniature chest.

Table 4-28.

Quantity	Description	Thick	Width	Length	Wood
1	Top	1/2	11	16	White pine
1	Bottom	1/2	11 1/2	16 1/2	White pine
2	Front and back	1/2	9 1/2	14	White pine
2	Ends	1/2	9 1/2	10	White pine
2	Front and back base rails	1/2	1 1/2	15	White pine
2	End base rails	1/2	1 1/2	10 1/2	White pine
Standard 11/16 in x 3/4 in. cove molding, approx. 40 linear feet					White pine
Standard 1 1/8 in. x 3/4 in. cove molding, approx. 40 linear feet					White pine
1/2 in. Half-round molding, approx. 100 in.					
2	Small brass hinges				

Note: Measurements in inches

Procedure:

1. *Cut* a piece of 1/2 in. *stock* 9 1/2-in. wide and at least 50 in. long. This amount will provide stock for the front, back and two ends. *Set saw* at 45 degrees. *Miter* one end of the stock. *Flip the stock over* and cut one length (front, back or ends) of the stock to correct length. *Continue measuring and flipping stock over* until all cuts are made for the four pieces (5 cuts total). This method will not only save stock but will also eliminate almost one-half the number of cuts.

233

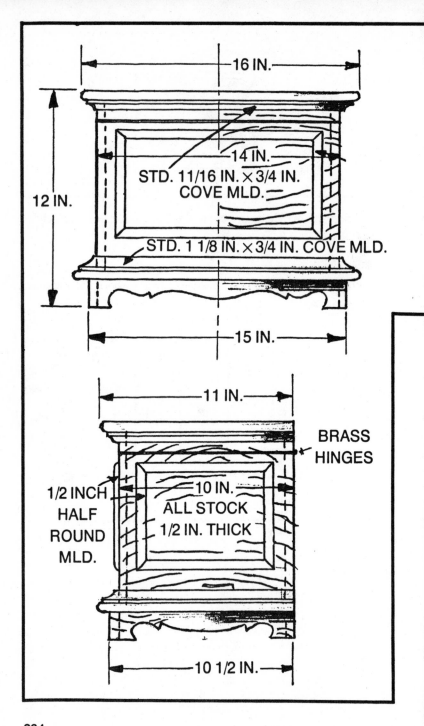

16 IN.

12 IN.

14 IN.

STD. 11/16 IN. × 3/4 IN. COVE MLD.

STD. 1 1/8 IN. × 3/4 IN. COVE MLD.

15 IN.

11 IN.

BRASS HINGES

10 IN.
ALL STOCK
1/2 IN. THICK

1/2 INCH HALF ROUND MLD.

10 1/2 IN.

234

Fig. 4-36. A versatile and beautiful miniature chest that can serve a purpose in any room.

2. *Fasten* these four pieces together with glue and small brads. **Note:** Stock is too thin to use splines.
3. When glue is dry, *cut* a 1 in. *section* from the box. This section will become a part of the top as demonstrated in Fig. 4-36.
4. *Cut* 1/2-in. half-round *molding* in the miter box (45 degree mitered corners) and *attach* to the front and two ends of the box with glue and small brads. (See Fig. 4-36.)
5. *Cut the top* to the required dimensions. *Roll the edges* with a plane and sandpaper. *Attach* this to the small section of the box.
6. *Cut the bottom* to the required dimensions. Roll the edges with a plane and sandpaper.
7. *Cut* a piece of *stock* 1/2 in. thick by 1 1/2 in. wide and 54-in. long; this is sufficient for the *four base rails. Cut to lengths* in a meter box by flip-flopping as was done in Step 1. *Make patterns* for the curved parts and *mark stock. Cut the curved portions* with any curve-cutting saw. *Fasten the four base rail parts* together with glue and small brads.
8. *Fasten the base* to the larger section of the box with glue and small brads driven down through bottom. Brad heads will be covered with cove molding.
9. *Attach* the two small *brass hinges* to the smaller section of the box and *attach the top* with glue and small brads. Around

three sides of top, attach standard 11/16 in. × 3/4 in. cove molding, mitered at corners, with glue and small brads. Attach the other half of the hinges to the larger section of the box.

10. *Attach* standard 1 1/8 in. × 3/4 in. cove molding to the bottom on three sides, mitered at corners, with glue and small brads.

POWDER MIRROR

The classically designed powder mirror of Fig. 4-37 will fit into any lady's boudoir. The drawer will provide space for many toilet articles. This piece may become a wonderful family heirloom to hand down to future generations.

Material:

Materials needed to complete the classic powder mirror are listed in Table 4-29.

Table 4-29.

Quantity	Description	Thick	Width	Length	Wood
1	Drawer compartment top	7/16	6 1/2	14 1/8	White pine
1	Drawer compartment bottom	7/16	6 1/2	14 1/8	White pine
2	Drawer compartment sides	7/16	2 3/4	6 1/2	White pine
2	Uprights (to hold mirror)	7/16	7/8	9 5/8	White pine
1	Mirror frame top	7/16	1 1/2	9 5/8	White pine
2	Mirror frame sides	7/16	7/8	12	White pine
1	Mirror frame bottom	7/16	7/8	9 5/8	White pine
2	Turned mirror pins	5/8	5/8	1 1/4	Birch
2	Turned drawer knobs	3/4	3/4	1 1/4	Birch
4	Turned feet	3/4	3/4	1	Birch
1	Mirror		8 1/2	10 3/4	Mirror glass
2	Small, thin washers				
1	Drawer front	13/16	2 3/4	13 3/8	White pine
2	Drawer sides	5/16	2 3/4	5 5/8	White pine
1	Drawer back	3/8	2 3/4	12 5/8	White pine
1	Drawer bottom	1/8	5 1/2	13	Hardboard
1	Dust cover	1/4	3 1/2	14 1/8	Plywood

Note: Measurements in inches

Procedure:

1. With trammel points or pencil-string-thumbtack compass, *swing an arc* of 36-in. radius on heavy paper. *Mark off two points* on the arc which will be exactly 14 1/8 in. on a straight line (cord of circle). *Draw a straight line* between the two points. Then *draw* a *right angle* perpendicular to the two points of a 6 in. length. *Draw a line* between the ends of the perpendiculars. *Cut* out the *pattern* with shears. This will be the pattern to use on the drawer compartment top and bottom and the drawer front.

2. *Cut the drawer compartment top* and *bottom* to squared dimensions. *Mark curved portions* with the pattern just made. *Cut the curved portions* with a band saw. Bore 1/4 in. holes 1/4-in. deep in the four corners of the bottom for feet.

3. *Cut the drawer compartment sides* to dimensions. **Note:** The length should be slightly longer to allow for the curved front.

4. *Make a pattern* for the top of the uprights. Cut the uprights to squared dimensions. *Mark the curved part* on the top of the uprights and saw on a band saw or other curved tool. On the other end of the uprights cut the angles (Fig. 4-37). Drill 1/4 in. hole 1 1/2 in. down from the top of the uprights.

5. *Make a pattern* for the mirror-frame top. *Cut the piece* to squared dimensions. *Miter corners* (45 degrees).

6. *Cut the two mirror side frames* to the required dimensions. *Miter corners* (45 degrees).

7. *Cut the mirror bottom frame* to the required dimensions. *Miter corners* (45 degrees).

8. *Cut rabbets* 7/16 in. wide and 3/16 in. deep on the inside of all four pieces. Do not change saw or dado setting until all four cuts are made.

9. *Assemble the mirror* with glue and small brads. It might be necessary to clamp.

10. *Cut the mirror glass* to the size of the rabbets in the frame. Cut a back-up piece of 1/8 in. thick standard hardboard. *Do not install* the glass in the frame until after the finishing process is completed.

11. Accurately *mark* the centers for the turned-mirror pins 5 in. down from the top of the frame. *Drill* 1/4 in. holes.

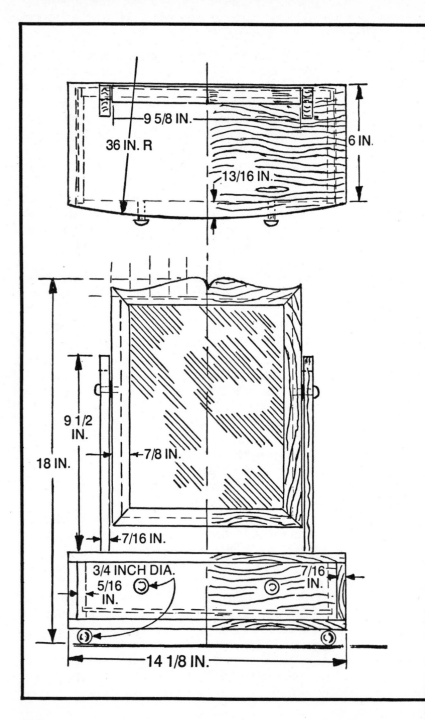

9 5/8 IN.

36 IN. R

6 IN.

13/16 IN.

9 1/2 IN.

18 IN.

7/8 IN.

7/16 IN.

3/4 INCH DIA.

5/16 IN.

7/16 IN.

14 1/8 IN.

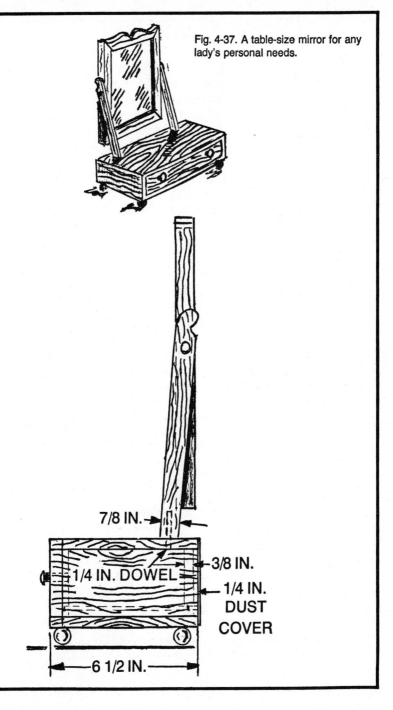

Fig. 4-37. A table-size mirror for any lady's personal needs.

7/8 IN.

3/8 IN.

1/4 IN. DOWEL

1/4 IN. DUST COVER

6 1/2 IN.

12. *Turn the mirror pins* (Fig. 4-37). The dowel part is 1/4 in. in diameter and the head of the pin is about 5/8 in. in diameter.

13. *Attach the mirror frame* to the uprights with the pins just turned. A small thin metal washer should be between the uprights and the frame. If the mirror turns hard *sand down* the mirror pins. Do not sand to the point where the mirror will not stay in position when adjusted for the angle.

14. *Cut a stick* (from a scrap box) equal in length to the width of the mirror frame plus the thickness of the two washers. *Clamp this stick* between the two uprights just below the mirror-frame bottom. *Set* this assembly *on top* of the drawer-compartment top. *Mark around the bottom* of the uprights as they sit on the drawer compartment top. In the center of this rectangle, *bore* a 1/4 in. *dowel hole* through the drawer-compartment top. *Drill corresponding* 1/4 in. *holes* in the lower ends of the uprights. *Cut the dowels* to fit. Apply glue to the dowels and ends of the supports. *Attach* the *compartment top* to the upright/frame subassembly.

15. *Drawer compartment sides, bottom and top* are assembled with glue and brads. *Turn* the four feet to 3/4 in. in diameter with a 1/4 in. diameter by 1/4 in. long dowel turned to enter the drawer-compartment bottom. *Place glue on the dowels* on the feet and insert them into the holes already drilled.

16. *Accurately measure the drawer opening. Cut the drawer front* to squared dimensions. *Mark the curved portion* on the edge of the drawer front with the pattern previously made. (It is the same pattern used with the drawer-compartment top and bottom.) *Cut a rabbet* in each end 1/8 in. deep and 5/16 in. wide. *Cut the drawer sides* to dimensions. *Cut a rabbet* in one end of each side 1/8 in. deep by 3/8 in. wide. *Saw the drawer back* to the required dimension. *Cut a saw kerf* 1/8 in. wide and 3/16 in. deep around a 11 four drawer parts 1/4 in. up from the bottom edge. Do not change saw settings until all four grooves are cut. *Measure carefully* for the drawer bottom and cut a piece of 1/8 in. standard hardboard to fit. *Assemble the drawer* with glue and clamp. Brads may be used on the back corners. *Turn knobs.* The knob should be 3/4 in. in diameter with the dowel part 1/4 in. in diameter and 1 in. long. *Drill* 1/4 in. *holes* in the drawer front. *Place glue on the dowel part* of the knobs and insert them into the holes.

17. *Cut* 1/8 in. thick *hardboard* to size for a dust cover and fasten to the back of the drawer compartment with glue and brads.
18. *Insert the mirror glass* and back up piece of hardboard in the frame after finishing process has been completed.

SERVING CART

The cart demonstrated in Figs. 4-38 and 4-39 has the advantage of being able to be stored in a small space. A bonus is the fact that the butler's tray may be used separately from the cart.

Material:

Table 4-30 gives materials needed to complete a versatile serving cart.

Table 4-30.

Quantity	Description	Thick	Width	Length	Wood
1	Butler tray base	1/2	18 3/4	36 1/2	White pine
2	Butler tray handles	5/8	4 1/2	17	White pine
2	Butler tray sides	1/2	2	35 3/4	White pine
2	Butler tray retainer strips	1/2	1/2	35 3/4	White pine
2	Butler tray retainer strips	1/2	1/2	17	White pine
4	Serving cart wheels	3/4	4	4	White pine
4	Serving cart long members	3/4	1 1/2	37 1/2	White pine
4	Serving cart short members	3/4	1 1/2	12 1/2	White pine
2	Serving cart cross members, Dowels		1/2	15	Birch Birch
6	Serving Cart Cross Members, Dowels		1/2	16 1/2	Birch Birch
2	Thin metal washers				
4	Round head screws 7-1 1/2				
4	Small washers to fit shank of round head screws				

Procedure:

1. *Cut the butler-tray base* to size. *Roll the edges* with a plane and sandpaper.
2. *Make patterns* for the handles and sides.

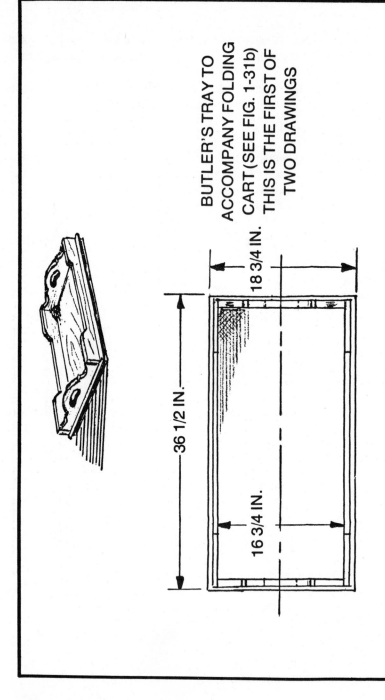

BUTLER'S TRAY TO ACCOMPANY FOLDING CART (SEE FIG. 1-31b) THIS IS THE FIRST OF TWO DRAWINGS

18 3/4 IN.

36 1/2 IN.

16 3/4 IN.

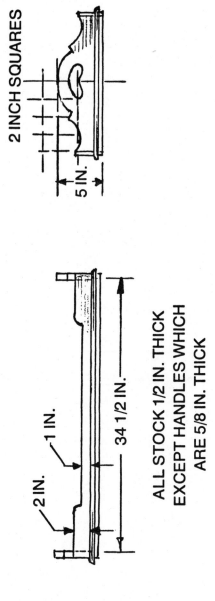

2 INCH SQUARES

5 IN.

1 IN.

2 IN.

34 1/2 IN.

ALL STOCK 1/2 IN. THICK
EXCEPT HANDLES WHICH
ARE 5/8 IN. THICK

Fig. 4-38. This serving cart has a removable butler's tray.

243

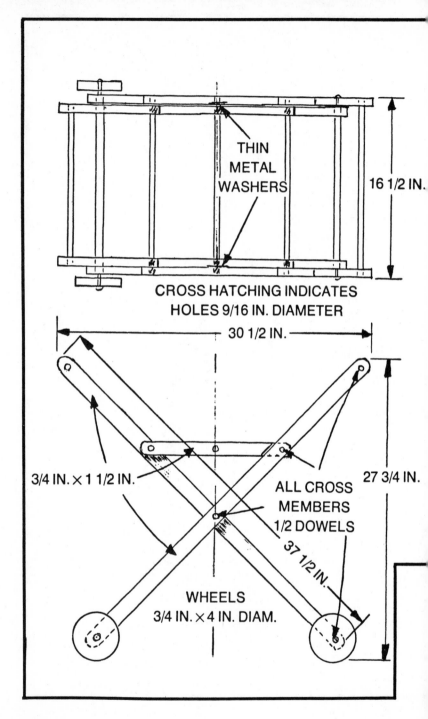

THIN METAL WASHERS

16 1/2 IN.

CROSS HATCHING INDICATES HOLES 9/16 IN. DIAMETER

30 1/2 IN.

3/4 IN. × 1 1/2 IN.

ALL CROSS MEMBERS 1/2 DOWELS

27 3/4 IN.

37 1/2 IN.

WHEELS 3/4 IN. × 4 IN. DIAM.

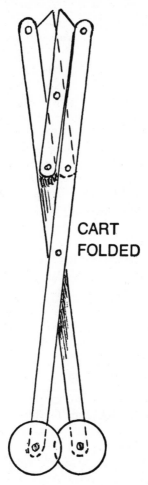

Fig. 4-39. A view of the serving cart demonstrating its ability to fold to a narrow, easy-to-store piece.

3. *Cut the handles* to the squared dimensions. *Mark the curved parts* with a pattern. *Cut* the outside *curves* with a band saw or other curve-cutting saw. *Cut the handle hole* with a jigsaw, coping saw, or saber saw.
4. *Cut the sides of the tray* to squared dimensions. *Mark the curved part* with a pattern. *Cut the curved parts* with a band saw or other curve-cutting saw.
5. *Cut* all four *retainer strips* to dimensions.

6. *Assemble the tray* with glue and brads.

7. *Cut the cart-wheel stock* to the squared size given in Table 4-30. *Cut a wheel* to round on a lathe or with a band saw. *Bore a hole* to take the shank of round-head screw No. 7-1 1/2 in.

8. *Cut the long members* of the cart to size. Round both ends as shown in Fig. 4-39. *Bore 1/2 in. holes* about 1 in. from the ends in the center of the stock. Bore 1/2 in. holes 20 in. from the ends of the four pieces in the center of the stock. Some holes must be rebored to 9/16 in. diameters. (See the crosshatched holes in Fig. 4-39.) *Bore* another *dowel hole* in the four members 11 1/2 in. from the end and between the 20 in. hole and the end.

9. *Cut the short members* of the cart to size. *Saw one end* at a 45 degree angle. *Round* the other ends. On the rounded end, *bore a dowel hole* about 1 in. from the end in the center of the stock.

10. *Cut* all *dowel cross members* to length. *Assemble* the cart by gluing the dowels into the dowel holes. *Do not* glue dowels where cross hatching is shown.

11. *Drill pilot holes* for the round head screws in the ends of the dowels which carry the wheels. Place small washers under the heads of the screws. Insert screws through the holes in the wheels and drive in with a screwdriver.

SPICE-DRAWER CABINET WITH RECESSED KNOBS

The superb adaptation of an apothecary cabinet into a spice drawer cabinet draws "Ohs" and "Ahs" from those who see it the first time. Originally this cabinet (Fig. 4-40) was built by the author for his basement woodshop. In it were stored nails, screws, washers, brads, tacks, nuts, bolts, etc. After two years and pressure from the distaff side of the family, it now occupies a favorite spot on the dining room wall. Today, no hardware will be found in the drawers.

Material:

Table 4-31 lists all materials required to complete the spice-drawer cabinet.

Procedure:

1. *Cut the top* and *bottom* to correct size. *Cut* the 1/4 in. deep, 1/2 in. wide *dadoes*. Use the same fence stop when sawing corresponding dadoes on both pieces.

Table 4-31.

Quantity	Description	Thick	Width	Length	Wood
2	Top and bottom	9/16	4 7/8	20	White pine
5	Vertical partitions	1/2	4 7/8	19 1/8	White pine
20	Horizontal partitions	3/8	4 7/8	4 1/4	White pine
24	Drawer fronts	1/2	2 11/16	3 15/16	White pine
48	Drawer sides	1/4	2 11/16	4 1/8	White pine
24	Drawer backs	1/4	2 11/16	3 5/8	White pine
24	Drawer bottoms	1/8	3 3/4	3 5/8	Hardbound
1	Dust cover	1/8	18	19 3/4	Hardbound

Note: Measurements in inches

2. *Cut* all five *partitions* and sides at the same time. Use the same cross cut fence stop for all five pieces.

3. *Cut dadoes* 1/8 in. deep, 3/8 in. wide on all five pieces. Keep in mind that dadoes will be cut on only *one* side of the two outside pieces, while dadoes will be cut on *both* sides of the other three pieces. Use the same fence stop when sawing corresponding dadoes on all five pieces.

4. *Assemble* all the *pieces* constructed so far with glue only.

5. *Cut a piece* of *standard hardboard* to size for a dust cover. Attach this to the back with glue and brads.

6. *Cut drawer fronts* to size. Turn recess knobs. Refer to Chapter 3, "How To Turn Recessed Knobs in Spice Drawer Fronts." *Cut* a 1/8 in. wide by 1/4 in. *deep dado* in the ends of the drawer fronts 1/4 in. from the ends of the fronts. *Make all 48 cuts* with the same saw setting. *Cut drawer sides* to correct dimensions. *Make* a 1/8 in. deep, 1/4 in. wide *rabbet* across one end of the sides. Make all 48 cuts with the same saw setting *Cut* a 1/8 in. deep 1/4 in. wide *dado* on the other end of the drawer sides. Make all 48 cuts with the same setting. *Cut* the *backs* to size. *Cut a groove* 1/8 in. deep, 1/4 in. from the bottom of all fronts, sides and backs. This groove will contain the drawer bottoms. Do not change the setting of the saw until all 96 cuts have been made. *Measure accurately* and *cut* the 24 bottoms from standard 1/8 in. hardboard. The size should be 3 3/4 in. × 3 5/8 in. *Assemble the drawers* with glue only.

SPICE-DRAWER CABINET WITH PORCELAIN KNOBS

Perhaps the woodworking craftsman might shy away from the spice drawer cabinet with twenty-four drawers shown in Fig. 4-40.

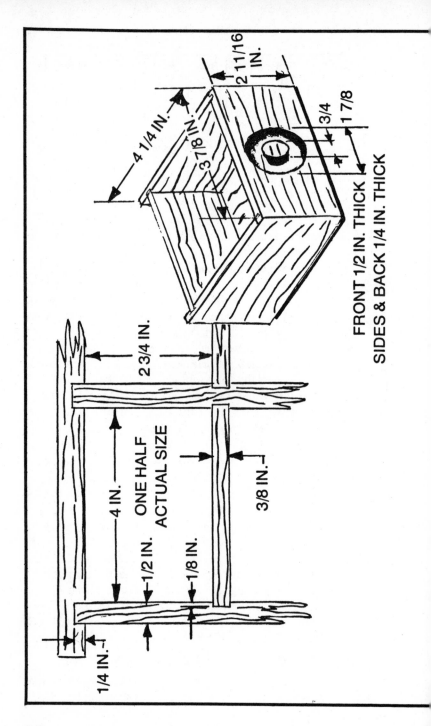

2 11/16 IN.

1 7/8

3/4

4 1/4 IN.

3 7/8 IN.

3 7/8

FRONT 1/2 IN. THICK
SIDES & BACK 1/4 IN. THICK

2 3/4 IN.

4 IN.

ONE HALF
ACTUAL SIZE

3/8 IN.

1/2 IN.

1/8 IN.

1/4 IN.

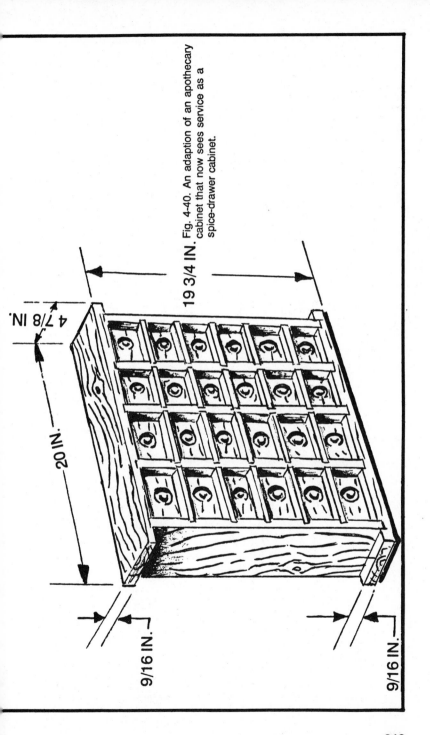

4 7/8 IN.

20 IN.

19 3/4 IN. Fig. 4-40. An adaption of an apothecary cabinet that now sees service as a spice-drawer cabinet.

9/16 IN.

9/16 IN.

He may particularly shy from the responsibility of turning the recessed knobs. This project (Fig. 4-41) is a very fine alternative. The porcelain knobs give this cabinet a distinctive Dutch flavor.

Material:

Materials needed to complete the spice-drawer cabinet are listed in Table 4-32.

Table 4-32.

Quantity	Description	Thick	Width	Length	Wood
1	Back	1/2	9 1/2	12 1/2	White pine
2	Sides	1/2	4 1/2	9 1/4	White pine
2	Top shelves	1/2	4 1/2	9	White pine
1	Bottom shelf	1/2	4 1/2	9 1/2	White pine
4	Drawer fronts	1/2	2 7/8	3 3/4	White pine
8	Drawer sides	1/4	2 7/8	3 3/4	White pine
4	Drawer backs	1/4	2 7/8	3 1/2	White pine
2	Vertical partitions	1/2	3 1/4	4 1/2	White pine
4	Porcelain knobs approx. 3/4 inch in diameter				

Note: Measurements in inches

Procedure:

1. *Make a pattern* for the curved portion of the back. *Cut the back* to squared dimensions. *Mark the curved portion* with the pattern. *Cut the back* on a bandsaw.

2. *Make a pattern* for the curved portions of the sides. *Cut the sides* to squared dimensions. *Mark the curved portion* with the pattern. *Cut the curved portion* of the sides on a band saw. *Cut 1/4 in. deep, 1/2 in. wide dadoes* for the *two top shelves only.*

3. *Cut the two top shelves* to dimensions. *Cut a 1/4 in. deep, 1/2-in. wide dado* in the center of *one* side of the uppermost top shelf. *Cut 1/8 in. deep, 1/2 in. wide dadoes* in *both* sides in the center of the middle shelf. See Fig. 4-41.

4. *Cut the bottom shelf* to dimensions. Cut rabbets in ends 1/2 in. × 3/8 in., *cut a 1/4 in. deep, 1/2-in. wide dado* in the center of *one* side (same side that rabbets are cut).

5. *Cut the vertical partitions* to size.

6. *Assemble* these eight *pieces* with glue. One-inch brads may be used on the back only.

7. *Cut drawer fronts* to size. *Cut a dado* on each end 1/8 in. wide, 1/4 in. deep and 1/8 in. in from the ends. *Cut drawer sides* to dimensions. On one end cut a rabbet 1/8 in. deep,

250

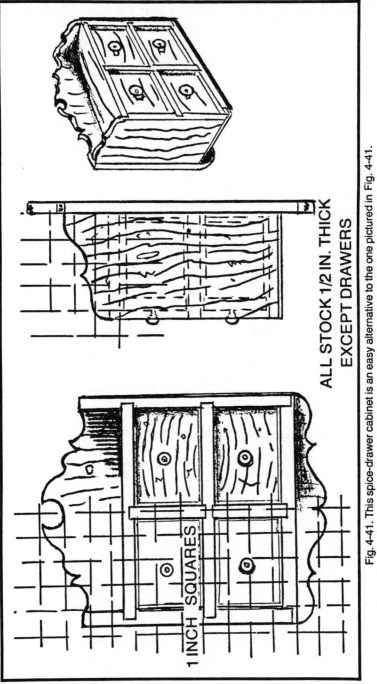

ALL STOCK 1/2 IN. THICK
EXCEPT DRAWERS

1 INCH SQUARES

Fig. 4-41. This spice-drawer cabinet is an easy alternative to the one pictured in Fig. 4-41.

1/4 in. wide. On the other end of the side, cut a dado 1/8 in. deep, 1/2-in. wide and in from the end 1/4 in. *Cut the back* to size. *Cut* a 1/8 in. *wide groove* 1/8 in. deep on all parts of the drawer 1/4 in. up from the bottom edge. Cut all 16 grooves at the same saw setting. *Measure the bottom opening* and *cut* the four bottoms to fit. If care has been taken in previous operations, the bottoms should be 1/8 in. × 3 1/4 in. × 3 1/2 in. *Assemble the drawers* with glue only. The back of cabinet will act as drawer stop. When the drawer is in place, it will be back into the sides about 3/8 in. This will cause some very interesting shadow designs.

SPICE RACK

This little beauty (Fig. 4-42 and Fig. 4-43) might rightly be called a "more than one project on a weekend." Fitted with small square spice jars, this wall or countertop ornament is not only a pleasure to look at but is practical as well. What a wonderful gift at Christmas or for a birthday!

Material:

Table 4-33 lists all materials needed to create the decorative spice rack.

Table 4-33.

Quantity	Description	Thick	Width	Length	Wood
1	Top back rail	5/16	2 1/4	13 1/2	White pine
1	Bottom	5/16	2 7/8	13 1/2	White pine
1	Front rail	3/16	1	13 1/2	White pine
2	Ends	5/16	2 5/8	5	White pine
2	Thin metal hangers				

Note: Measurements in inches

Procedure:

1. *Make* heavy *paper patterns* of all curved parts.
2. *Cut the top back rail* to squared dimensions. *Mark* the *curved portion* with the appropriate pattern. *Cut the curved part* with a band saw, saber saw, jig saw, or coping saw.
3. *Cut the bottom* to the required dimensions. *Roll* the front edge and two ends with sandpaper.
4. *Cut the front rail* to squared dimensions. *Mark the curved portion* with the appropriate pattern. *Cut the curved part* with any curve-cutting saw.

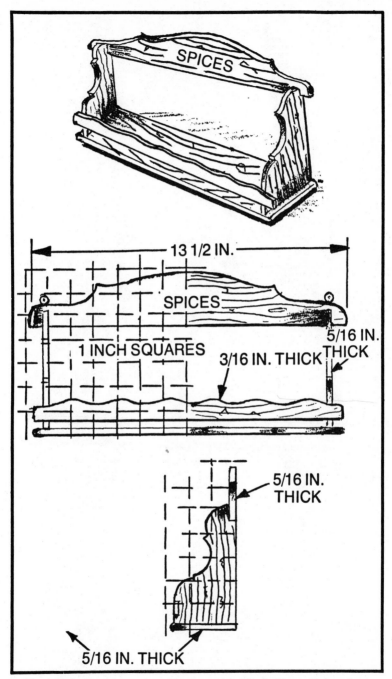

SPICES

13 1/2 IN.

SPICES

1 INCH SQUARES

3/16 IN. THICK

5/16 IN. THICK

5/16 IN. THICK

5/16 IN. THICK

Fig. 4-42. A decorative and useful spice rack to blend with any kitchen decor.

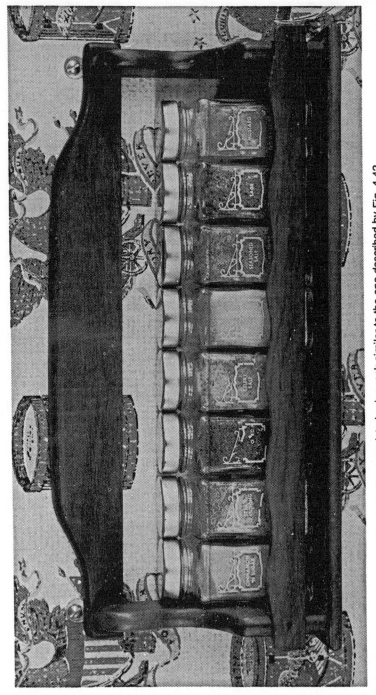

Fig. 4-43. The completed spice rack similar to the one described by Fig. 4-42.

5. *Cut the ends* to squared dimensions. With the proper pattern, *mark* the *curved portions. Cut the curves* with a band saw, coping saw, saber saw or jigsaw.
6. *Roll all front edges* a small amount. *Assemble* the *spice rack* with glue and small brads. *Attach* small *metal hangers.* (Distressing and glazing may be somewhat overemphasized without destroying the character of the project.)

CARD TABLE

The card table shown in Fig. 4-44, which also doubles as a console table, gets plenty of attention around the house. Birch or maple might be substituted for white pine if it is anticipated that the table will receive severe usage.

Material:

Table 4-34 lists materials necessary to complete a card table.

Table 4-34.

Quantity	Description	Thick	Width	Length	Wood
2	Top leaves	3/4	18	36	White pine
2	Front and back rails	3/4	3 3/4	30	White pine
		(Add 3 in. if blind mortise and tenon points are to be used)			
2	End rails	3/4	3 3/4	13	White pine
		(Add 3 in. to length if blind mortise and tenon joints are to be used.)			
4	Legs	2	2	28 1/4	White pine
1	Outside pivot member	3/4	4	16	Maple or birch
1	Inside pivot member	1 1/2	1 1/2	1 1/4	Maple or birch

Note: Measurements in inches

Procedure:

1. *Cut the top leaves* to required dimensions.
2. *Cut all four rails* with the same setting of the saw for width. Be sure to add 3 in. to rail length if *blind mortise* and *tenon joints* are to be used. (See half-size drawing of Fig. 1-44.) If blind mortise and tenons are to be used, cut the tenons on the rails by cutting rabbets on each side of the end 3/16 in. deep and 1 1/2 in. wide. The tenon should be exactly

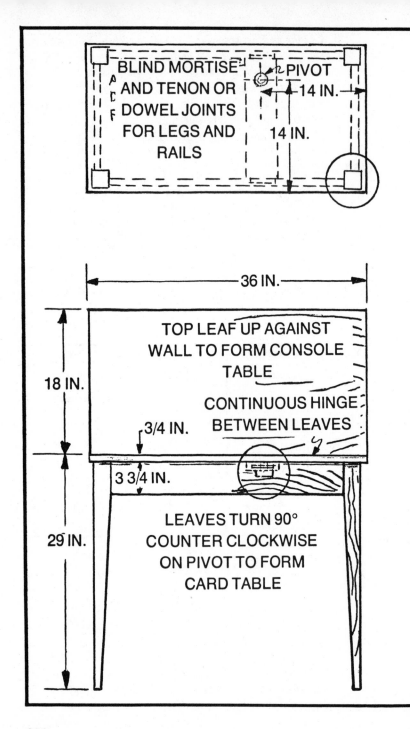

BLIND MORTISE AND TENON OR DOWEL JOINTS FOR LEGS AND RAILS

PIVOT

14 IN.

14 IN.

36 IN.

18 IN.

3/4 IN.

3 3/4 IN.

29 IN.

TOP LEAF UP AGAINST WALL TO FORM CONSOLE TABLE

CONTINUOUS HINGE BETWEEN LEAVES

LEAVES TURN 90° COUNTER CLOCKWISE ON PIVOT TO FORM CARD TABLE

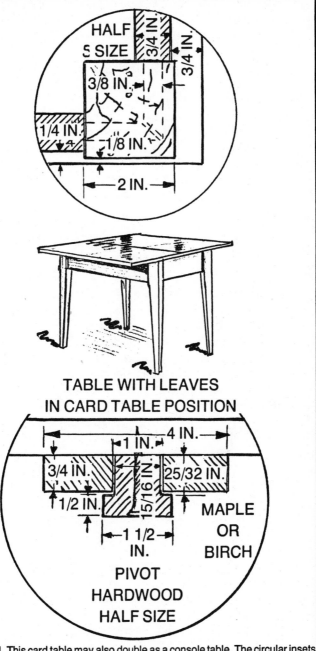

HALF SIZE

3/4 IN.

3/4 IN.

3/8 IN.

3/4 IN.

1/4 IN.

1/8 IN.

2 IN.

TABLE WITH LEAVES
IN CARD TABLE POSITION

4 IN.

1 IN.

3/4 IN.

15/16 IN.

25/32 IN.

1/2 IN.

MAPLE
OR
BIRCH

1 1/2
IN.

PIVOT
HARDWOOD
HALF SIZE

Fig. 4-44. This card table may also double as a console table. The circular insets are scaled for a closer view.

3/8 in. thick if a 3/8 in. hollow-chisel mortiser is used to cut mortise. If mortise is hand-bored and chiseled, accuracy is not quite as important. The mortise can simply be cut until the tenon fits into it snugly. The tenon (and the mortise) should be 2 3/4 in. wide. The tenon and mortise starts 1/2 in. down from the top of the rail and ends 1/8 in. from the bottom of rail. A mortise that starts less than 1/2 in. down from the top of the rail and leg is apt to break in the assembly process. The tenons are mitered (45 degrees) on the ends. The rabbets that are cut to form tenons are best cut with a dado head.

3. *Cut* four *legs* to dimensions given in Table 4-33. *Start taper* cut 4 in. from the end of the leg. The taper is best done with successive cuts on the jointers, but they can also be cut with a plane. (The fore plane and jointer plane are better than the jack plane.) *Cut mortises* in all four legs if mortise and tenon joints are to be used.

4. *Cut stock* for the *inside pivot member* (bearing) to make a 1 3/4 in. cube. *Turn the bearing* to size on a lathe. (See Fig. 4-44. The bearing-dowel diameter should be between 15/16 in. and 31/32 in. in diameter.

5. *Cut stock* for the *outside pivot member* (3/4 in. × 4 in. × 16 in.) *Cut rabbets* to form a 3/8 in. thick tenon on each end. Although the drawing calls for a 1/2 in. long tenon, it is best to make tenons at least 9/16 in. long. This is to allow for adjustments to the table top before final gluing.

6. *Cut* 3/8 in. *grooves* 3/16 in. from the top of the rails for the tenon on the outside pivot member. This groove should be at least 4 1/4 in. long to allow for table top adjustment.

7. *Bore* a 1 in. *hole* in the center of the outside pivot member, *exactly* 3 in. from the end.

8. On the *underside of leaf* that will eventually rest directly on the rails and legs when the leaves are folded, *mark a point, very accurately*, 14 in. from one end and 14 in. from one side as in Fig. 4-44.

9. *Clamp legs and rails* with the outside pivot in place. *Do not glue.*

10. *Drill a hole* in the center of the *inside pivot member* (bearing) for a flat head screw.

11. *Drill a pilot hole* for this same screw in the underside of the top.

12. *Align the table top* so the screw will find the pilot hole through the bearing. At the same time, the bearing (inside pivot member) must be through the 1 in. hole in the outside pivot member.

13. *Drive in a screw securely.* If the table top does not line up correctly, make corrections by moving the tenons on the outside pivot members in the rail groove. After corrections are made, mark grooves and tenons carefully.

14. *Remove the clamps* and *disassemble* all parts.

15. *Attach a continuous hinge* between the two top leaves.

16. *Glue the legs, rails, and outside pivot member.* The outside pivot member must be lined up with correction marks.

17. *Rub paraffin* on the *bearing surface* of the inside pivot member. *Insert a bearing* through the 1 in. hole in the outside pivot member. *Put the table top* in place. *Place a screw* in the pilot hole in the table top and *drive* the *screw* down securely with a screwdriver. It will probably be necessary to disassemble a second time while finish material is being applied.

CONSOLE TABLE

A console table is a table used against a wall (see Fig. 4-45). It is often used in an entrance way as a surface on which to place gloves, a hat, calling cards, etc. temporarily. Quite often a mirror is hung above the console table.

Material:

Materials needed to complete a console table are given in Table 4-35.

Table 4-35.

Quantity	Description	Thick	Width	Length	Wood
1	Top	3/4	18	40	White pine
1	Back rail	3/4	4	36	White pine
1	Front rail	3/4	4	21 1/2	White pine
2	Side rails	3/4	4	13 1/2	White pine
4	Legs	2	2	28 1/4	White pine

Note: Measurements in inches

Procedure:

1. *Cut the top* to squared dimensions. *Make a pattern* for the *curved part* and mark it on the top. *Cut the curved parts* with a band saw, saber saw or jigsaw.

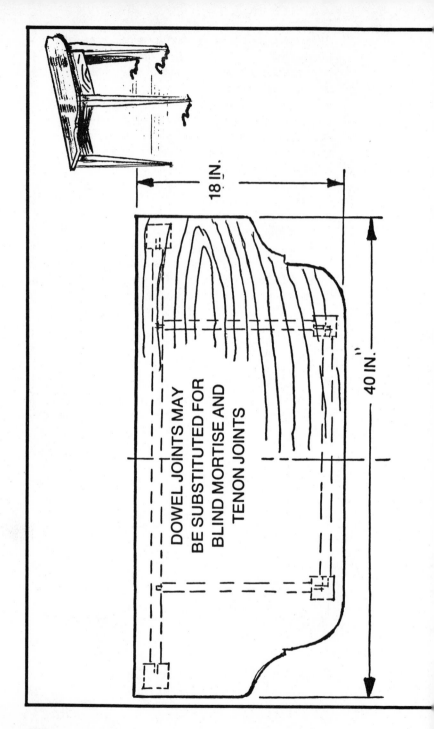

18 IN.

40 IN.

DOWEL JOINTS MAY
BE SUBSTITUTED FOR
BLIND MORTISE AND
TENON JOINTS

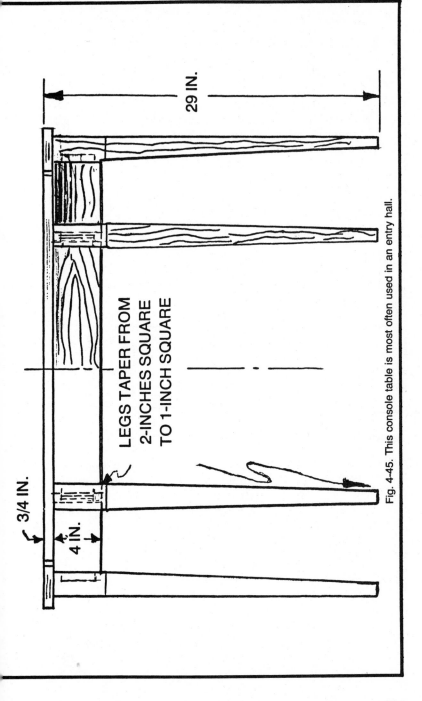

29 IN.

3/4 IN.

4 IN.

LEGS TAPER FROM
2-INCHES SQUARE
TO 1-INCH SQUARE

Fig. 4-45. This console table is most often used in an entry hall.

2. *Cut the four rails* with the same setting of the saw width as in Step 1. *Cut the rails* to correct lengths. *Cut two rabbets* on each end with a dado head to form the tenons.
3. *Cut the four legs* to squared dimensions. *Cut mortises* with a hollow-chisel mortiser, drill-press mortiser attachment, or by hand.
4. *Cut a taper* on the legs starting at 4 1/4 in. from the end. *Cut a taper on the jointer* or with a fore plane or jointer plane.
5. *Glue, assemble and clamp* all the parts together.

CORNER TABLE

Figure 4-46 demonstrates a small table that feels right at home in a small room where space is at a premium. It is ideal in a nursery, boy's or girl's room, den, or small bedroom.

Material:

Materials to complete a corner table are given in Table 4-36.

Table 4-36.

Quantity	Description	Thick	Width	Length	Wood
1	Top	3/4	13	21 3/4	White pine
1	Front rail	3/4	4	17 3/4	White pine
2	Back rails	3/4	4	11 1/4	White pine
3	Legs	1 1/2	1 1/2	25	White pine

Note: Measurements in inches

Procedure:

1. *Make a pattern* for the entire top (curve and 90-degree corner). On heavy paper, *lay out a right angle* with a framing square. *Lay out a point* 15 1/2 in. out on each leg of the 90 degree angle. *Erect a right angle* to each of these two points. On these two legs, *make a point* 2 1/4 in. On a center line bisecting the original 90 degree angle (corner of table), *fold over the pattern.* Between the open ends of the last two 2 1/4 in. lines, *lay out one-half of the curved portion. Cut out the entire top pattern* with shears.
2. *Cut the top* to squared dimensions. *Place the pattern* on squared stock and *mark the outline* of top. The grain of the wood *must* run *parallel* to the front of the table top. The table will always be an eyesore if the grain runs in any other direction. See Fig. 4-46.

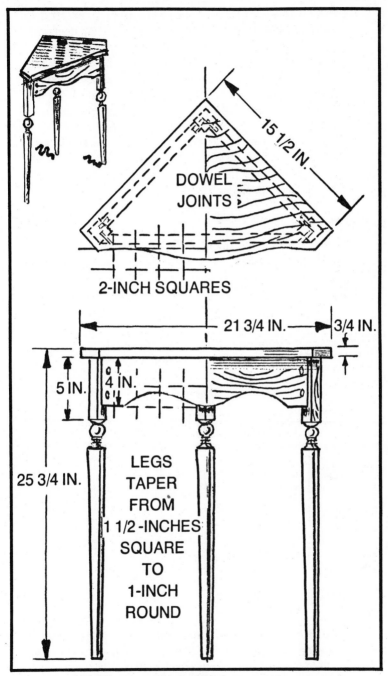

DOWEL JOINTS

15 1/2 IN.

2-INCH SQUARES

21 3/4 IN.

3/4 IN.

5 IN.

4 IN.

25 3/4 IN.

LEGS
TAPER
FROM
1 1/2 -INCHES
SQUARE
TO
1-INCH
ROUND

Fig. 4-46. This corner table is ideal where space is a premium.

3. *Cut all three rails* with the same setting of the saw for the correct width. *Cut the rails* to length. Miter (45 degrees) the *front rail*.
4. *Cut the legs* to squared dimensions. *Turn* 20 in. of the leg on the lathe using a round-nose, diamond point, skew, square point, and other lathe tools. Sand the leg with narrow strips of sandpaper while lathe is revolving.
5. *Bore holes* for 1/4 in. dowels using a doweling jig.
6. *Place glue* on *dowels* and the *ends of the rails. Assemble* and *clamp*. Special blocks with a "V" cut in them will have to be used with the clamps across the front of the table. When glue is dry, *attach the table top*.

DROP-LEAF TABLE

The general utility table of Fig. 4-47 will find many uses around the home. Although too small for a dining table, it can be used in a breakfast nook, dining alcove or any other place where two people eat together: but many other uses will be found for it as well.

Material:

Table 4-37 gives materials to complete a drop-leaf table.

Table 4-37.

Quantity	Description	Thick	Width	Length	Wood
1	Center top	3/4	14	36	White pine
2	Top leaves	3/4	11	36	White pine
2	Front and back rails	3/4	3 1/2	31	White pine
2	End rails	3/4	3 1/2	9	White pine
4	Legs	3/4	1 3/4	25 3/4	White pine
1	Leaf support (stationary)	1	3 1/2	11	White pine
1	Leaf support (moveable)	1	3 1/2	10 1/4	Birch or maple
2	Leaf support stops	1/2	1	2	Birch or maple

Note: Measurements in inches

Procedure:

1. *Cut the three top leaves* to squared dimensions. On the outside corners of the two outer (11 in.) leaves, *swing* a 2 1/4 in. radius *quarter circle* (see Fig. 4-47). *Cut the quarter circles* with a band saw. *Bore holes* for the six invisible

hinges and *insert* the hinges in the leaves as in Fig. 4-47. *Set this top assembly aside* until later.

2. *Cut the front rails, back rails* and *end rails* with the same setting width of the saw. *Cut the rails* to the proper length.

3. *Cut the four legs* to squared dimensions. *Cut tapers*, starting 4 in. from the end, with jointer, fore plane or jointer plane.

4. *Cut four pieces* of birch or maple for *leaf supports*. *Cut the four pieces one inch wider* than called for in Fig. 4-47 and Table 4-37. In the ends of the four pieces, *cut 1/2 in. dadoes* 1/2-in. apart and 1-in. deep. *The accuracy of the distance between dadoes is very important.* Cut dadoes on both ends with the same saw or dado setting. *Insert* the dadoed "fingers" of one end into the dadoed end of the other. *Lay this flat* on a bench top. Naturally, the sides of the supports are mismatched. The sides do not form a straight line. With a straight edge, *extend the edge* of one piece onto the other. *Measure* 3 1/2 in. in width and straighten the other edge and mark. *Cut off excess* so that the two pieces will line up as in Fig. 4-47. *Mark and cut* the curved portion on the leaf support (movable). *Round the ends* of the dadoed "fingers" and drill a hole for 1/4 in. or 3/8-in. dowel. While "fingers" are interlocked (see circular inset of Fig. 4-47) *insert a dowel* in the hole and *attach* the *leaf support* (stationary) to the front and back rails with flat head screws from inside.

5. *Drill holes* for 1/4-in. dowels in the rail ends and in the legs.

6. *Glue, assemble* and *clamp the legs* and *rails*.

7. When glue is dry, *attach table-top* assembly.

GATELEG TABLE

This simplified version of the classical and ever-present gateleg table (Fig. 4-48) is probably as much, or more, contemporary in design than Early American. As such, it is a wonderful space-saver in a small home or small apartment.

Material:

Materials needed to complete a gate leg table are listed in Table 4-38.

Procedure:

1. *Glue up stock* for a piece of wood 3/4 in. × 14 1/2 in. × 85 in.

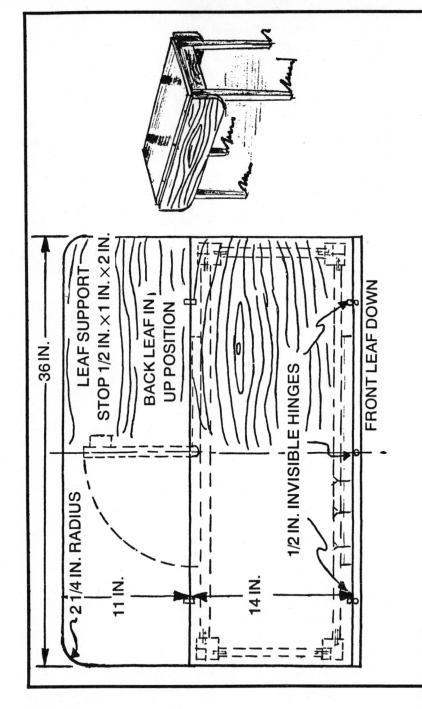

36 IN.

LEAF SUPPORT
STOP 1/2 IN. × 1 IN. × 2 IN.

BACK LEAF IN, UP POSITION

2 1/4 IN. RADIUS

11 IN.

14 IN.

1/2 IN. INVISIBLE HINGES

FRONT LEAF DOWN

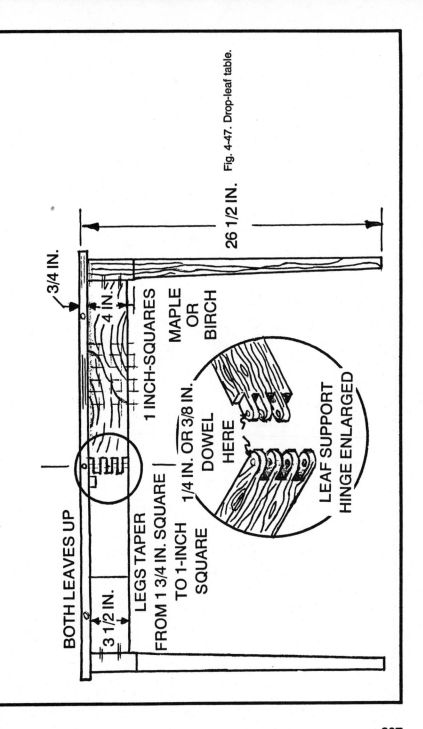

BOTH LEAVES UP

3 1/2 IN.

LEGS TAPER
FROM 1 3/4 IN. SQUARE
TO 1-INCH
SQUARE

3/4 IN.

4 IN.

1 INCH-SQUARES

MAPLE
OR
BIRCH

1/4 IN. OR 3/8 IN.

DOWEL
HERE

LEAF SUPPORT
HINGE ENLARGED

26 1/2 IN.

Fig. 4-47. Drop-leaf table.

267

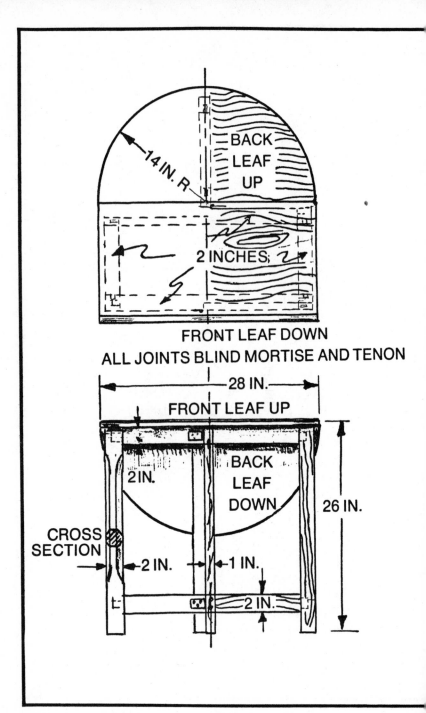

14 IN. R

BACK
LEAF
UP

2 INCHES

FRONT LEAF DOWN

ALL JOINTS BLIND MORTISE AND TENON

28 IN.

FRONT LEAF UP

2 IN.

BACK
LEAF
DOWN

26 IN.

CROSS
SECTION

2 IN.

1 IN.

2 IN.

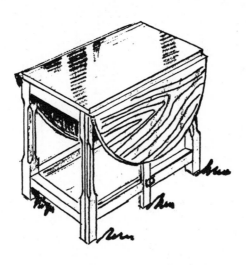

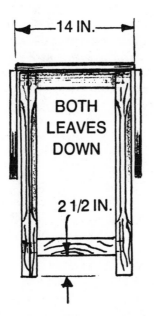

‹— 14 IN. —›

BOTH
LEAVES
DOWN

2 1/2 IN.

Fig. 4-48. A contemporary gateleg table.

Table 4-38.

Quantity	Description	Thick	Width	Length	Wood
2	Semicircular top leaves	3/4	14	28	White pine
1	Center top section	3/4	14	28	White pine
4	Front and back rails	2	2	24 3/4	White pine
4	End rails	2	2	10 3/4	White pine
2	Center section uprights	1	2	23 1/4	White pine
4	Legs	2	2	25 1/4	White pine
4	Table hinges 1 1/2-in. × 3 1/8-in.				
2	28-in. Continuous hinges				

Note: Measurements in inches

2. *Joint one edge* and cut it exactly 14 in. wide.
3. *Cut three sections* exactly 28 in. long.
4. On two of these 14 in. × 28 in. sections, *swing a half circle*, 14 in. radius, with trammel points or pencil-string-thumbtack compass. *Cut curves* on the band saw.
5. *Cut* the *four front* and *back rails* to size. From each rail *cut out* a *section* 1 in. × 2 in. × 13 in. These smaller sections will become a part of the "swinging gate." On one end of the swinging-gate section and the end of the smaller section of remaining rails, *cut tenons* (8 altogether) 1/4 in. × 1 in. On the larger end of the rails, *cut tenons* (4 altogether) 1- 1/2 in. wide and 1 in. long.
6. *Cut four end rails* to size. Cut 3/8 in. wide and 1/2 in. tenons on the end of the rails.
7. *Cut the center section uprights* to size.
8. *Cut four legs* to size (see Table 4-38). *Cut* off the corners of each leg, extending 3 in. from the top of the leg to 6 in. from the bottom. *Form* an *octagonal cross section* using a spokeshave, wood rasp and sandpaper (see Fig. 4-48). *Split two* of the four legs exactly in the center lengthwise. One-half of the two legs will become part of the swinging gate.
9. *Cut off two inches* of two of the cut out sections (1 in. × 2 in. × 13 in.) on the ends opposite the tenon ends. These (1 in. × 2 in. × 11 in.) cut out sections will become the lower horizontal cross members of the two swinging gates. *Drill* two 1/4 in. *dowel holes* in the upper ends of the center section uprights and corresponding holes in the underside

of the upper horizontal cross member (1 in. × 2 in. × 13 in.). *Drill* two 1/4 in. dowel holes in the side of the center section uprights near the bottom (Fig. 4-48) and corresponding dowel holes in the end of the lower cross members (1 in. × 2 in. × 11 in.). *Cut mortises* (1/4 in. × 1 in.) in the upper and lower parts of the split section of the legs. All lower members (rails and lower member of the swinging gate) should start 2 1/2 in. from the bottom of the legs (see Fig. 4-48).

10. *Glue, assemble*, and *clamp* all the parts of the swinging gates. *Set this aside* for the glue to dry.
11. *Cut mortises* in the 2 in. × 2 in. legs, 1/2 in. wide and 1 in. deep. *Cut mortises* in the split sections of the legs (1 in. × 2 in.) 1/4 in. wide and 1 in. deep. *Cut 1/2 in.* wide and 3/8 in. deep *mortise* in the legs to accept the two end-rail tenons.
12. *Glue, assemble,* and *clamp* all the *rails* and *legs*.
13. When glue is dry on this lower assembly, *attach swinging gates* to the lower assembly with the four table hinges.
14. *Attach* the continuous *hinges* to the three tabletop sections and *attach* this to the lower assembly.

HARVEST TABLE

These long, narrow tables were put to good use on the farm during harvesting and threshing time when additional help was needed. The farmer's wife was under considerable pressure to provide bountiful and nourishing food for the hard-working, outdoor help. Today, these tables (Fig. 4-49) can be used to advantage in a family room or basement recreational room.

Material:

Table 4-39 lists materials for the harvest table of Fig. 4-49.

Table 4-39.

Quantity	Description	Thick	Width	Length	Wood
1	Center top	3/4	17	74	White pine
2	Drop leaves	3/4	10 1/2	74	White pine
2	Front and back rails	1 1/8	5	65 1/2	White pine
2	End rails	1 1/8	5	13 1/2	White pine
4	Legs	2	2	27 1/4	White pine
4	Leaf supports	1 1/2	5	9 1/2	Maple or birch
8	Heavy brass hinges 2-in. long				
8	Table hinges 1 1/2-in. × 3 1/8-in.				

Note: Measurements in inches

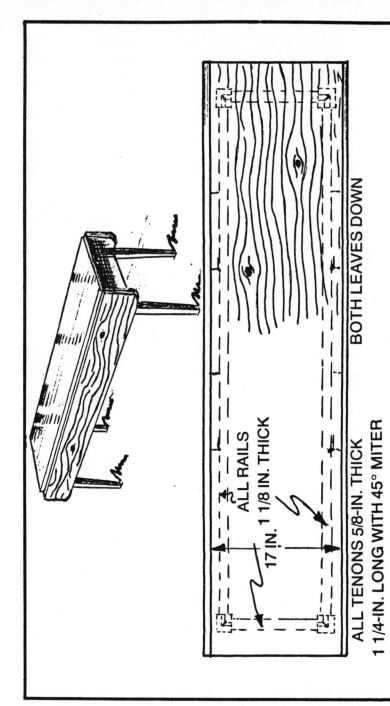

ALL RAILS
1 1/8 IN. THICK

17 IN.

BOTH LEAVES DOWN

ALL TENONS 5/8-IN. THICK
1 1/4-IN. LONG WITH 45° MITER

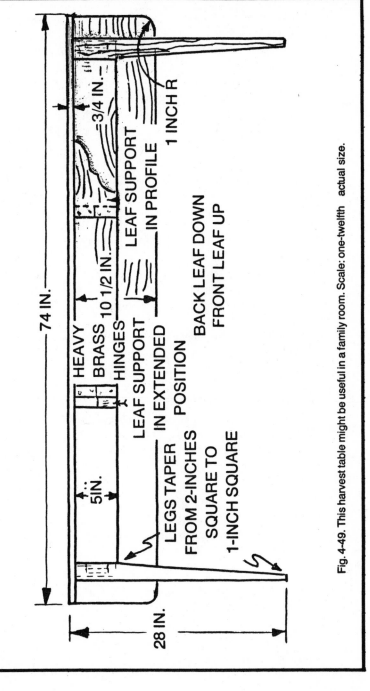

Fig. 4-49. This harvest table might be useful in a family room. Scale: one-twelfth actual size.

74 IN.

3/4 IN.

HEAVY
BRASS
HINGES

10 1/2 IN.

LEAF SUPPORT
IN PROFILE

1 INCH R

LEAF SUPPORT
IN EXTENDED
POSITION

BACK LEAF DOWN
FRONT LEAF UP

5 IN.

LEGS TAPER
FROM 2-INCHES
SQUARE TO
1-INCH SQUARE

28 IN.

Procedure:

1. *Cut the center top* to size. (Stock will probably have to be glued up for width.)

2. *Cut* two *drop leaves* to squared dimensions. *Swing* a 1 in. radius on two corners with a compass. *Saw* the curves with a band saw.

3. *Cut* four *rails* with the same setting of the saw for the appropriate width. *Cut* the *rails* to length. *Cut* 5/8 in. thick, 1 1/4 in. long *tenons* on the end of the rails. Miter (45 degree) on the end of the tenons.

4. With the same width setting of the saw, *cut* a piece of *stock* 1 1/2 in. × 5 in. × 30 in. By making a full-size pattern of the entire leaf supports, a considerable savings in lumber can be achieved. The pattern is flopped over as patterns are marked. The slanting curved parts overlap each other and the straight parts are butted together on two of the parts. This method will save 8 in. of 5 in. wide stock. *Cut* the four *supports* with a circular saw and bandsaw.

5. *Cut* the four *legs* to squared size. *Cut* the 5/8 in. × 1 1/4 in. *mortises* in the ends of the four legs with a hollow-chisel mortiser, drill press mortiser attachment, or by hand. *Cut* the necessary *tapers*, starting at 5 in. from the end, using a jointer, fore plane, or jointer plane.

6. *Attach* two of the heavy *brass hinges* to each of the leaf supports. *Attach* the *other half* of the hinges to the front and back rails, approximately 19 in. from the end of the rail.

7. *Glue, assemble,* and *clamp* the *rails* and *legs*.

8. *Attach* the four table *hinges* to each drop leaf and to the center. *Attach* the center top and drop leaves to the lower assembly.

CHECKER TABLE

The table of Fig. 4-50 and Fig. 4-51 has only one purpose—a game table. Chessmen can be left in place if there is an interruption in a game, and there usually is. The unique marquetry of two contrasting shades of wood is an excellent conversation topic.

Material:

Materials necessary to complete the chess/checker table of Fig. 4-50 are listed in Table 4-40.

Procedure:

1. Make the chess/checkerboard of Fig. 4-51.

Table 4-40.

Quantity	Description	Thick	Width	Length	Wood
4	Table border pieces	3/4	5 1/2	26	White pine
1	Chess/Checkerboard				
2	Drawer rails	3/4	3 1/2	19 1/2	White pine
2	Curved rails	3/4	4	19 1/2	White pine
4	Legs	1 1/2	1 1/2	28 1/4	White pine
2	Drawer fronts	3/4	2	10	White pine
2	Drawer backs	1/2	2	9 3/4	White pine
2	Curved drawer sides	2	2	9	White pine
2	Drawer bottoms 1/8-in. hardboard cut to fit drawer				
2	Wrought brass butt hinges, Ht. 2 in., width open 1 3/8 in.				
2	Small brass knobs.				

Note: Measurements in inches

2. *Make patterns* for the table border pieces. *Cut* the *table border pieces* to squared dimensions. *Cut* a 45 degree *miter* on each end. *Mark* the *curved portions* with the pattern. *Cut* the *curves* on band saw. *Cut saw kerfs* in the face of the miter for the splines. *Cut* the *splines*. *Place glue* on the splines and miter faces and on the edges of the chess/checkerboard. *Clamp* these together using special cut-out blocks on the corners to protect the curved portions.

3. *Cut* two *drawer rails* to size. Cut 1/4 in. thick, 3/4 in. long tenons on the ends. *Cut* 1/2 in. off *one edge* (top edge). *Cut* out the *opening* for the drawer front. *Cut* a piece of *stock* 1/2 in. × 3/4 in. × 18 in. and glue to the top edge of the drawer front over the drawer front opening (see Fig. 4-50).

4. *Make* a *pattern* for the curved *rails*. *Cut* the *two rails* to squared dimensions. *Cut* 1/4 in. thick by 3/4 in. long *tenons* on the ends. *Mark* the *curved portion* with the pattern. *Cut* the *curves* with a band saw.

5. *Cut four legs* to squared dimensions. *Start* a *taper* 5 in. from the end. *Cut* a *taper* with a jointer, fore plane or jointer plane. *Cut mortises* to accept 1/4 in. thick, 3/4 in. long tenons.

6. *Cut pieces* for the drawer fronts 3/4 in. × 2 in. × 10 in. *Cut pieces* for the drawer backs 1/2 in. × 2 in. × 9 3/4 in. On a piece of heavy paper, *strike two arcs* of a circle, one arc with a 10 in. radius, the other arc with a 9 1/2 in. radius. *Cut* out the *arc* between the two arcs. The arc should be

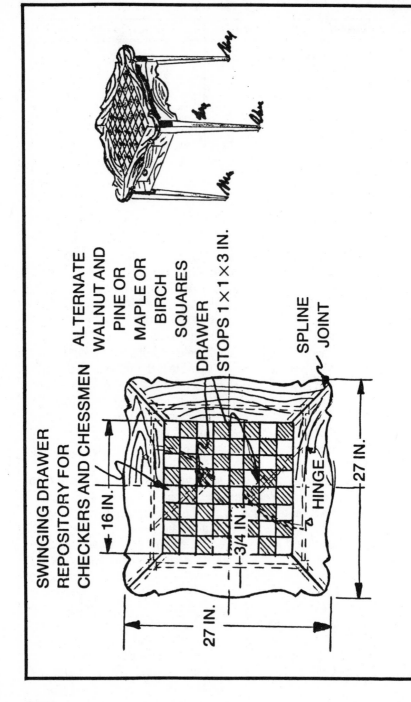

SWINGING DRAWER REPOSITORY FOR CHECKERS AND CHESSMEN

ALTERNATE WALNUT AND PINE OR MAPLE OR BIRCH SQUARES

DRAWER STOPS 1×1×3 IN.

SPLINE JOINT

16 IN.

3/4 IN.

HINGE

27 IN.

27 IN.

27 IN.

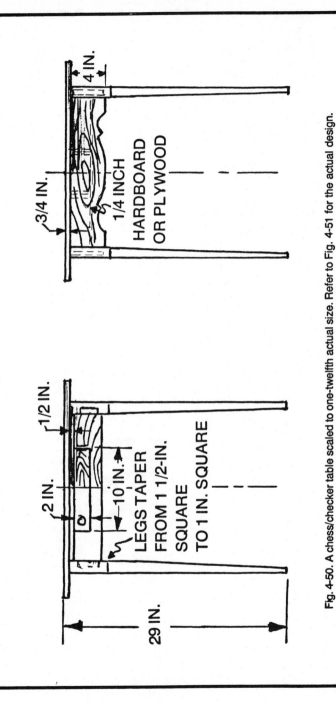

4 IN.

3/4 IN.

1/4 INCH
HARDBOARD
OR PLYWOOD

1/2 IN.

2 IN.

10 IN.

LEGS TAPER
FROM 1 1/2-IN.
SQUARE
TO 1 IN. SQUARE

29 IN.

Fig. 4-50. A chess/checker table scaled to one-twelfth actual size. Refer to Fig. 4-51 for the actual design.

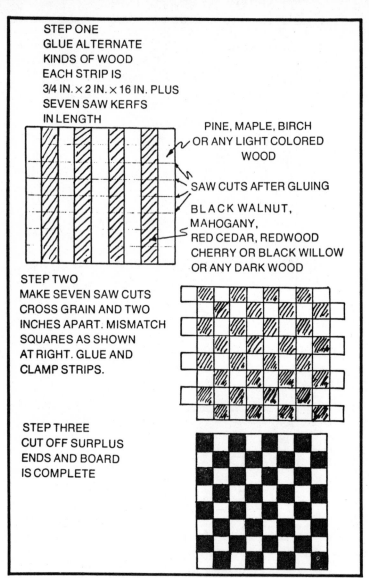

STEP ONE
GLUE ALTERNATE
KINDS OF WOOD
EACH STRIP IS
3/4 IN. × 2 IN. × 16 IN. PLUS
SEVEN SAW KERFS
IN LENGTH

PINE, MAPLE, BIRCH
OR ANY LIGHT COLORED
WOOD

SAW CUTS AFTER GLUING

BLACK WALNUT,
MAHOGANY,
RED CEDAR, REDWOOD
CHERRY OR BLACK WILLOW
OR ANY DARK WOOD

STEP TWO
MAKE SEVEN SAW CUTS
CROSS GRAIN AND TWO
INCHES APART. MISMATCH
SQUARES AS SHOWN
AT RIGHT. GLUE AND
CLAMP STRIPS.

STEP THREE
CUT OFF SURPLUS
ENDS AND BOARD
IS COMPLETE

Fig. 4-51. Steps for making the checkerboard design for the table of Fig. 4-50.

9 in. long. *Lay* the 1/2 in. wide *arc* on the 2 in. × 2 in. × 9 in. stock and mark the curved drawer sides. *Cut* the *sides* on a bandsaw. *Cut* a 1/8 in. × 1/8 in. *groove*, 1/4 in. from the bottom of the drawer front and back. The 1/8 in. × 1/8 in. groove on the curved side will have to be cut by hand. With a sharp marking gauge *score lines* 1/8 in. apart,

1/4 in. up from the bottom inside edge of the curved sides. *Cut out* the *wood* between the scored lines with a narrow chisel. Cut a piece of 1/8 in. thick hardboard to fit the bottom of the drawer. *Attach* a small *brass knob* to the drawer front on the end opposite the hinge end. *Glue, assemble* and *clamp* the drawer parts. Special blocks will have to be cut to aid in clamping.

7. *Cut a piece* of 1/4 in. standard *hardboard* to extend between the four rails. *Cut out corners* around the legs.
8. *Attach brass hinges* to the end of the drawer front. The other half of the hinges is attached to the edge of the drawer opening.
9. *Glue, assemble* and *clamp* the rails (with drawers attached) and legs.
10. When glue is dry, *put* the 1/4 in. *hardboard bottom in place.* It should fit lightly against the bottom of the drawers. When the drawers are opened and closed, they will slide on the 1/4 in. hardboard bottom. The bottom will be held in place with 1 in. × 1 in. × 3 in. right-angle triangular glue blocks.
11. *Attach* the *top* to the lower assembly.

TIER TABLE

The tier table pictured in Fig. 4-52 can be used for a multitude of purposes. It might be used for papers and magazines, family albums, genealogies, family Bibles or for books and references that are currently being read. It can be used in most any room, but would be particularly valuable in a boy's or girl's room, where studying takes place.

Material:

The materials needed to complete a tier table are listed in Table 4-41.

Table 4-41.

Quantity	Description	Thick	Width	Length	Wood
1	Top	3/4	18	28	White pine
2	Shelves	1/2	12	22	White pine
2	Front/Back rails	3/4	3	21	White pine
2	End rails	3/4	3	11	White pine
4	Legs	1 1/2	1 1/2	26 1/2	White pine

Note: Measurements in inches

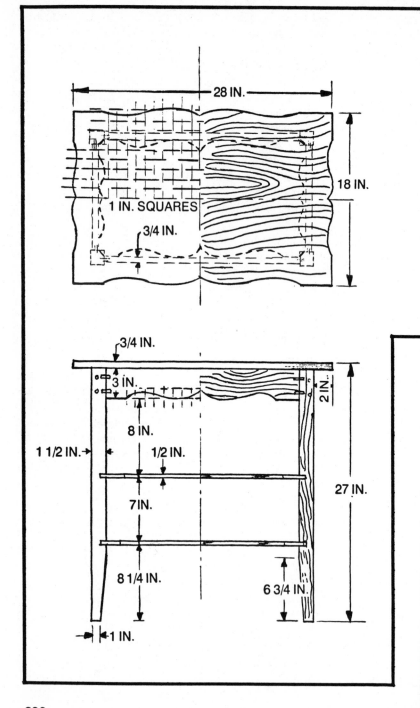

28 IN.

18 IN.

1 IN. SQUARES

3/4 IN.

3/4 IN.

3 IN.

2 IN.

8 IN.

1 1/2 IN.

1/2 IN.

27 IN.

7 IN.

8 1/4 IN.

6 3/4 IN.

1 IN.

Fig. 4-52. Tier table.

Procedure:

1. *Glue up* and *clamp stock* for the top. When the glue is dry, cut the top to squared dimensions. *Make patterns* for the curved parts of the top. *Mark* the *curved parts* using the patterns as guides. *Cut* the *curved portions* with any curve cutting saw (band saw, saber saw, or jigsaw).

2. *Cut* the two *shelves* to squared dimensions. *Make patterns* for the curved parts and *mark* the *curved parts* on the shelf stock. Note in particular the small (1/2 in. × 1/2 in.) 45 degree mitered corners. These corners will fit into cross-corner dadoes on each leg and will provide the only support for the shelves (see Fig. 4-52). *Cut* the *curved sections* of the shelves with any curve cutting tool.

3. *Cut all rails* with the same width setting of the saw. *Saw* the *rails* to length and bore holes for 3/8 in. dowels using a doweling jig. *Make* a *pattern* for the curved parts. *Use* the *pattern to mark* the curved portions on the rails. Saw the *curved portions* with any curve cutting saw.

4. *Cut* the *four legs* to squared dimensions. *Bore four holes* near the top end to receive 3/8 in. dowels (see Fig. 4-52).

Make a *"V" shaped trough jig* to hold the legs while the cross-corner dadoes are being cut. *Cut* the *cross-corner dadoes* 1/2 in. wide. These dadoes will support the shelves (see Fig. 4-52). *Cut* the *tapers* on the lower ends of the legs starting 6 3/4 in. up on the legs. The taper is from 1 1/2 in. to 1 in. Use a jointer, fore plane or jointer plane to cut the paper.

5. *Place glue* on the dowels, end of rails, and corners of the shelves. *Assemble* and *clamp*. When glue is dry, *attach the top*.

TIP-TOP TABLE

Many of the Early American tip-top tables were modified and simplified versions of the European; nevertheless, they were clean-cut and artistic and in many cases surpassed the European design. The simple tilting mechanism permits the top to be placed in a vertical position so that the table may be set against the wall where it will occupy little space. See Fig. 4-53.

Material:

Table 4-42 lists all materials needed to create a tip-top table.

Procedure:

1. *Glue* up-and *clamp stock* for the top. When glue is dry, *cut* the *top* to squared dimensions. *Make* a *pattern* of heavy paper for the curved portions. *Mark* the *curved portions* with the pattern.

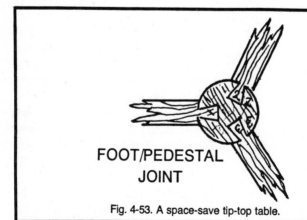

FOOT/PEDESTAL
JOINT

Fig. 4-53. A space-save tip-top table.

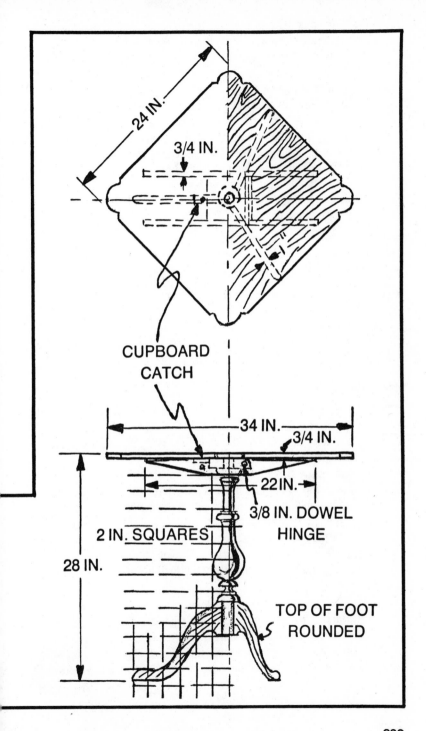

24 IN.

3/4 IN.

CUPBOARD
CATCH

34 IN.

3/4 IN.

22 IN.

3/8 IN. DOWEL
HINGE

2 IN. SQUARES

28 IN.

TOP OF FOOT
ROUNDED

2. *Glue* up and *clamp stock* for the pedestal. When the glue is dry, *cut* and *corner off* with a drawshave forming a rough octagon in cross-section. *Make* a *pattern* of the outline of a turning of Masonite, hardboard or thin wood. *Place* the *stock in the lathe* and turn, check frequently with the pattern. The dowel at top end must be exactly 1 in. in diameter. *Measure frequently* with calipers. The lower portion of the turning must be exactly 3 in. in diameter and straight, because the three feet fit onto this part. *Sand* while the pedestal is turning, but be careful not to sand off the tops of the beads and the sharp edges.

3. *Make* a *pattern* for the feet. *Cut* the *stock* for the feet to the squared dimensions. *Mark* the *pattern* on the feet. Be sure

Table 4-42.

Quantity	Description	Thick	Width	Length	Wood
1	Top	3/4	24	24	White pine
1	Pedestal		4 1/4	22	White pine
3	Feet	1	4	15	White pine
2	Table top supports	3/4	2	22	White pine
1	Bearing/Catch block	1 1/4	5 1/2	5 1/2	Birch
1	3/8-in. Dowel, 7-in. long				Birch
1	Cupboard catch				

Note: Measurements in inches

that the grain runs as shown in Fig. 4-53; that is, parallel to the general contour of the feet. *Cut* the *curved portions* on a band saw. Be sure to leave the stock necessary for dovetails. *Make* the *outside pattern* of the dovetail from aluminum. The narrow part of the dovetail should be about 3/8 in., the wide part about 5/8 in., and the length of the dovetail 7/8 in. The cutting of the dovetails on the ends of the feet will really challenge your skill in the use of a chisel and gouges. *Check frequently* with the outside aluminum pattern.

4. *Make* an *inside pattern* of a dovetail from aluminum. *Pad the pedestal turning* and place it in a vise with the lower portion at the top. *Divide* the *circumference* of the pedestal base into three equal parts and mark. From this mark, *draw* a *line* to the center of the base circle. *Center* the *aluminum dovetail pattern* over each line and *scribe around* with a very

sharp knife point. *Sharpen* a *pencil* to a chisel point and darken the knife point lines by letting the pencil point follow in the trough made by the knife. (This method of scribing lines is much more accurate than using a pencil alone.) With a piece of aluminum 2 in. wide and 3 in. long bent to a right angle, *lay out* the *lines* leading up from the base of the pedestal. The right angle device will follow around the circumference of the turning where the feet are attached. Lines made with this device will always be parallel to the longitudinal center of the pedestal. *Bore* 1/4 in. holes, 3/4 in. deep, between the lines which outline the dovetails. The bit or drill *must* always *point toward* the center of the turning while drilling or boring is taking place. From the bottom of the turning *start chiseling* the dovetail. Chisels must be very sharp. Before chiseling very far, *assign* and *mark* a number by placing a 1, 2 or 3 on the base of the pedestal next to the dovetail being cut. Also *assign* and *mark* the same numbers on the dovetail tenons on the three feet. As the chiseling progresses, *check* not only with the aluminum pattern, but also check by inserting the dovetail tenons on the feet into the dovetail mortises on the pedestal. The assigned corresponding numbers must be adhered to. The dovetail tenons should slide in and out of the dovetail mortises with little difficulty, but the joints should not be sloppy. Glue is a miracle liquid but it will never compensate for sloppy or loose-fitting joints.

5. *Place glue* on the dovetail tenons, dovetail mortises, and the part of the feet that come in contact (shoulder) with the pedestal. If joints are snug, clamps will not be necessary. Set this assembly aside for the glue to dry.

6. *Cut* the *table top supports* to squared dimensions. *Taper* 8 in. on each end from 2 in. wide to 1/4 in. at the end. *Bore* a *hole* for a 3/8 in. dowel, 9 in. from the end.

7. *Cut* the *bearing/catch block* to size. Bore a 3/8 in. dowel hole, 5/8 in. from the end of the block through the width of the block. Round over the corner on the end where the hole is located so that the corner of the block will not catch on the top when the top is moved to a vertical position. *Bore* a 1 in. *hole* in the center of the block to receive the 1 in. dowel on the end of the pedestal. *Bore* a *hole* in the side of the block to receive the bolt from the cupboard catch. Check the diameter of the bolt and the distance bolt

is from the base of the catch. The cupboard catch will hold the top in place when the top is in a horizontal position.

8. *Assemble* the *bearing/catch block, dowel* and *tabletop* supports. The dowel bearing should work freely in the hole in the bearing/catch block. If it binds, *sand* that portion of the dowel. *Do not sand the ends.* They must be glued into the table-top supports. *Fasten the table-top supports* to the top with glue and brads. *Attach* the *cupboard catch* and *check*.

TRESTLE TABLE

The trestle table of Fig. 4-54 is identified by the horizontal feet. The trestle (little crossbeam) acts as a batten and support for the ends. A heavy crossbeam can absorb considerable punishment.

Material:

Materials necessary to complete a sturdy trestle table are listed in Table 4-43.

Table 4-43.

Quantity	Description	Thick	Width	Length	Wood
1	Top	1 1/4	32	50	White pine
2	Ends	1 1/8	13	25	White pine
2	Feet	2	3	29	White pine
1	Stretcher	1 1/8	5	40	White pine
2	Top/End supports	1 1/2	1 1/2	13	Birch
2	Keys	5/8	2	6	Birch
6	Carriage bolts 3/8 × 3 1/2				
4	FHB No. 12-2 1/2 in. screws				

Note: Measurements in inches

Procedure:

1. *Glue* up and *clamp stock* for the top. When the glue is dry, *saw* to correct dimensions.
2. *Glue* up and *clamp stock* for the ends. *Make* a *pattern* on heavy paper of the curved parts. When the glue is dry, *mark* the *curves* using the pattern. This is done after the stock has been cut to squared dimensions. *Cut* the *curved parts* with a band saw. *Cut* 1/2 in. by 1 1/4 in. *tenons* on the bottom of the legs.
3. *Cut* the *feet* to squared dimensions. *Cut mortises* (1/2 in. × 1 1/4 in.) to accept the tenons on the bottom end of

286

the ends. *Make* a *pattern* for the curved parts. *Mark* the *curved parts* with the pattern. *Cut* the *curved parts* with a band saw.

4. *Cut* a *stretcher* to squared dimensions. *Cut tenons* on the ends of the stretcher to measure 3 1/2 in. wide and 4 1/8 in. long. On the tenon, 1 1/16 in. for the shoulder, *cut* a *hole* for the key 5/8 in. × 1 1/2 in. *Make* a *pattern* for the curved parts. *Mark* the *curved parts* with a pattern. *Saw* the *curved parts* with a band saw.

5. *Cut* a *key* 5/8 in. thick and 6 in. long, tapering from 2 in. at one end to 3/4 in. on the other.

6. *Cut* the *top/end supports* to size. *Clamp* the *supports* to the top of the ends. *Bore three* 3/8 in. holes for carriage bolts (see Fig. 4-54). *Drill vertical holes* for the shank of FHB No. 12-2 1/2 in. screws. There will be two holes in each support. *Countersink* for the screw heads. *Glue* and *bolt* the *supports* to the ends with 3/8 in. × 3 1/2 in. carriage bolts. Place the head of the bolts on the outside.

7. *Assemble* the *feet* to the ends with glue. *When the glue* is dry, *assemble* the *ends* to the stretcher and drive in the key securely. With the table top on low sawhorses, *tip* the *assembled stretcher* and *ends* upside down on the underside of the top. *Position* the *top/end supports* correctly with regard to the sides and the end of the top. *Mark* pilot *holes* on the underside of the top with an awl extending down through the shank holes for the four FHB No. 12-2 1/2 in. screws. *Move* the *top-end supports* and the lower assembly to one side and *drill pilot holes* (slightly smaller in diameter than the spiral portion of the screws). *Move* the *top/end supports* and *lower-assembly back* over the pilot holes and *drive* the screws into the top with a screwdriver.

TV TRAY

A few of these TV trays (Fig. 4-55) would certainly earn their way in a home setting. When folded, they occupy little space. They are just the thing when guests drop in at lunch or snack time.

Material:

Table 4-44 lists materials needed to complete the TV tray pictured in Fig. 4-55.

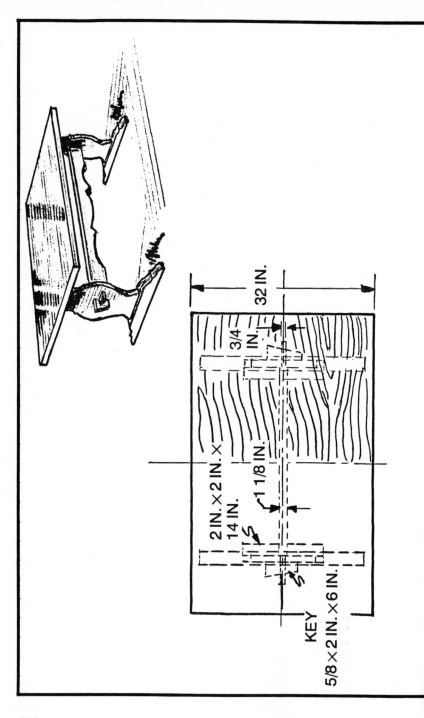

32 IN.

3/4 IN.

2 IN. × 2 IN. × 14 IN.

1 1/8 IN.

KEY
5/8 × 2 IN. × 6 IN.

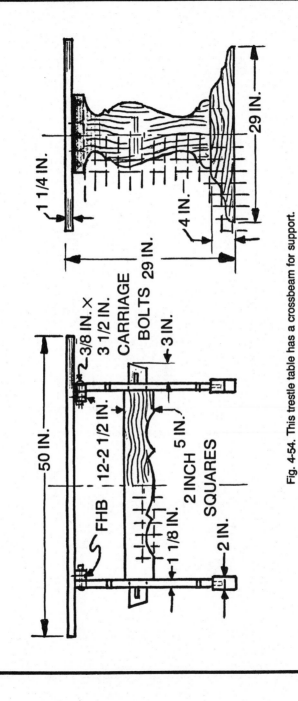

Fig. 4-54. This trestle table has a crossbeam for support.

1 1/4 IN.

29 IN.

4 IN.

29 IN.

CARRIAGE
BOLTS

3 IN.

3/8 IN. ×
3 1/2 IN.

50 IN.

FHB   12-2 1/2 IN.

5 IN.

2 INCH
SQUARES

1 1/8 IN.

2 IN.

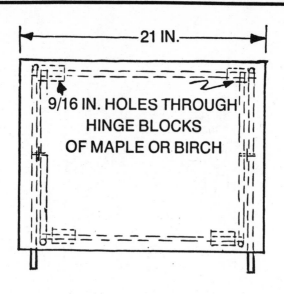

21 IN.

9/16 IN. HOLES THROUGH
HINGE BLOCKS
OF MAPLE OR BIRCH

LEGS OF MAPLE OR BIRCH
PINE TOP

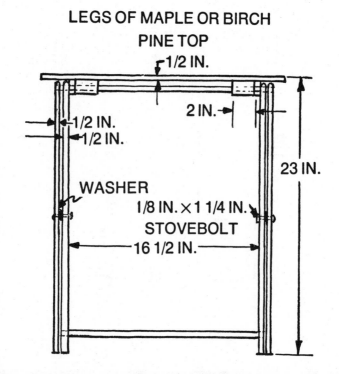

1/2 IN.

2 IN.

1/2 IN.
1/2 IN.

23 IN.

WASHER

1/8 IN. × 1 1/4 IN.
STOVEBOLT
16 1/2 IN.

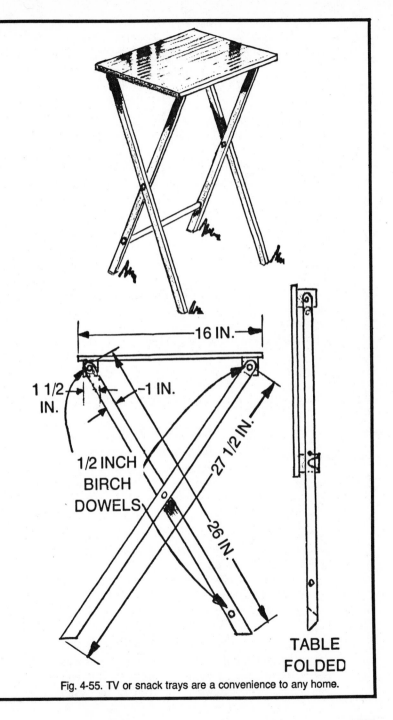

16 IN.

1 1/2 IN.

1 IN.

1/2 INCH BIRCH DOWELS

27 1/2 IN.

26 IN.

TABLE FOLDED

Fig. 4-55. TV or snack trays are a convenience to any home.

Table 4-44.

Quantity	Description	Thick	Width	Length	Wood
1	Top	1/2	16	21	White pine
2	Legs	1/2	1	26	Birch or maple
2	Legs	1/2	1	27 1/2	Birch or maple
2	1/2-in. dowels, 17 1/2-in. long				Birch
1	1/2-in. dowel, 19 1/2-in. long				
4	Blocks (2 hinge, 2 retainer)	1 1/4	1 1/4	2	Birch or maple
2	Stove bolts 1/8 in. × 1 1/4 in.				
2	Washers, 1/8-in. hole				

Note: Measurements in inches

Procedure:

1. *Glue* up *stock* for the top. When the glue is dry, *cut* the *stock* to dimensions.

2. *Cut* all *four legs* to proper thickness and width, using the same setting of the saw. *Cut* the *legs* to length. *Saw* an *angle* of approximately 35 degrees on one end of each leg. On the other end of the legs, *bore* a 1/2 in. *hole* for the dowels, 1/2 in. from the end and one the flat side. Round over the ends of the legs to a semicircile (1/2 in. radius). Near the ends of the two shorter (26 in.) legs where the angle is located, *bore* two 1/2 in. holes for the dowels (see Fig. 4-55).

3. *Cut* the four *hinge* and *retainer blocks* to size. *Bore* a 9/16 in. *hole* longitudinally through two blocks. These are the bearing blocks and the dowel must turn freely in the holes. *Bore* a 1/2 in. *hole* longitudinally in the other two blocks. *Make* two *cuts* with a band saw on an angle to meet the hole. This will allow the dowel to fit in and out when folding or unfolding, and acts as retainers when the table is set up. (See the table-folded section on Fig. 4-55 to note the shape of the retainer blocks.)

4. *Assemble* the *legs* with stove bolts and washers. *Bore* 1/8 in. *holes*, 13 1/2 in. down from the top of the 27 1/2 in. legs and 12 in. down on the 26 in. legs, to receive the stove bolts.

5. *Run* a 1/2 in. *dowel* through the hole in the 27 in. piece, through the two hinge blocks. Just before the dowel enters the second leg, *put glue* on the inside of the hole and on the end of the extended dowel before it enters the first leg. *Put*

glue on the ends of the 17 1/2 in. dowel. *Spring* the lower ends of the 26 in. legs apart and insert dowels into the holes. *Attach blocks* to the top with glue and small brads.

WALL BRACKET OR SCONCE

The sconce (literal meaning "hiding place") was always somewhat of a mixed blessing. The main function in pioneering days was to hold a candlestick and candle. But if the sconce was built to shut out most of the wind that drifted through the early log cabins, it also shut out the light it was supposed to shed. Many revisions in design were experimented with to achieve a balance between protection from drafts and the emitting of light.

Today the sconce (or wall bracket) of Fig. 4-56 is mostly for ornamental purposes. On it might be found trinkets, small ceramic pieces, and occasionally an actual candlestick and candle. In that event, if the electricity were cut off, the sconce would function in the same capaicity that it did over 200 years ago.

Material:

Materials to complete a wall bracket are contained in Table 4-45.

Table 4-45.

Quantity	Description	Thick	Width	Length	Wood
1	Back	3/8	6	11 1/2	White pine
2	Sides	5/16	2 13/16	7 1/4	White pine
1	Bottom	1/2	4 1/2	5 3/8	White pine

Note: Measurements in inches

Procedure:

1. *Make patterns* for the back and sides.
2. *Cut* the *back* to squared dimensions. *Mark* the *curved portions* with the appropriate pattern. *Cut* the *curved portions* of the back with any curve-cutting saw (band saw, jigsaw, saber saw, or coping saw).
3. *Cut* the *sides* of the sconce to squared dimensions. However, stock can be saved by overlapping the narrow parts of the sides. *Mark* the *curved portions* with the appropriate pattern. *Cut* the *curved parts* with any curve-cutting saw.

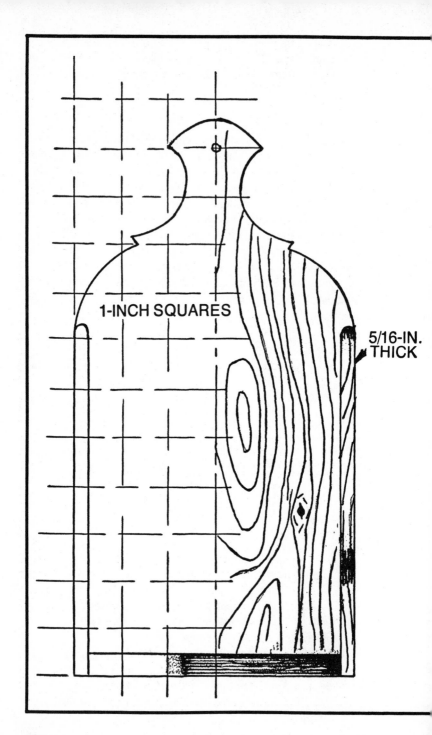

1-INCH SQUARES

5/16-IN. THICK

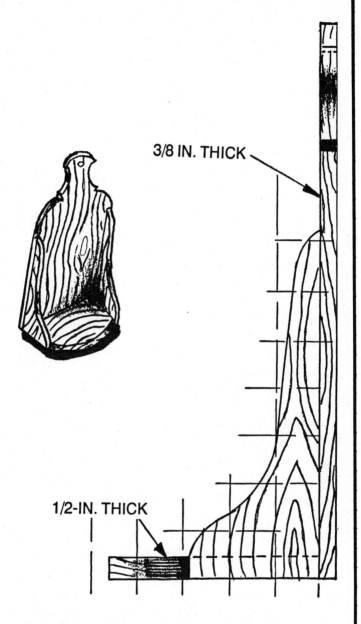

3/8 IN. THICK

1/2-IN. THICK

Fig. 4-56. This wall bracket or sconce can still be used as it was yesterday—as a candleholder.

4. On heavy paper or cardboard, *draw a straight line* 5 in. or 6 in. long. At about the 2 1/2 in. or 3 in. point, *draw a line* about 6 in. long at right angles to the first line. *Put a point* on the first line 1 11/16 in. from the second line (the difference in width between the bottom and side piece). On the second line, mark off 2 11/16 in. each way from where the first and second lines cross. *Set a compass* at 2 15/16 in. *Place* the *pencil end* on the point on the first line 1 11/16 in. from the second line. The other point of the compass will also be placed on first line on the opposite side of second line. Now, *swing* an *arc* through the three points (the two points on the second line and the one point on the first line). It might be necessary to adjust the compasss slightly to hit all three points. *Cut out* the *segment* of the circle formed. This will be the pattern for the curved part of the bottom. *Cut* the *bottom* of the sconce to squared dimensions. *Place* the *pattern* on one side of the bottom and *mark*. *Cut* the *curved portion* with a bandsaw.

5. *Assemble* all *four pieces* with glue and brads.

WALL BRACKET OR SCONCE

The design of Fig. 4-57 is simpler in construction than the one described in Fig. 4-56, but in some ways it has a classical elegence that might appeal to more craftsmen.

Material:

Table 4-46 contains all necessary materials to complete the wall sconce of Fig. 4-57

Table 4-46.

Quantity	Description	Thick	Width	Length	Wood
1	Back	3/8	6	11	White pine
1	Shelf	1/2	3	6	White pine

Note: Measurements in inches

Procedure:

1. On heavy paper, *make a pattern* for the back. *Cut the back* to squared dimensions. *Mark* the *curved parts* with the pattern. *Cut* the *curved parts* with a band saw, jigsaw, saber saw, coping saw, or turning saw.

2. On a piece of 1/2 in. stock, *swing a semicircle* of 3 in. radius with a compass. *Cut* the *curve* with any curve-cutting saw. *Sand* the *curved edge* smooth and *cut* the *molded edge* with a router or shaper.

3. *Assemble* the sections with glue and brads.

WALL CUPBOARD

The cupboard of Fig. 4-58, meant to hang on the wall, could also be used as the top portion of a breakfront, "Welsh dresser," or Pennsylvania Dutch free-standing cupboard. The lower part of these breakfront cabinets were generally "drawers over doors." The lower part was built separately from the shelf assembly above.

In the early pioneering days, wall cupboards were always open, but as glass became more available and less expensive, doors were added to keep out dust.

This cupboard is designed to be used either open or with glass doors.

Material:

All necessary materials for the wall cupboard of Fig. 4-58 are listed in Table 4-47.

Table 4-47.

Quantity	Description	Thick	Width	Length	Wood
2	Top and bottom	13/16	15 1/2	49	White pine
2	Sides	13/16	13	40 3/8	White pine
1	Top shelf	13/16	5 1/2	42	White pine
1	Bottom plate groove shelf	13/16	10	42	White pine
2	Middle shelves	13/16	9 3/4	42	White pine
3	Guard rails	5/8	1 1/4	42	White pine
	Back (Enough pieces—the widths generally vary—40 3/8-in. long—of tongue-and-groove stock to cover the back. One piece of T and G stock will probably have to be split to fit.)				
	Standard cove molding	11/16	1 1/8	14 ft	
2	Hinge strips	13/16	5/8	40 3/8	White pine
1	Center muntin	13/16	2	40 3/8	White pine
2	Vertical supports	1/2	1	40 3/8	White pine
2	Outside curved parts	1/2	4 1/2	9	White pine
1	Center curved part	1/2	4 1/2	19 1/2	White pine

Note: Measurements in inches

Procedure:

1. *Cut* the *top* and *bottom* to dimensions. It probably will be necessary to glue up stock first. *Roll* the *front* and two *end edges* with a plane and sandpaper.

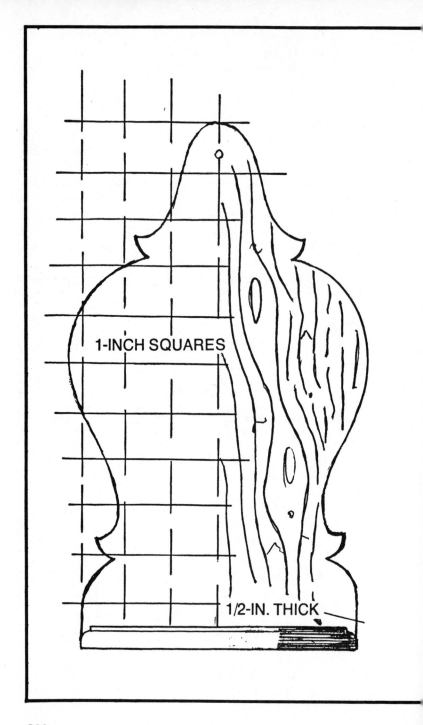

1-INCH SQUARES

1/2-IN. THICK

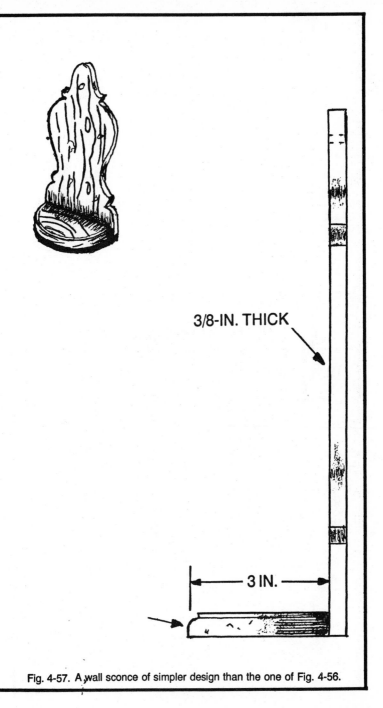

3/8-IN. THICK

3 IN.

Fig. 4-57. A wall sconce of simpler design than the one of Fig. 4-56.

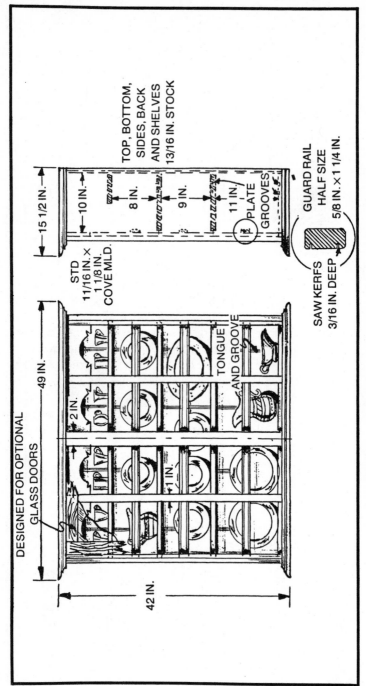

TOP, BOTTOM, SIDES, AND SHELVES 13/16 IN. STOCK

15 1/2 IN.

10 IN.

8 IN.

9 IN.

11 IN.

PLATE GROOVES

STD 11/16 IN. × 1 1/8 IN. COVE MLD.

GUARD RAIL HALF SIZE 5/8 IN. × 1 1/4 IN.

SAW KERFS 3/16 IN. DEEP

DESIGNED FOR OPTIONAL GLASS DOORS

49 IN.

2 IN.

1 IN.

TONGUE AND GROOVE

42 IN.

Fig. 4-58. An Early American wall cupboard with a closer view of circular insert.

300

2. *Cut* the *two sides* to dimensions.
3. *Cut* all *shelves* to proper dimensions.
4. *Cut* the three *guard rails* to dimensions.
5. *Cut hinge strips* to dimensions.
6. *Cut* the center *muntin* to dimensions.
7. *Cut* the *vertical supports* to dimensions.
8. *Assemble* the top and sides with glue and long brads, dowels, or dowel-covered flat head screws. *Check* the *corners* for squareness. *Measure accurately* between the top and bottom and *cut* the tongue-and-groove material to length. *Slide* the material in between the top and bottom and *anchor* it with long brads driven in from the top and bottom.
9. Accurately *measure* the *shelf length. Attach* the three *top shelves* to the sides and back with brads and glue. *Attach* the *bottom-plate groove* shelf to the bottom with glue and brads (driven down through the top of the bottom-plate groove shelf).
10. *Measure carefully* and *install* the three *guard rails* with glue and brads through the side. The front of the rail should measure 10 in. from the back.
11. *Measure accurately* the length of *vertical supports. Slide* these in between the top and bottom and anchor between the top and bottom with long brads. The *vertical supports* should be *flush* against the guard rails and should be *anchored* to the guard rails with brads. Although the vertical supports will not actually touch (about a 1/4 in. gap) the edges of middle shelves, a long brad through the vertical supports into the front edge of the middle shelves will greatly improve their sturdiness.
12. *Measure between* the *vertical supports* and between the vertical supports and sides to establish the length of the curved pieces. *Make paper patterns* for the curved pieces. *Cut curved pieces* to squared dimensions. *Mark* the *curved portions* with the pattern. *Cut* the *curves* with any curve-cutting saw. *Install* the *center curved part* between vertical supports. Install the outside curved part between the vertical supports and sides. *Cut* two pieces of *stock* 1/4 in. × 3 in. × 4 1/2 in.: *put glue* on *one face* and slip it in behind the top of each vertical support and overlapping curved piece. Brads from the outside of the side pieces can help anchor the two outside curved parts.

13. *Attach* the *two hinge strips* to the side with glue and brads. The hinge strip must be flush with the front edge of the sides.

14. *Attach* the *center muntin strip*. It must be set evenly with the front edge of the sides and hinge strips as it will become the separating member between the two doors. The top is anchored by long brads down through top. At the bottom, a piece 1/2 in. × 1/2 in. × 2 in. is glued to the bottom and the bottom plate-groove shelf, directly behind the center muntin and is anchored with long brads through the bottom.

15. *Cut* the *standard* 11/16 in. × 1 1/8 in. *cove molding* to length. *Molding* must be *mitered* (45 degrees) at the front corners both on the top and the bottom. *Attach* this with glue and brads.

16. If doors are to be added, *cut four top* and *bottom rails* 13/16 in. × 2 in. × 19 in. and *four vertical stiles* 13/16 in. × 2 in. × 39 1/2 in. *Corners* are *joined* by mortise and tenons. *Cut rabbets* for glass and *attach hinges* and a *knob*. *Attach doors* to the hinge strips.

WALL SHELVES

Wall shelves are a suitable project for the beginning craftsman. Figure 4-59 shows a light, delicate piece, but it is by no means weak. It will hold many art objects, small ceramic pieces, wood carvings, Hummels, miniatures, and other ornamental pieces. The wall shelves will fit into almost any room setting.

Material:

Table 4-48 lists materials needed to complete the beginner's wall shelves.

Table 4-48.

Quantity	Description	Thick	Width	Length	Wood
2	Sides	5/16	5 1/2	26	White pine
1	Shelf	1/4	5 1/2	11 5/8	White pine
1	Shelf	1/4	4 3/4	11 5/8	White pine
1	Shelf	1/4	3 3/4	11 5/8	White pine
2	Thin metal hangers				

Note: Measurements in inches

Procedure:

1. On heavy paper, *make a pattern* for the sides. *Cut* the *sides* to squared dimensions. *Mark* the *curved* portions with the pattern. *Cut* the *curves* with a band saw or any other curve cutting saw. *Roll edges* slightly with sandpaper. *Cut* 1/4 in. *dadoes*, 1/8 in. deep.
2. *Cut* the *shelves* to dimensions.
3. *Apply glue* to the shelf ends, *assemble* and *clamp*.
4. When glue is dry, *attach thin metal hangers* on the back and at the top of the sides.

SAWBUCK TABLE

Figure 4-60 is a sketch of a sturdy, attractive table that may be used as a dining table either with two benches or with traditional chairs. The sawbuck table is so named because of the cross-lapped end members. This piece of furniture expresses the designing ability and craftsmanship of our Early American forefathers.

Material:

Materials needed to create an attractive sawbuck table are given in Table 4-49.

Table 4-49.

Quantity	Description	Thick	Width	Length	Wood
1	Top	1 1/8	36	60	White pine
4	Half lap members	1 1/2	5 1/2	48	White pine
1	Stretcher	1 1/2	3 1/2	48	White pine
2	Keys	1/2	2	6	White pine
2	Top end rails	2	2	32	White pine
4	Lag screws 3/8-in x 3-in				

Note: Measurements in inches

Procedure:

1. *Glue up stock* for the table top and clamp. When glue is dry, *cut table top* to size.
2. *Cut half-lapped cross members* to squared dimensions. *Cut* the *half-lap joints* with dado blades and head. *Make* a *pattern* for the *curved portions* of the cross members. *Mark* the *curved portions* of the stock for the cross members. *Cut* the *curved portions* on a bandsaw. In an overlapped position, *cut* the 1 1/2 in. × 1 1/2 in. *mortise hole*.
3. *Cut* the *top end rails* to dimensions. *Glue* the *half-lapped cross members* together and clamp. When glue is dry, *bore*

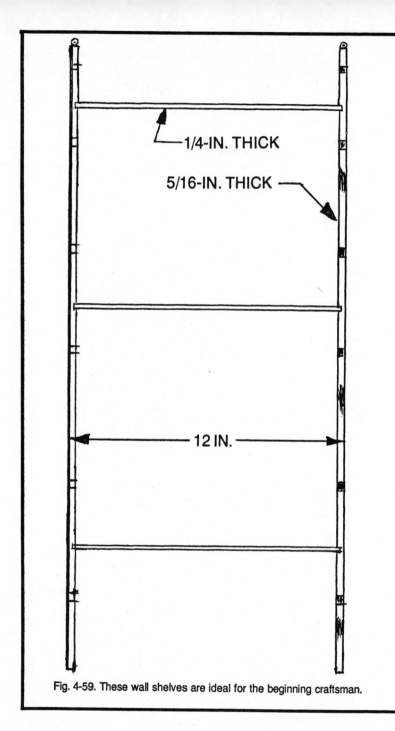

1/4-IN. THICK

5/16-IN. THICK —

12 IN.

Fig. 4-59. These wall shelves are ideal for the beginning craftsman.

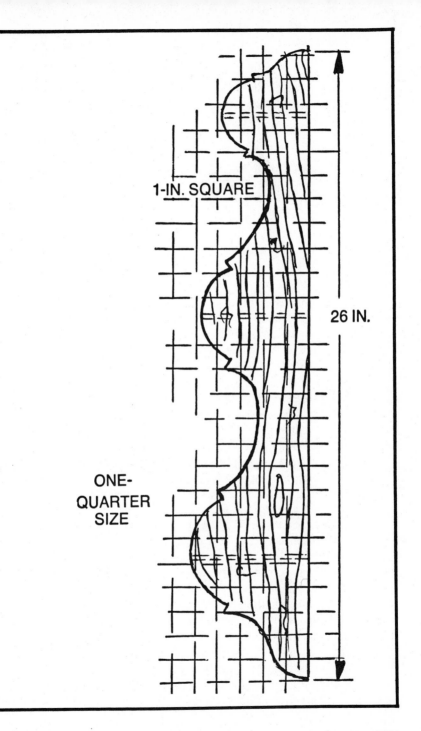

1-IN. SQUARE

26 IN.

ONE-
QUARTER
SIZE

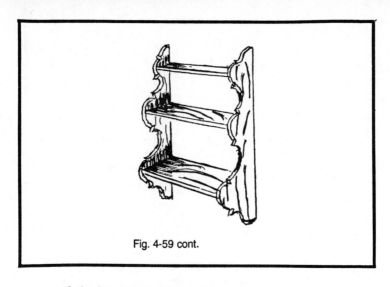

Fig. 4-59 cont.

holes for the lag screws. *Clamp* the *top end rails* to the top of the assembled cross members (see Fig. 4-60). In clamped position, *bore pilot holes* for the lag screws. *Drive lag screws* with a wrench applied to the square head.

4. *Cut* the *stretcher* to squared dimensions. *Cut rabbets* to form a 1 1/2 in. × 1 1/2 in. × 5 1/2 in. tenon on both ends of the stretcher. Out on the tenon, 1 7/16 in. from the shoulders, *cut* a *hole* through the tenon 1/2 in. wide and 1 1/2 in. long.

5. *Cut* the *key* of maple or birch 1/2 in. thick, 6 in. long, and tapering from 2 in. wide at the top to 3/4 in. at bottom.

6. *Drill holes*, at right angles to lag screws, for the shank of FHB No. 12-2 1/2 in. screws in the top end rails (4 holes in each rail) and *countersink*.

7. *Extend* the *tenon ends* of the stretchers through a mortise hole in each pair of the cross members and drive the key in. With the table top on low sawhorses, *tip* the *assembled stretcher* and cross members upside down on the underside of the top. *Position* the *top end rails* correctly with regard to the sides and the end of the top. *Mark pilot holes* on the top with an awl extending down through the shank holes for the eight FHB No. 12-2 1/2 in. screws. *Move* the *top rails* and lower assembly to one side and *drill* pilot holes (slightly smaller in diameter than the spiral part of the screws). *Move* the *top rails* and lower assembly back over the pilot holes and drive the screws into the top.

TAVERN TABLE

The original tavern table was not used as a regular table—it was a little too low—but as a platform on which to place a stein of beer or ale, or a jug of cider while one talked with his friends. The lower stretchers had to be replaced periodically because they were used as abbreviated footstools. The "double bottle" turnings add greatly to the design. See Fig. 4-61.

Material:

Table 4-50 lists materials needed to complete the tavern table of Fig. 4-61.

Table 4-50.

Quantity	Description	Thick	Width	Length	Wood
1	Top	1	22	31	White pine
2	Front and back top rails	3/4	3 3/4	15	White pine
2	End rails	3/4	3 3/4	11	White pine
2	Front and back lower stretchers	1	2	15	White pine
2	End lower stretchers	1	2	11	White pine
4	Legs	1 3/4	1 3/4	23	White pine

Note: Measurements in inches

Procedure:

1. *Glue* up *stock* for the top and clamp. When the glue is dry, *cut* the *top* to size.
2. *Cut all rails* to size. Do not change the saw setting for the width. If blind mortise and tenons joints are to be used, add 2 in. to the length.

Fig. 4-60. This sawbuck table may be used as a dining table.

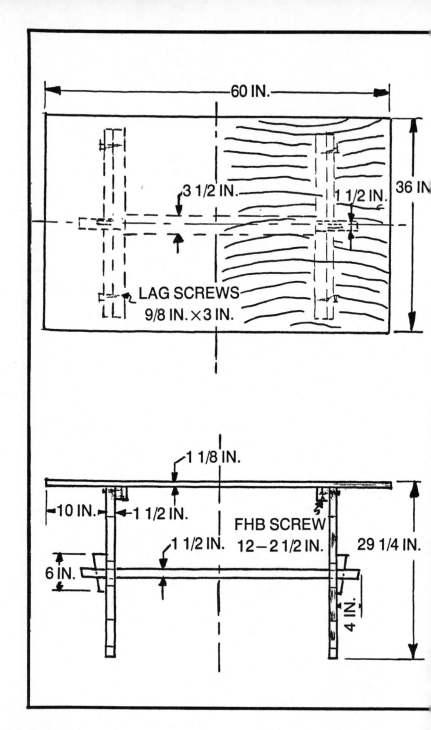

60 IN.

36 IN.

3 1/2 IN.

1 1/2 IN.

LAG SCREWS
9/8 IN. × 3 IN.

1 1/8 IN.

10 IN.

1 1/2 IN.

FHB SCREW
12 − 2 1/2 IN.

29 1/4 IN.

1 1/2 IN.

6 IN.

4 IN.

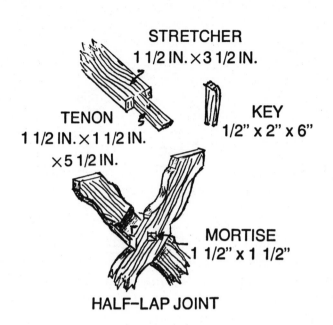

STRETCHER
1 1/2 IN. × 3 1/2 IN.

KEY
1/2" x 2" x 6"

TENON
1 1/2 IN. × 1 1/2 IN.
× 5 1/2 IN.

MORTISE
1 1/2" x 1 1/2"

HALF–LAP JOINT

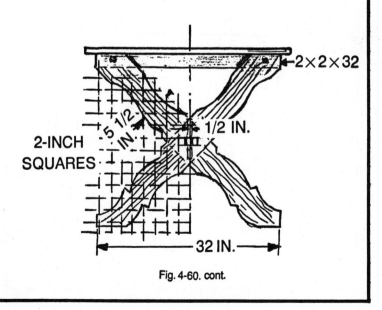

2×2×32

1/2 IN.

5 1/2 IN.

2-INCH
SQUARES

32 IN.

Fig. 4-60. cont.

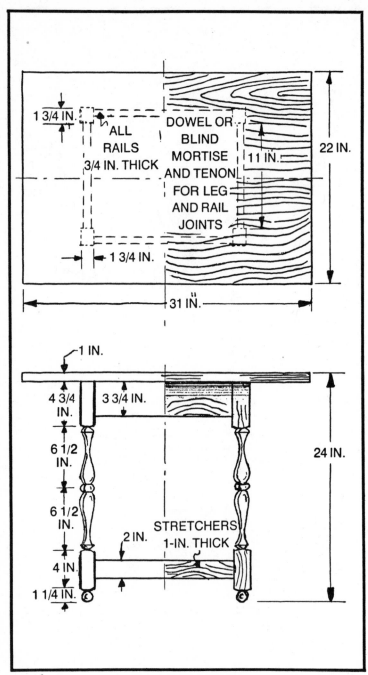

Fig. 4-61. A tavern table.

3. *Cut* the *lower stretchers* to size. Do not change the setting of the saw for the width. If blind mortise and tenons joints are to be used, add 2 in. to the length.
4. *Cut* the *four legs* to squared dimensions. *Turn* the "double bottle" *turnings* on the lathe with round nose, diamond point and skew lathe turning tools. *Cut* in the *mortises,* or drill holes for the dowels depending on which method of joinery is selected and used.
5. *Cut* the *tenons,* or drill holes for dowels, on all rails and stretchers.
6. *Glue, assemble* and clamp the legs, rails and stretcher.
7. When glue is dry, *attach* the *lower assembly* to the top of the table.

Chapter 5
Modern and
Contemporary Projects

MODERN AND CONTEMPORARY PROJECTS

The projects contained within this chapter emphasize sleek, modern design. These furniture pieces add interesting accents to any room featuring contemporary tastes.

A few of the projects at the beginning of the chapter stress furniture suitable for both indoor and outdoor use. They are included because of their design charateristics. The remainder of the chapter's projects are devoted to furniture for indoor use only.

Again, each project features an introductory description, listing of material (table form), step-by-step instructions and accompanying figures sketched to scale.

CAMP FURNITURE—FOLDING CAMP TABLE

The lightweight, easily protable space-saver of Fig. 5-1 can be used out-of-doors in almost any weather because of the redwood construction. It is surprising how sturdy this table becomes when the stiff but bendable ash "bow" snaps into place in the rabbets in the cross rails.

Material:

Materials necessary to complete the folding camp table are contained in Table 5-1.

Procedure:

1. *Glue* up *stock* for the *top*. *Waterproof glue* must be used. When the glue is dry *cut* the stock to dimensions.

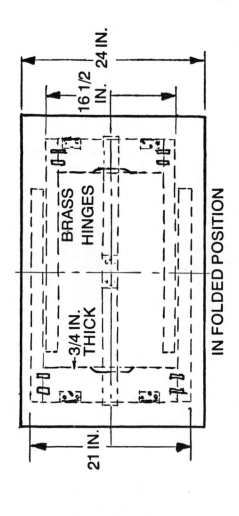

24 IN.

16 1/2 IN.

21 IN.

BRASS HINGES

3/4 IN. THICK

IN FOLDED POSITION

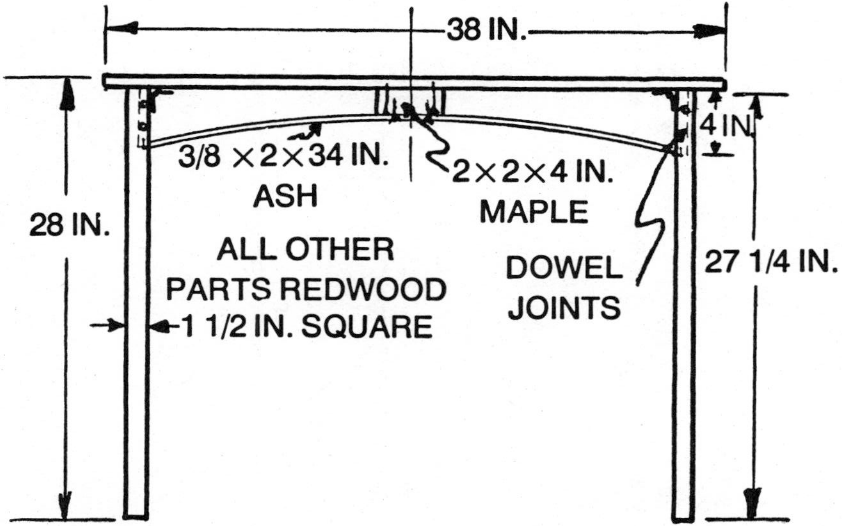

Fig. 5-1. A folding camp table.

38 IN.

4 IN.

27 1/4 IN.

2×2×4 IN.
MAPLE

DOWEL
JOINTS

3/8 × 2×34 IN.
ASH

ALL OTHER
PARTS REDWOOD
1 1/2 IN. SQUARE

28 IN.

317

Table 5-1.

Quantity	Description	Thick	Width	Length	Wood
1	Top	3/4	24	38	Redwood
4	Legs	1 1/2	1 1/2	27 1/4	Redwood
1	Cross rail	3/4	4	13 1/2	Redwood
1	Cross rail	3/4	4	18	Redwood
1	Center anchor block	2	2	4	Maple
1	"Bow" leg support	3/8	2	34	Ash
4	Brass hinges, 3" long			3 inches	

Note: Measurements in inches

2. *Cut* the four *legs* to dimensions.

3. *Cut* the *cross rails* to dimension. *Cut* a *rabbet* about 5 in. long, 3/8 in. wide and 3/8 in. deep in the center of one edge of the cross rails. The ash "bow" will snap into these rabbets with an audible click to assure the camper that the table is ready to be used.

4. *Cut* the center *anchor block* to size.

5. *Cut* the *"bow" leg support* to size.

6. *Attach* the *legs* to the rails with glue and 1/4 in. or 3/8 in. dowels.

7. *Attach brass hinges* to the rails and then attach the other half of the hinges to the top.

8. With the tabletop upside down and the legs folded as in the top view of Fig. 5-1, bore four *shank holes* through both the "bow" and the center anchor block. Mark pilot holes in the top and drill anchor holes. Countersink for screws in the "bow." Use FHB No. 12-2 1/2 in. screws. If the screws should tear out due to the tremendous pressure put upon them, it might be necessary to put in carriage or stove bolts extending completely through the top of the table.

9. Lift legs to the upright position and check to see if the *"bow" snaps into position* satisfactorily. Then check to see how much effort it takes to lift up the end of the "bow" 3/8 in. to allow the legs to be folded in. If the effort is too great, take out the screws holding the "bow" to the anchor block and remove 1/32 of an inch at a time from the thickness until the effort is about right for the camp table owner.

CAMPAIGN CHEST

A chest of similar design to the one pictured in Fig. 5-2 was a favorite of the British Army. The brass corners and recessed pulls helped protect it while being transported on the campaign trail.

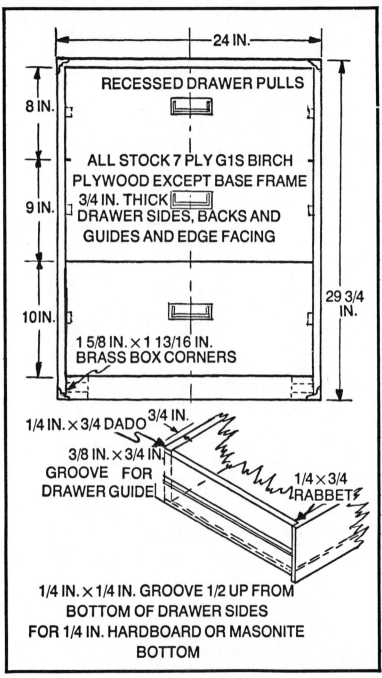

Fig. 5-2. A campaign chest is versatile and sturdy. (Continued on page 320.)

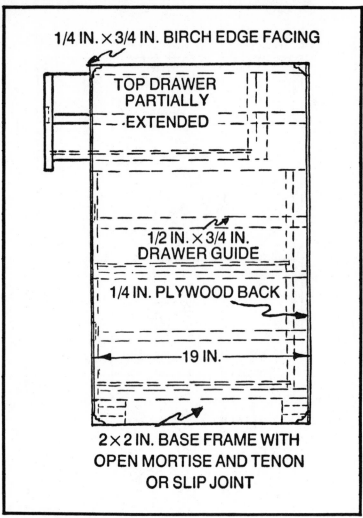

1/4 IN. × 3/4 IN. BIRCH EDGE FACING

TOP DRAWER
PARTIALLY
EXTENDED

1/2 IN. × 3/4 IN.
DRAWER GUIDE

1/4 IN. PLYWOOD BACK

19 IN.

2 × 2 IN. BASE FRAME WITH
OPEN MORTISE AND TENON
OR SLIP JOINT

Fig. 5-2. (Continued from page 3-19.)

Material:

All materials needed to complete this versatile chest are listed in Table 5-2.

Procedure:

1. *Cut* the *top* to dimensions.
2. *Cut* the *bottom* to correct dimensions.
3. *Cut* the two *sides* to dimensions.

Table 5-2.

Quantity	Description	Thick	Width	Length	Wood
1	Top	3/4	19	22 1/2	7 Ply, Birch plywood G1S
1	Bottom	3/4	18	22 1/2	7 Ply, Birch plywood G1S
2	Sides	3/4	19	29 3/4	7 Ply, Birch plywood G1S
1	Plywood Back	1/4	24	29 3/4	Birch plywood
1	Drawer Front	3/4	8	22 1/2	7 Ply, Birch plywood G1S
1	Drawer Front	3/4	9	22 1/2	7 Ply, Birch plywood G1S
1	Drawer Front	3/4	10	22 1/2	7 Ply, Birch plywood G1S
6	Drawer guides	1/2	3/4	18	Maple or birch
2	Drawer sides	3/4	7	18 1/2	Birch
2	Drawer sides	3/4	8 1/2	18 1/2	Birch
2	Drawer sides	3/4	9 1/4	18 1/2	Birch
1	Drawer back	3/4	7	21 1/2	Birch
1	Drawer back	3/4	8 1/2	21 1/2	Birch
1	Drawer back	3/4	9 1/4	21 1/2	Birch
3	Drawer bottoms	1/4	17 1/4	21 1/2	Hardboard or Masonite
2	Front/Back base frame	2	2	22 1/2	Birch or maple
2	End base frame	2	2	18	Birch or maple
2	Birch edge facing	1/4	3/4	29 3/4	Birch
1	Birch edge facing	1/4	3/4	22 1/2	Birch
1	Base frame cover	3/4	2	22 1/2	Birch
8	Brass box corners 1 5/8 × 1 13/16				
3	Recessed drawer pulls				

Note: Measurements in inches

4. *Cut* the four *base frame* pieces. Cut through the mortise and tenons for corner joining. Glue and assemble the base from pieces.

5. *Assemble* the *top, sides* and *base frame.* Use only *waterproof glue* throughout the project.

6. Put glue on the top of the base frame and slide the bottom into place. Drive in ten (3 on front and back and 2 on each end) FHB No. 7-1 1/2 in. screws through the bottom into the base frame.

7. *Tack drawer guides* into place temporarily. Do not glue.

8. *Cut* the *drawer fronts* to fit the openings. Cut a 1/4 in. × 3/4 in. dado 3/4 in. from the end of the drawer sides. *Cut* a 3/8 in. × 3/4 in. *groove,* longitudinally, in the exact center of each drawer side. *Set* a 1/4 in. *dado blade* to cut 1/4 in. deep. *Saw* the *bottom groove* 1/2 in. up from the

bottom of the sides and backs. With the same dado blade set at the same depth, *saw* the *bottom groove* 1 1/4 in. up from the bottom of the drawer front. *Glue, assemble,* and *brad.* Clamp.

9. When the glue is dry try out the drawers with the drawer guide. When the right place for guides is found, where the drawers slide in and out freely, *mark* the *guides*, place glue on the guides and brad them into place.
10. *Install pulls* in the recesses already made.
11. *Install* the *base frame* cover with glue and finishing nails.
12. *Attach* eight 1 5/8 in. × 1 13/16 in. brass box corners on the corners of the chest.

CUTTING BOARD

The cutting board illustrated in Fig. 5-3 can be used for multiple purposes, but is specifically designed for chopping ingredients for salads. Chopped bits of vegetables, nuts and meats are easily pushed toward the curved end of the board where they fall into the salad bowl below. Whether for home use, or as a gift, it is difficult to find a more practical project.

Material:

Table 5-3 lists materials needed to complete the salad cutting board.

Table 5-3.

Quantity	Description	Thick	Width	Length	Wood
1	Top	2	10 1/2	15	Maple
4	Dowels	1-D		6 1/4	Birch
3	Hexagonal head bolts and hex nuts	3/8-D		10 1/2	

Note: Measurements in inches

Procedure:

1. To make the cutting top, *glue up* 7 pieces of end grain *maple* in slabs about 2 1/8 in. × 2 1/8 in. × 15 1/4 in. Each piece in the slab should not be over 4 in. or 5 in. wide and the grain should be reversed so as to reduce warpage as much as possible. Run each slab through a planer to take the width of the slab down to exactly 2 in. Clamp the 7 *slabs*

together and with a 1 in. counterbore, bore three holes 1/2 in. deep in the sides of the clamped slabs. In the center of each counterbore, *bore* a 3/8 in. *hole* about two-thirds of the way. Do the same on the other side. If the holes do not line up correctly, try a 7/16 in. bit. After a hole is bored that is deep enough to allow the bolts to go completely through the top, *mark* the *pieces* so they will go together in the same manner. Unclamp the top and place *glue* on all surfaces that require it. *Clamp* the pieces together again, checking the line-up marks that have been made. Thrust the three bolts through the holes and thread on the hex-nut bolt. With a box wrench, *tighten* the *bolts* as tightly as possible. When the glue is dry, *sand* the *top* surface with coarse sandpaper—preferably with a portable belt sander. If a belt sander is not available, plane the surface with a sharp plane blade and follow with succeedingly finer grades of sandpaper. *Cut* a 1/4 in. *chamfer* on all the top edges. Cut the 4 in. radius circle segment on the end with a band saw. Turn the top over and *plane* the *bottom surface.* It is not necessary to sand.

2. *Cut* four 1 in. *dowels*, 6 in. long. *Sand* the dowels except for the part that goes into the hole. *Make* a *boring jig* for boring holes at the right angle. (Refer to the Cobbler's Bench of Chapter 4.) *Bore* the four 1 in. *holes*, 1 1/4 in. deep. Place glue on the ends of the dowels and drive them into the holes.

Make a simple *surface gauge* with a block of scrap wood. Cut a wooden cube about 1 1/2 in. on a side. Drill a hole through the block the size of a lead pencil so that the point of the pencil will be exactly 1/2 in. above the base. Set the four legs with the cutting board on the table of a circular saw, or any other perfectly flat surface. Extend the pencil point out through the hole in the block. Set the block so that pencil point is touching the dowel. Move the block and pencil around the dowel scribing a line completely around it. In the same manner, scribe lines on the other three dowels. Saw off the dowels on the scribed line with a back saw. If the cutting board does not sit quite level, sandpaper the ends of the longest legs. Do not put any finish on the cutting board. It is permissible to put a finish on the dowel legs. A bright colored enamel or lacquer on the legs would add a great deal to the project.

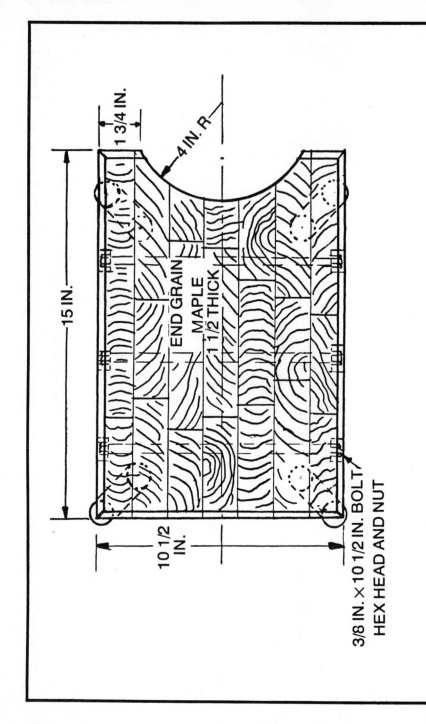

1 3/4 IN.

4 IN. R.

END GRAIN
MAPLE
1 1/2 THICK

15 IN.

10 1/2 IN.

3/8 IN. × 10 1/2 IN. BOLT
HEX HEAD AND NUT

324

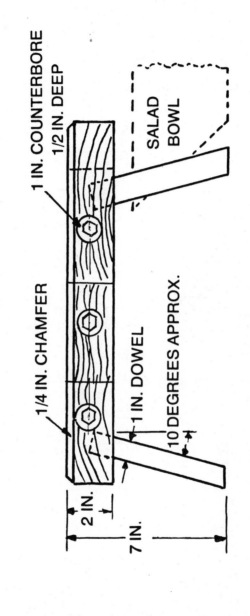

1 IN. COUNTERBORE 1/2 IN. DEEP

SALAD BOWL

1/4 IN. CHAMFER

1 IN. DOWEL

10 DEGREES APPROX.

2 IN.

7 IN.

Fig. 5-3. A handy salad cutting board.

DESK

The unique distinction of the large work desk sketched in Fig. 5-4 is that it uses a standard interior birch door for the top. The cost of this ready-made top is less than if the top was made of solid birch glued up. The cost of building this modern desk is only a fraction of what a commercial ready-made desk would be.

Material:

The materials needed to create a large work desk are listed in Table 5-4.

Table 5-4.

Quantity	Description	Thick	Width	Length	Wood
1	Top (purchased door)	1 1/4	36	84	Birch
4	Legs	1 1/2	2 1/2	31	Birch
2	Top leg rails	1 1/2	3	18	Birch
1	Back stretcher	3/4	2	68	Birch
2	Dowel stretchers 3/4-in. diam. × 30-in. long		4 inch D	30-inches	
4	Drawer compartment sides	3/4	13	26	Birch plywood
8	Open frame end rails	3/4	2 1/2	11 1/2	Birch
8	Open frame side rails	3/4	2 1/2	25	Birch
1	Drawer front (file cabinet)	3/4	11 1/2	14	Birch
1	Drawer front (middle)	3/4	3	32	Birch
1	Drawer front (upper right)	3/4	4 1/2	14	Birch
2	Drawer sides (lower right)	3/4	7	24	Birch
2	Drawer sides (middle)	3/4	3	19	Birch
1	Drawer back (file cabinet)	3/4	9	13	Birch
	Approx. 48 inches of 1/8 inch × 3/4-inch Birch to cover edges of plywood				
1	Drawer back (middle)	3/4	3	32	Birch
1	Drawer back (upper right)	3/4	4 1/2	13	Birch
1	Drawer back (lower right)	3/4	7	13	Birch
1	Drawer bottom (file cabinet)	1/4	13	28 1/8	Hardboard or Masonite
1	Drawer bottom (middle)	1/4	18 1/2	31	Hardboard or Masonite
1	Drawer bottom (upper right)	1/4	13	28 1/8	Hardboard or Masonite
1	Drawer bottom (lower right)	1/4	13	28 1/8	Hardboard or Masonite
5	Contemporary drawer pulls				
1	Card identification (file) holder				
6	Drawer guides	3/8	1 1/4	24	Birch
2	Drawer guides	3/8	7/8	19	Birch

Note: Measurements in inches

Procedure:

1. *Purchase* the *door* for the top.

2. *Cut* four *legs* to squared dimensions. *Taper* legs from 2 1/2 in. to 1 in. *Cut* out the *corners* on the wider end to receive the squared end of the 3 in. top leg rails. *Bore holes* for the dowels. *Cut recesses* for the back stretcher on two legs only (3/8 in. deep, 2 in. wide). *Roll corners* (except top 3 in.) with a plane, wood rasp and sandpaper.

3. *Cut* the two *top leg rails* to dimensions. *Bore holes* for end dowels 3/8 in. to match holes in the legs. *Drill 4 holes*, 2 in each rail, for the shank of FHB No. 18-4 in. screws to attach the door to the legs.

4. To construct the drawers and drawer compartments, *cut open frame parts* (8 end rails, 8 side rails) to dimensions. *Cut* a *dovetail tenon* on the end rails and *dovetail mortises* on side rails. Glue and clamp. When dry, drill 6 shank holes for FHB No. 6-1 1/2 in. screws in each frame. Countersink all holes. *Cut 4 drawer compartment sides* to dimensions. *Assemble* the drawer compartment sides and open rails with glue and long brads. Clamp until glue is dry. *Cut* and *tack* in the *drawer guides* temporarily. Do not glue. Be sure to tack (temporarily) the two drawer guides for the middle drawer on the outside. **Note:** If the desk is to be used constantly, it is recommended that ball-bearing, nylon-wheel drawer slides be used—particularly on the file cabinet drawer.

5. To construct the drawer for the file cabinet, *cut* the *drawer front* to size. *Cut* a 1/4 in. wide, 1/4 in. deep *dado*, 1/2 in. in from the ends. *Cut* the *drawer sides* to dimensions. Note that the sides are much shallower (or narrower) than the drawer front which is typical of all drawer file cabinets. *Cut* 1/2 in. × 1/4 in. *rabbets* in the ends of each side piece. The tongue formed (1/4 in. × 1/4 in.) will fit into the drawer front. On the other end of the drawer sides, *cut* a 3/4 in. wide by 1/4 in. deep *dado* 3/8 in. in from the end. *Cut grooves* (3/8 in. × 1 1/4 in.) in the center of the sides for the drawer guides. *Cut* the *drawer back* to size.

6. The middle drawer construction begins by *cutting* the *front* to size. *Cut* a 1/2 in. × 3/4 in. *rabbet* in each end of the drawer front. *Cut* the *drawer sides* to dimensions. *Cut* a 3/8 in. × 7/8 in. *groove* in the center of each side for the

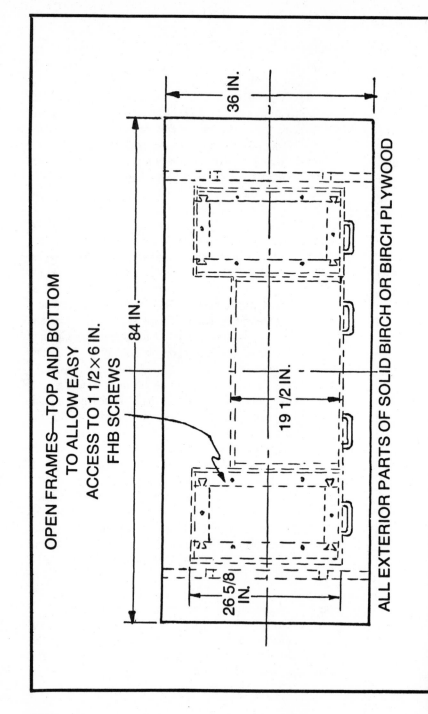

OPEN FRAMES—TOP AND BOTTOM TO ALLOW EASY ACCESS TO 1 1/2 × 6 IN. FHB SCREWS

36 IN.

84 IN.

19 1/2 IN.

26 5/8 IN.

ALL EXTERIOR PARTS OF SOLID BIRCH OR BIRCH PLYWOOD

328

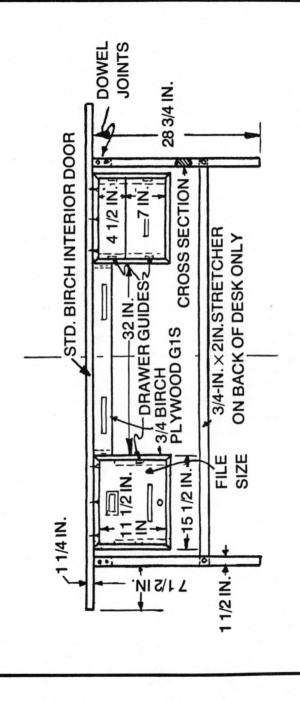

Fig. 5-4. An inexpensive, easily constructed desk. The scale drawing represents one-sixteenth second the actual size.

329

drawer guides. *Cut* the *drawer back* to size. Cut a 1/2 in. × 3/4 in. *rabbet* on each end.

7. Cut the front to size for the upper right and lower right drawer. *Cut* a 1/4 in. wide, 1/4 in. deep *dado*, 1/2 in. in from the ends. *Cut* the *drawer sides* to dimension. *Cut* 1/2 in. × 1/4 in. *rabbets* in the ends of each side piece. The tongue formed (1/4 in. ×1/4 in.) will fit into the drawer front. On the other end of the drawer sides, *cut* a 3/4 in. wide by 1/4 in. *dado* 3/8 in. in from the end. *Cut grooves* (3/8 in. × 1 1/4 in.) in the center of the sides for the drawer guides. *Cut* the *drawer back* to size.

8. *Cut* a 1/4 in. × 1/4 in. *groove*, 3/8 in. from the bottom on all *drawer fronts, sides* and *back* with the same setting of the saw or dado head.

9. *Cut* the *bottoms* for all drawers and fit to drawers.

10. *Glue, assemble* and *clamp* all the drawers.

11. *Lay* the *top* (door) on two low saw horses. Place the two drawer compartments in their relative positions with the center drawer in place. The center drawer should move rather easily on the guides. With an awl, *mark* the *six pilot holes* of each frame by extending the awl down through the shank holes in the top open-frame ends and sides. *Drill* the *pilot holes* and fasten the drawer compartments to the top (door) with screws. Check again for proper fit of the middle drawer. It may be necessary to make adjustments with the guides. When the right place is found for the *guides, attach* the permanently with glue and brads. *Cut* and *miter* the 1/8 in. × 3/4 in. *edge covering birch* to cover the core material of the plywood and end of open frames on the front of the drawer compartments. *Slide* the other three drawers into the drawer compartments. Make the necessary adjustments with guides until the drawer moves easily. *Attach* the *guides* permanently with glue and brads.

12. Remove the five drawers and attach the pulls and the identification card holder.

13. While the top is in this same position, *attach* the *legs* to the top with the FHB No. 18-4 in. screws by marking pilot holes on the door, drilling pilot holes, and driving screws into the door with a screwdriver.

14. *Tip* the *table* on its side with the back in the top position. *Attach* the *stretcher* to the legs with dowels or round head (brass) screws.

LAWN FURNITURE—TABLE

The easy-to-make, easy-to-take-down, storable loose-top table of Fig. 5-5 is specially designed for outdoor use. This is another example of a one weekend project.

Material:

Materials needed to complete a table for outdoor use are listed in Table 5-5.

Table 5-5.

Quantity	Description	Thick	Width	Length	Wood
1	Top	3/4	34	50	Douglas fir
2	Ends	3/4	26	29 1/4	Exterior G2S
1	Top rail (support)	3/4	6	47	Exterior G2S
1	Lower stretcher	3/4	5	45	Exterior G2S
4	Retaining blocks	1 1/2	4	4	Birch

Note: Measurements in inches

Procedure:

1. *Cut* the *top* to size.
2. *Make* a *pattern* for the curved portion of the ends. *Cut* the *ends* to squared dimensions. *Mark* the *curved portions* with the pattern. *Cut* the *curved portions* on a bandsaw.
3. *Cut* the *top rail* to size. The top edge should be 47 in. long and the bottom edge 44 in. long.
4. *Cut* the *lower stretcher* to size. The upper edge should be 45 in. long and the bottom edge 42 in. long.
5. *Cut* all *half-lap joints* (ends, top rail and lower stretcher). Make sure that the holes in the end pieces are long enough to accept the ends of the lower stretcher.
6. *Assemble* the ends, top rail and lower stretcher.
7. *Place* the *top* on low saw horses. Position the lower assembly in proper relationship to the top. *Mark* the outline of the *retaining blocks*. *Cut* the triangular *retaining blocks*. *Drill* three *holes* in each block for the shank of FHB No. 8-2 in. screws. *Mark pilot holes* with awl on the top by inserting the awl through the shank holes in the retaining blocks. Move the blocks aside and *drill pilot holes*. Put *glue*—water glue only—on the *retaining blocks* and drive in the screws. Retaining blocks are to keep the top from shifting around. They are not attached to the top rail or ends.

8. Disassemble the table and cover all raw and exposed edges of the plywood with 1/8 in. × 3/4 in. birch. *Attach* these pieces with glue and small brads. Use only waterproof glue. *Finish* with spar varnish, epoxy finish, polyurethane, waterlox, or any other weather-resistant finish or paint.

MAGAZINE RACK

The interesting, modern project illustrated in Fig. 5-6 is made more attractive by the use of a plastic clothesline. The open and airy design is unique and appealing.

Material:

Table 5-6 lists materials needed to complete a handsome magazine rack.

Table 5-6.

Quantity	Description	Thick	Width	Length	Wood
4	End Uprights	3/4	2 1/2	20	Birch or maple
1	Dowel		1-D	17	Birch
1	Dowel		1/2-D	15 1/2	Birch
1	Dowel		1/2-D	16 1/2	Birch
1	Plastic Clothesline				

Note: Measurements in inches

Procedure:

1. *Cut* the four *end uprights* to squared dimension. *Taper* on one side of each piece, from 1-in. wide at the two ends to 2 1/2 in., eight inches from the lower end. *Cut* the 1/4 in. *dadoes* in each piece to form the partial half laps. *Bore* 1/2 in. *holes* near the top end and a 1 in. dowel hole in the center of the half-lap section. (This is done only after partial half laps have been glued and clamped and the glue has dried.) *Round* the *ends* of all dowels. Place glue on the inside of the dowel holes. *Insert* the *dowels*. After the glue is thoroughly dry, wind on the plastic clothesline as shown in Fig. 5-6.

MIRROR

The contemporary mirror of Fig. 5-7 is simple to make because only standard commercial widths and thicknesses are used. This is yet another example of a one weekend project.

Material:

Materials needed to complete a contemporary mirror design are listed in Table 5-7.

Table 5-7.

Quantity	Description	Thick	Width	Length	Wood
2	Side pieces	3/4	3 1/2	29	White pine
2	Side pieces	3/4	3 1/2	36	White pine
2	Top -/Bottom pieces	3/4	3 1/2	24	White pine
2	Top/Bottom pieces	3/4	3 1/2	17	White pine
4	Small turnings of mahogany, walnut, or any other dark wood 3/8 inch in thickness, 1 inch in diameter				
1	Mirror glass, 18 inch x 30 inch				
1	Plywood backup	1/4	18	39	Fir

Note: Measurements in inches

Procedure:

1. *Cut* all *eight pieces* to the lengths indicated in the Table 5-7.
2. On the two longest side pieces (36 in. long) and the two shortest top/bottom pieces, *cut* 1/2 in. × 1/2 in. *rabbets*. Start and stop the rabbets about 2 in. from each end.
3. *Glue, assemble,* and *clamp* together all eight pieces. Be sure to have enough clamps ready when you start applying glue.
4. When the glue is dry *sand* the *front* and *back faces* until they are flush. *Plane* and *sand* all *outer edges*.
5. On each corner, *draw* two *squared lines* that intersect 2 in. from each side of the corner. At these four points, *bore* a 1 in. diameter *hole*, 3/8 in. deep with a Forstner bit.
6. *Turn* a *dowel* of dark wood 1 in. in diameter and about 2 1/4 in. long. After the dowel is turned, *cut* off four 7/16 in. thick *slices*. Put *glue* on these *slices* and *drive* them into the four corner holes. When the glue is dry, sand the slices down to the surface of the mirror frame.
7. *Mark* a 2 in. *radii* on the corners and *cut* on a bandsaw.
8. *Apply finish*, insert a mirror and backup piece.

SERVING CART

The combination serving cart sketched in Fig. 5-8 plays a dual role. With the cover down, an ample area of 15 1/2 in. × 55 in. can be used as a buffet table for cold foods. With the cover up, hot foods can be served for any length of time. When not in use the end leaves fold down to conserve space. This serving cart is just the thing for impromptu parties or when a few unexpected guests drop in.

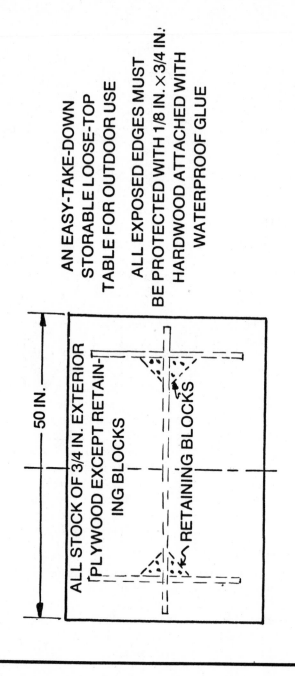

AN EASY-TAKE-DOWN
STORABLE LOOSE-TOP
TABLE FOR OUTDOOR USE

ALL EXPOSED EDGES MUST
BE PROTECTED WITH 1/8 IN. × 3/4 IN.
HARDWOOD ATTACHED WITH
WATERPROOF GLUE

50 IN.

ALL STOCK OF 3/4 IN. EXTERIOR
PLYWOOD EXCEPT RETAIN-
ING BLOCKS

RETAINING BLOCKS

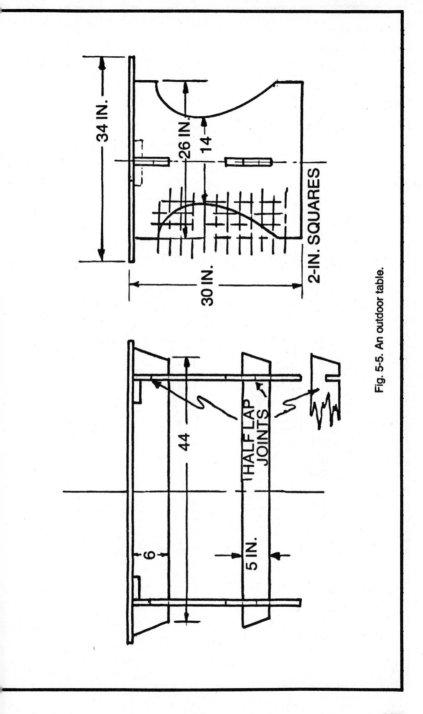

34 IN.

26 IN.

14

30 IN.

2-IN. SQUARES

44

6

5 IN.

HALF LAP JOINTS

Fig. 5-5. An outdoor table.

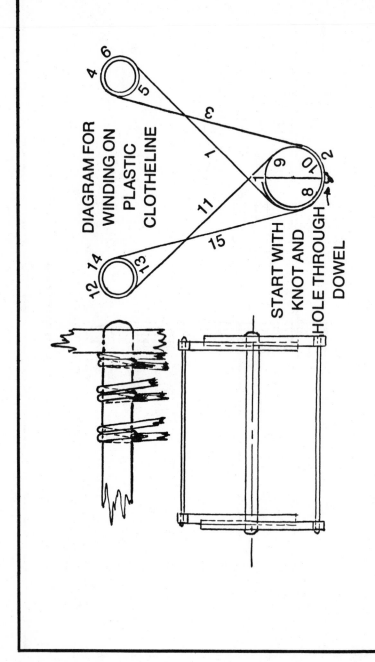

DIAGRAM FOR
WINDING ON
PLASTIC CLOTHELINE

START WITH
KNOT AND
HOLE THROUGH
DOWEL

336

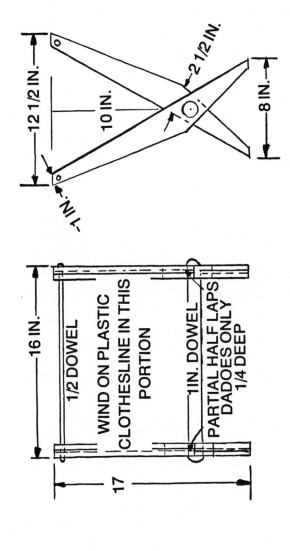

12 1/2 IN.

10 IN.

2 1/2 IN.

8 IN.

1 IN.

16 IN.

1/2 DOWEL

WIND ON PLASTIC
CLOTHESLINE IN THIS
PORTION

1IN. DOWEL

PARTIAL HALF LAPS
DADOES ONLY
1/4 DEEP

17

Fig. 5-6. A contemporary magazine rack with a design difference—a plastic clothes line.

337

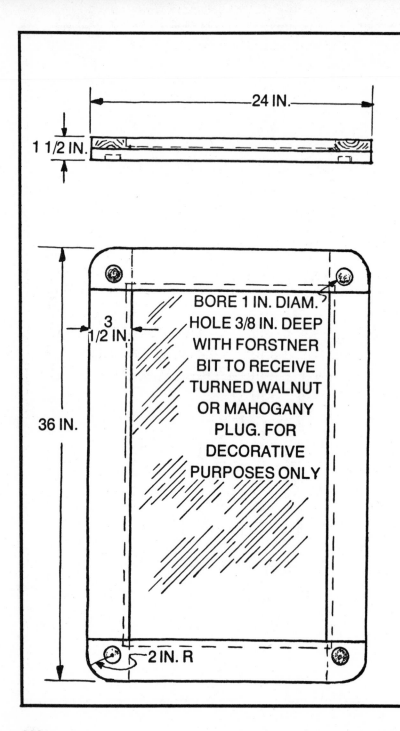

24 IN.

1 1/2 IN.

3 1/2 IN.

36 IN.

BORE 1 IN. DIAM. HOLE 3/8 IN. DEEP WITH FORSTNER BIT TO RECEIVE TURNED WALNUT OR MAHOGANY PLUG. FOR DECORATIVE PURPOSES ONLY

2 IN. R

ALL STOCK STANDARD
1 IN. × 4 IN. PINE COMMERCIAL
LUMBER. NO RIPPING
OF STOCK NECESSARY

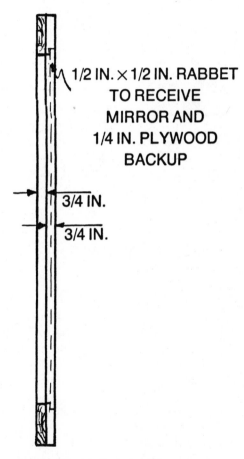

1/2 IN. × 1/2 IN. RABBET
TO RECEIVE
MIRROR AND
1/4 IN. PLYWOOD
BACKUP

3/4 IN.

3/4 IN.

Fig. 5-7. A contemporary mirror.

Material:

Table 5-8 lists all materials necessary to complete a versatile serving cart.

Table 5-8.

Quantity	Description	Thick	Width	Length	Wood
1	Cover	3/4	15 1/2	27	Birch plywood G1S or G2S
2	Leaves	3/4	10	15 1/2	Birch plywood G1S or G2S
2	Hinge members	3/4	4	15 1/2	Birch plywood G1S or G2S
1	Lower shelf	3/4	14	28 1/2	Birch plywood G1S or G2S
2	Leaf supports	3/4	5	6	Birch plywood G1S or G2S
2	Upper end rails	3/4	5	12 1/2	Birch plywood G1S or G2S
2	Upper side rails	3/4	5	27	Birch plywood G1S or G2S
1	Bottom	3/4	14	28 1/2	Birch plywood G1S or G2S
2	Leaf support hinges, brass			3-inch	
1	27-inch Continuous hinge				
4	3-in. Rubber casters				
4	Legs	1 1/2	1 1/2	26 1/4	Birch
4	Drop leaf table hinges				
	Formica or asbestos to line inside of tray compartment				

Note: Measurements in inches

Procedure:

1. *Cut* the *cover* to size.
2. *Cut* the *leaves* to dimensions.
3. *Cut* the *hinge members* to size.
4. *Cut* the *lower shelf* to size.
5. *Cut* the *leaf supports* to size.
6. *Cut* the *end* and *side rail* to dimensions.
7. *Cut* the *legs* to size. *Cut* a *cross-corner* 3/4 in. wide *dado* on one corner of each leg 7 in. from the bottom of the leg. *Bore dowel holes* 3/8 in. deep (to attach legs to rails).
8. *Bore holes* for 3/8 in. dowels in the ends of the rails.
9. *Glue, assemble* and *clamp* legs, rails and the lower shelf (after cutting off corners at 45 degrees).
10. *Cut* the *bottom* to fit inside the tray compartment. In one corner of the bottom, *cut* a 3 in. *hole* for an electric cord with a saber saw, jigsaw, coping saw, compass saw, or keyhole saw. *Anchor* the bottom with three round-head

brass screws No. 6-1 1/2 in. through the lower edge of the upper-end rails.

11. *Cut* the *angle* on the previously cut *leaf supports* to the correct size. *Attach* a *hinge* on the 5 in. side. *Attach* the other half of the hinge to the upper-end rails.

12. *Attach* the *leaves* to the hinge members with drop-leaf table hinges. *Attach* the *hinge members* in place, over the upper-end rails, with dowel-covered flat head screws into the upper-end rails.

13. *Attach* the *cover* to the upper back/side rail with a continuous hinge.

14. Turn the cart upside down and *bore holes* for *casters. Insert* the *casters* into these holes.

15. Turn the cart in the upright position and *line* the inside of the *tray compartment* with asbestos or Formica.

16. *Cut* strips of *birch* 1/8 in. × 3/4 in. and cover all exposed and unprotected edges. *Attach* these strips with glue and small brads. **Note:** If the craftsman has (or is going to purchase) an electric warmer tray other than the model shown in Fig. 5-5, of course he will have to adjust the dimensions accordingly.

ACCENT TABLE

A general utility table as shown in Fig. 5-9 may be used in many places and in many ways. An extra coffee table, cocktail table, TV table, book stand, or bedside stand always come in handy. In an emergency, this sturdily-built table could be used as a step stool. The use of commercial lumber sizes will eliminate considerable time in constructing this project.

Material:

Materials needed to complete an accent table are listed in Table 5-9.

Procedure:

1. *Glue* up and *clamp* stock for the top. When the glue is dry, *cut* the *top* to dimensions.

2. *Cut* the *top trim* pieces to length. Miter (45 degrees) on each end.

3. *Cut* the *leg pieces* to length.

4. *Cut* the *top rails* to length.

5. *Cut* the *bottom rails* to length.

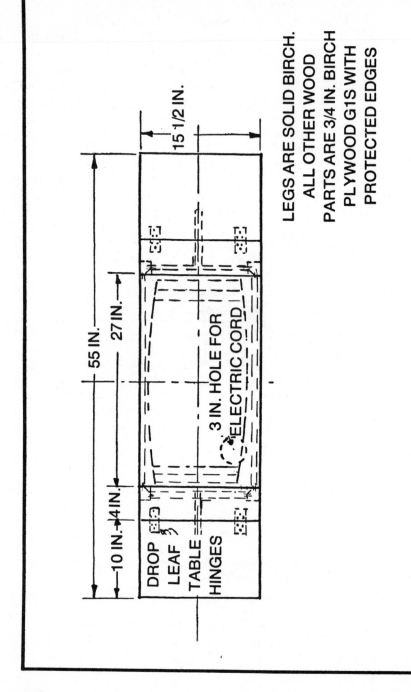

15 1/2 IN.

55 IN.

27 IN.

10 IN. 4 IN.

DROP
LEAF
TABLE
HINGES

3 IN. HOLE FOR
ELECTRIC CORD

LEGS ARE SOLID BIRCH.
ALL OTHER WOOD
PARTS ARE 3/4 IN. BIRCH
PLYWOOD G1S WITH
PROTECTED EDGES

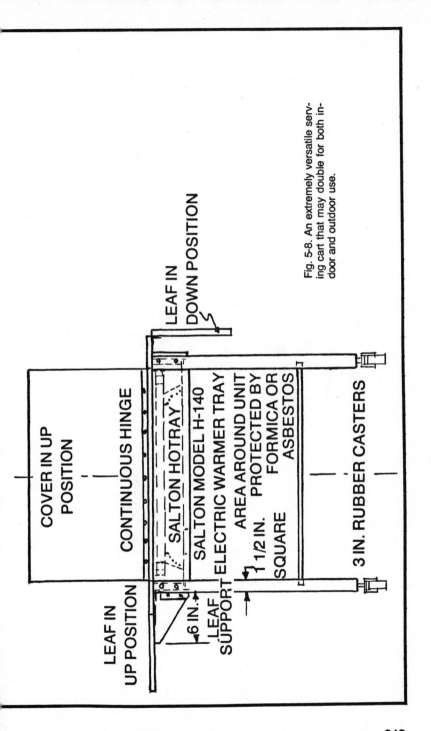

COVER IN UP POSITION

CONTINUOUS HINGE

LEAF IN UP POSITION

6 IN.

LEAF SUPPORT

SALTON HOTRAY

SALTON MODEL H-140 ELECTRIC WARMER TRAY

AREA AROUND UNIT PROTECTED BY FORMICA OR ASBESTOS

1/2 IN. SQUARE

LEAF IN DOWN POSITION

3 IN. RUBBER CASTERS

Fig. 5-8. An extremely versatile serving cart that may double for both indoor and outdoor use.

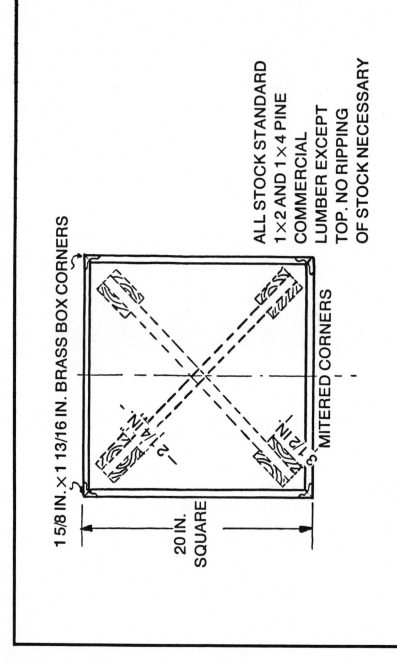

1 5/8 IN. × 1 13/16 IN. BRASS BOX CORNERS

ALL STOCK STANDARD
1 × 2 AND 1 × 4 PINE
COMMERCIAL
LUMBER EXCEPT
TOP. NO RIPPING
OF STOCK NECESSARY

MITERED CORNERS

20 IN.
SQUARE

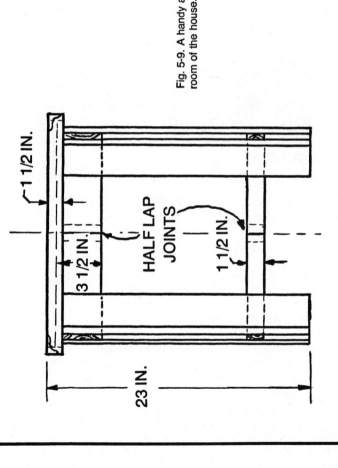

23 IN.

1 1/2 IN.

3 1/2 IN.

HALF LAP JOINTS

1 1/2 IN.

Fig. 5-9. A handy accent table that will find use in any room of the house.

Table 5-9.

Quantity	Description	Thick	Width	Length	Wood
1	Top	3/4	18 1/2	18 1/2	White pine
4	Top trim pieces	3/4	1 1/2	20	White pine
8	Leg pieces	3/4	3 1/2	22 1/4	White pine
2	Top rails	3/4	3 1/2	23	White pine
2	Bottom rails	3/4	1 1/2	23	White pine
4	Brass box corners, 1 5/8 inches × 1 13/16 inches				

Note: Measurements in inches

6. *Cut* the *half laps* in the center of the top and bottom rails.
7. *Glue* and *assemble* the top- and bottom-rail half laps.
8. *Glue* and *assemble* the top and bottom rails and legs. Make sure the corners are square. The bottom rails should be 4 in. up from the bottom of the legs. Use plenty of clamps and have them ready before the glue is applied.
9. *Fasten* the *trim pieces* to the top with glue and brads.
10. *Attach* the top to the legs with FHB No. 18-4 in. screws up through the top rails.
11. *Attach* 1 5/8 in. × 1 13/16 in. brass box corners to the corners of the table top.

BOOK-TROUGH TABLE

The sturdy but airy contemporary piece of furniture of Fig. 5-10 not only fits into a den or library, but into nearly every other room in the house. It is a handy place to keep books that you are currently reading.

Material:

Table 5-10 lists all materials needed to complete a book-trough table.

Table 5-10.

Quantity	Description	Thick	Width	Length	Wood
1	Top	3/4	14	22 1/2	Maple
4	Legs	1 1/4	2	30 1/2	Maple
2	Top leg rails	1 1/4	1 1/2	4	Maple
1	Shelf member	5/8	8 1/2	22 1/2	Maple
1	Shelf member	5/8	8 3/16	22 1/2	Maple

Note: Measurements in inches

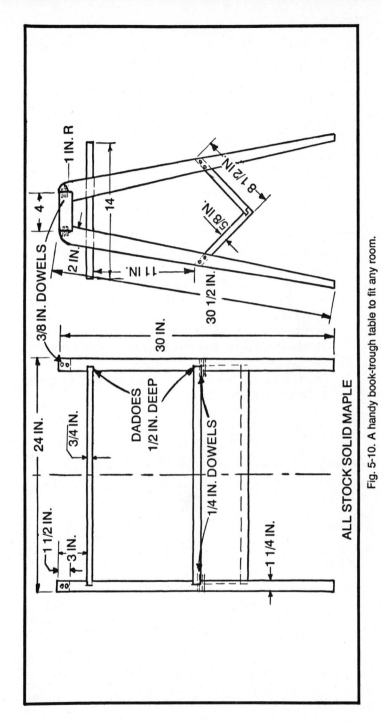

Fig. 5-10. A handy book-trough table to fit any room.

Procedure:

1. *Glue* and *clamp stock* for the top. When the glue is dry *cut* the *stock* to size.
2. *Cut* the four *legs* to squared dimensions. *Taper* the legs from 2 in. at one end to 3/4 in. at the other. *Mark* a 1 in. radius, *quarter-circle* on one corner of the upper leg. *Cut* with a band saw. *Cut* out the *other corner* to receive the top-leg rails. *Cut* a *dado* to receive the top and an *angled dado* to receive the shelf. *Bore* 3/8 in. *dowel holes* in the angled dadoes to receive the shelf and reinforce the dado joint. *Bore* 3/8 in. dowel holes in the corner to receive the top rails. **Note:** It is a good idea, when the position of angled legs is very important, to lay out on heavy paper the whole end section.
3. *Cut* the *top leg rails*. *Bore* 3/8-in. dowel holes in the ends.
4. *Cut* the *shelf members* to size. *Cut* the required *angle* on one side. On the other side of one shelf, *cut* a 5/15 in. × 5/16 in. *dado*, 5/16 in. from the end. On the other side of the other shelf, *cut* a 5/16 in. × 5/16 in. *rabbet* to form a 6/16 in. tongue. *Bore* 1/4 in. *dowels* in the ends of the shelf members. See Fig. 5-10.
5. *Glue, assemble* and *clamp* all parts of the table together. Use Jorgenson adjustable hand clamps, opened at an angle, to clamp the legs to the top-leg rails.

BUTLER-TRAY TABLE

There are three options when using the table of Fig. 5-11. The butler tray may be used alone or the butler tray can be used with a table or the butler table can be laid on its side (notice the option of two heights for the cocktail table) for a cocktail or coffee table.

Material:

Table 5-11 lists all materials needed to complete a combination butler-tray table.

Procedure:

1. *Cut* the 2 butler-tray *side rails* to squared dimensions. *Butt out* the *recessed sections* with a bandsaw or any curve-cutting saw. *Cut* 3/8 in. × 1/2 in. *rabbets* on each end which form a 1/8 in. × 1/2 in. tongue.
2. *Cut* the 2 butler-tray *end rails* (handles) to squared dimensions. *Cut* out the *curved section* around the handle

Table 5-11.

Quantity	Description	Thick	Width	Length	Wood
2	Butler-tray side rails	1/2	3	31	Cherry
2	Butler-Tray end rails (handle)	1/2	3 1/2	18 3/4	Cherry
1	Butler-Tray bottom	1/4	18 1/2	30 1/2	Cherry plywood
4	Legs	1 1/2	1 1/2	29 3/4	Cherry
4	Stretchers	3/4	1 3/4	15 1/2	Cherry
4	Stretchers	3/4	1 3/4	14	Cherry

Note: Measurements in inches

with a band saw or any curve-cutting saw. *Saw* out the *handle hole* with a coping saw, jigsaw, saber saw, keyhole saw or compass saw. These saws may be used only after holes are bored to admit the saw blade. *Saw* the *bottom groove* 1/4 in. × 1/4 in. up 1/4 in. from the bottom of the sides and ends with a dado head or saw. Do not change the setting of the dado or saw until all four grooves are cut.

3. *Glue, assemble* and *clamp* all parts of the butler tray.

4. *Cut* the *legs* to dimensions. *Bore* 3/8 in. *holes* deep enough to allow the top stretchers to be 2 in. down from the top of the legs. The bottom stretchers will be 2 in. up from the bottom of the legs.

5. *Cut* the eight *stretchers* to squared dimensions. *Bore* 3/8 in. *dowel holes* to match the corresponding holes in the legs. *Mark* the *legs* and *stretcher ends* so that they will always be assembled and disassembled with the parts in the same positions. *Cut out* the *recessed parts* with a band saw or other curve-cutting saw.

6. *Glue, assemble* and *clamp* the *shorter* stretchers to the corresponding legs.

7. When the glue is dry on these two subassemblies, *glue, assemble* and *clamp* the *longer* stretchers between these two subassemblies.

COCKTAIL TABLE

The cocktail table illustrated in Fig. 5-12 represents another project which eliminates all ripping operations by using standard commercial lumber sizes.

Material:

Materials necessary to construct a contemporary cocktail table are listed in Table 5-12.

349

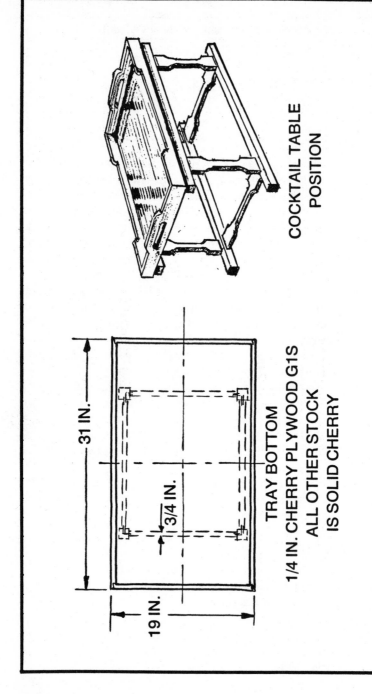

COCKTAIL TABLE
POSITION

TRAY BOTTOM
1/4 IN. CHERRY PLYWOOD G1S
ALL OTHER STOCK
IS SOLID CHERRY

31 IN.

19 IN.

3/4 IN.

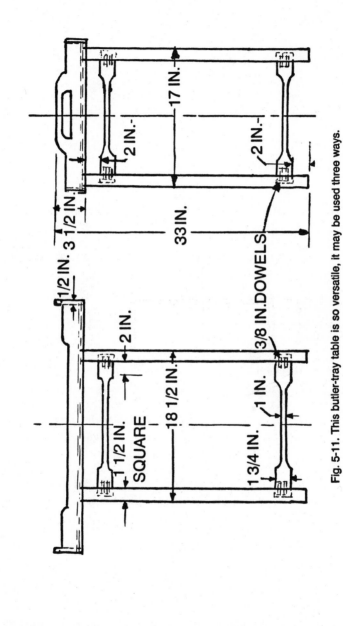

Fig. 5-11. This butler-tray table is so versatile, it may be used three ways.

Table 5-12.

Quantity	Description	Thick	Width	Length	Wood
13	Top strips	3/4	1 1/2	42	White pine
8	Leg strips	3/4	1 1/2	14 1/2	White pine
24	Filler blocks	3/4	1 1/2	3	White pine
16	Filler blocks	3/4	1 1/2	2	White pine
4	Filler blocks	3/4	1 1/2	1 1/2	White pine
4	3/8-inch Dowels			18 3/4	
4	3/8-inch Dowels			2 1/4	

Note: Measurements in inches

Procedure:

1. *Cut* the *top strips* to length.
2. *Cut* the *leg strips* to length.
3. *Cut* all *filler blocks* to length.
4. Carefully and accurately *measure* all the *dowel holes*. A marking gauge, with a spur sharpened to a chisel edge and a try square will aid in accurately locating the dowel holes. Use a sharp awl to prick a small hole where the lines of the marking gauge and try square intersect. The prick mark will help direct the point of the bit when boring the dowel holes.
5. The holes in the ends of the top strips should be exactly in the middle and 1 1/2 in. from the ends. The two other holes in top strips should be in the center and 8 1/4 in. from the ends. The holes in the bottom ends of the legs should be in the center and 3/4 in. from the end.
6. *Bore* all the *holes* for the dowels. Try out the dowels by assembling all the parts. Do not glue at this time. Small adjustments can be made by reboring the out-of-line holes 7/16 in. in diameter.
7. After adjustments have been made, *glue, assemble* and *clamp* all parts. Make sure you have plenty of clamps ready before gluing begins. Make sure that the legs are square with the top.

COFFEE TABLE

The streamline coffee table sketched in Fig. 5-13 has two unusual features: walnut dovetail keys and ash legs. The dovetail keys not only add to the strength of the top, but they are also decorative. The ash legs look fragile, but actually are very strong.

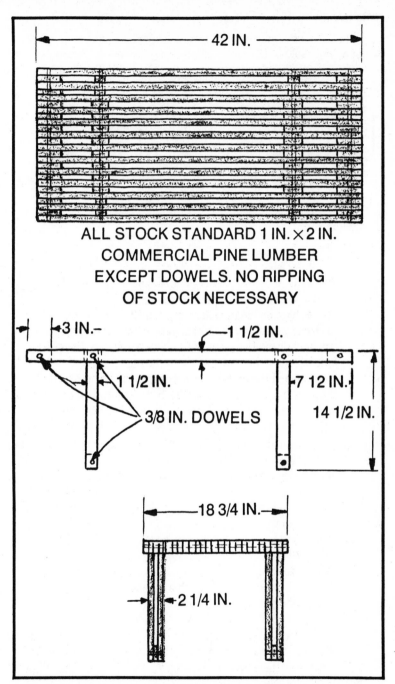

ALL STOCK STANDARD 1 IN. × 2 IN.
COMMERCIAL PINE LUMBER
EXCEPT DOWELS. NO RIPPING
OF STOCK NECESSARY

42 IN.

3 IN.—

1 1/2 IN.

1 1/2 IN.

3/8 IN. DOWELS

7 12 IN.

14 1/2 IN.

18 3/4 IN.

2 1/4 IN.

Fig. 5-12. A contemporary cocktail table using standard commercial sizes.

Material:

Materials needed to complete the ash and walnut coffee table are listed in Table 5-13.

Table 5-13.

Quantity	Description	Thick	Width	Length	Wood
1	Top	1 1/2	18	36	Maple
2	Top end battens	1 1/2	6	18	Maple
4	Legs	2	6	22	Ash
10	Dovetail keys	1 1/2	1	1 1/2	Walnut

Note: Measurements in inches

Procedure:

1. *Cut* three pieces of 1 1/2 in. maple that have a combined width of about 19 in. The length of the pieces should be about 37 in. *Joint* the edges and *clamp* the pieces together.

2. *Make* an *aluminum pattern* of the fullsize dovetail key. *Lay* the *pattern* on the top extending equally on both pieces, and *mark* closely around the aluminum with the point of a sharp knife. It is not necessary to space dovetail keys in as symmetrical a pattern as shown in Fig. 5-13. With a hard lead pencil sharpened to a chisel edge, *trace* the knife marks. The pencil should reach the bottom of the knife mark.

3. After the dovetail keys have been marked, *unclamp* the three boards and very carefully *cut* out the dovetail keys with a bandsaw, just barely touching the line on the *inside* of the dovetail key.

4. *Clamp* the three boards back together in their original position. On a 1 1/2 in. piece of walnut, *mark* the outlines for the dovetail keys with the aluminum pattern using the same knife point, chisel-edge pencil technique.

5. *Cut* out the dovetail keys with the band saw, this time barely touching the line on the *outside*.

6. *Mark* each dovetail key with a number, and assign a corresponding number to a dovetail-keyhole. Work down the outside of the key with the bandsaw, wood files, chisels and sandpaper. During the fitting process, rub the inside of the dovetail-keyhole with a soft art pencil. The portion to be taken off the key will show up as a dark spot during the fitting process.

7. After the six dovetail keys have been fitted, *unclamp* the boards. Put *glue* on the edges of the boards and dovetail keys, *assemble* and *clamp*. When the glue is dry, *cut* the *top* to length.

8. *Cut* the *end battens* to width, but cut the ends to a length equal to the rough width of the top (19 in.) *Joint* one edge of the battens so they fit closely to the ends of the tops. Mark and cut both dovetail-keyholes and dovetail keys as described above. *Glue, assemble* and *clamp* the battens to the top.

9. When the glue is dry on the top and the battens, *unclamp* and *cut* the complete *top* (battens and top) to size. *Sand* the top down with a belt sander. *Set* a circular saw at the proper angle and *cut* a *bevel* on the underside of the top. The edge of the top should be from 1/4 in. to 3/8 in. thick. Experiment on scrap stock before cutting the bevel. Do not change the saw setting until all bevels are cut. *Sand* the underside of the table.

10. *Make* a heavy paper *pattern* of the leg. *Lay* the *pattern* on 2 in. thick ash and *mark* the outline of the legs. Make sure the grain of the woods runs parallel to the sides of the lower part of leg. *Cut* the *legs* on a band saw.

11. *Drill* two holes in the under-table bracket of the leg. One hole—the one to take the longer screw—should be the size of the shank of a FHB No. 9-2 1/2 in. screw. The other hole is the shank size of a FHB No. 6-1 1/2 in. screw. See Fig. 5-13. *Countersink* the *screw holes* and *attach* the legs to the top with glue and screws.

LAMP TABLE

A person might think that the light, airy, gossamer-like table of Fig. 5-14 might blow away with the first sign of a breeze. Never think it. The strength of this dowel structured piece is surprising.

Material:

Table 5-14 lists materials to construct a strong lamp table.

Table 5-14.

Quantity	Description	Thick	Width	Length	Wood
1	Lamp shelf	3/4	11	17	Birch plywood
1	Table top	3/4	17	26	Birch plywood
4	Legs	1 1/2	1 1/2	17 1/2	Birch
8	Dowels		7/16-D	6	Birch
4	Dowels		1/2D	22	Birch
4	Dowels		1/2D	12 1/2	Birch

Note: Measurements in inches

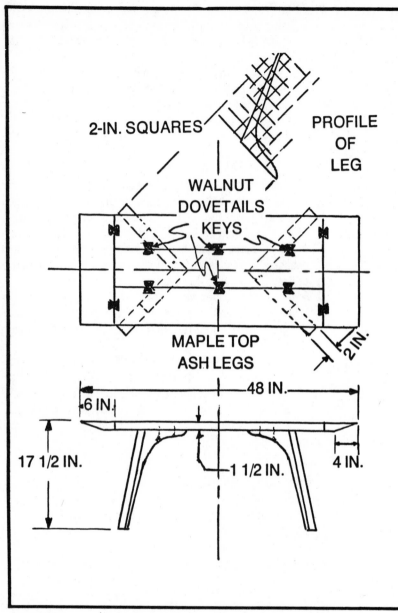

2-IN. SQUARES

PROFILE OF LEG

WALNUT DOVETAILS

KEYS

MAPLE TOP
ASH LEGS

2 IN.

48 IN.

6 IN.

17 1/2 IN.

1 1/2 IN.

4 IN.

Procedure:

1. *Cut* the *lamp shelf* to size. *Glue* and *brad* on 1/8 in. × 3/4 in. birch strips to protect the edges. *Bore* the eight 7/16 in. dowel holes.

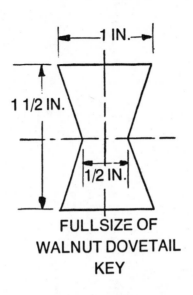

FULLSIZE OF
WALNUT DOVETAIL
KEY

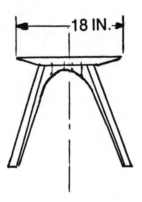

Fig. 5-13. A coffee table whose streamlined design hides its strength.

2. *Cut* the *table top* to size. *Glue* and *brad* on 1/8 in. × 3/4 in. birch strips to protect the edges. *Bore* the eight 7/16 in. dowel holes and the four 1/2 in. corner dowel holes to fasten the top to the legs.

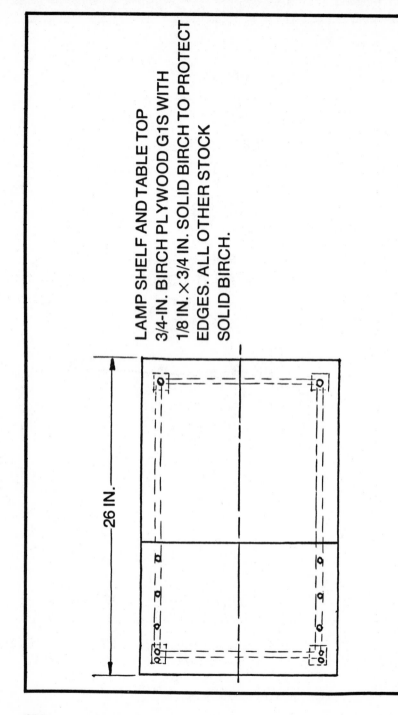

LAMP SHELF AND TABLE TOP
3/4-IN. BIRCH PLYWOOD G1S WITH
1/8 IN. × 3/4 IN. SOLID BIRCH TO PROTECT
EDGES. ALL OTHER STOCK
SOLID BIRCH.

26 IN.

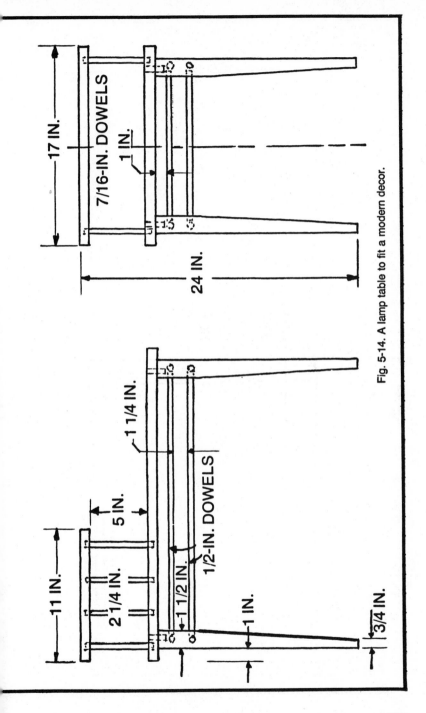

Fig. 5-14. A lamp table to fit a modern decor.

359

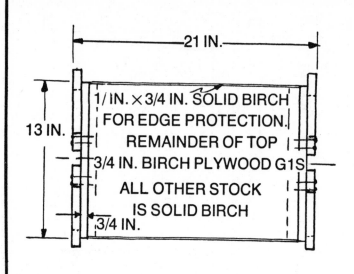

21 IN.

13 IN.

1/ IN. × 3/4 IN. SOLID BIRCH
FOR EDGE PROTECTION.
REMAINDER OF TOP
3/4 IN. BIRCH PLYWOOD G1S
ALL OTHER STOCK
IS SOLID BIRCH
3/4 IN.

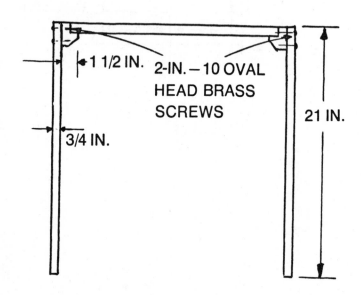

1 1/2 IN. 2-IN. – 10 OVAL
HEAD BRASS
SCREWS

3/4 IN.

21 IN.

Fig. 5-15. Nested tables are appropriate with any decor and can be a great asset for serving guests.

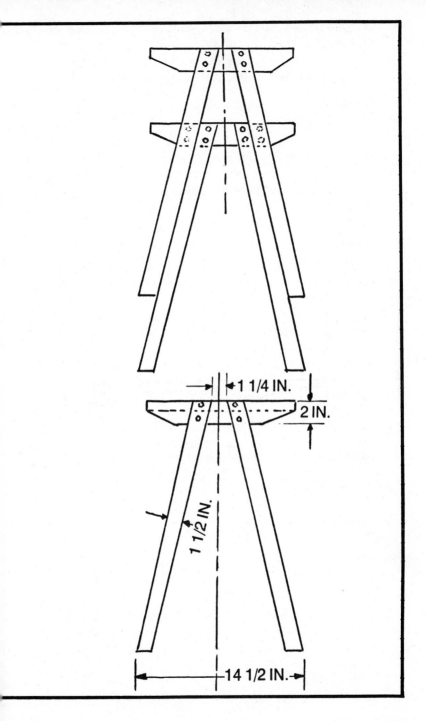

1 1/4 IN.

2 IN.

1 1/2 IN.

14 1/2 IN.

3. *Cut* the *legs* to squared dimension. *Bore* four 1/2 in. dowel holes in each leg (Fig. 5-14). *Taper* the *legs*, from 3 1/2 in. below the top end of the leg, to 3/4 in. square at the lower end. Use a jointer, fore plane or jointer plane to cut the taper.
4. *Cut* the dowels to the right length.
5. *Glue, assemble* and *clamp* the lamp shelf, table top and 7/16 in. dowels. Set this assembly aside to dry.
6. *Glue, assemble* and *clamp* the legs and 1/2 in. dowels and set aside to dry.
7. When both subassemblies are dry, *glue, assemble* and *clamp* the one subassembly to the other one.

NESTED TABLE

Nested tables take up little room, but have many uses. TV trays, snack trays, extra guest tables, and study or reading tables for the small fry are only a few of the uses that these general utility tables can perform. One table a weekend for six weeks will provide as many tables as normally would be needed. See Fig. 5-15 for the diagram of these nested tables.

Material:

Materials to complete the nested tables are listed in Table 5-15.

Table 5-15.

Quantity	Description	Thick	Width	Length	Wood
1	Top	3/4	13	18	Birch plywood
2	Top supports	1 1/2	2	13	Birch
4	Legs	3/4	1 1/2	22	Birch

Note: Measurements in inches

Procedure:

1. *Cut* the *top* to size. *Attach* 1/8 in. × 3/4 in. birch protective strips on the two long edges.
2. *Cut* the *top supports* to squared dimension. *Cut* 3/4 in. × 3/4 in. *rabbets* on the corners (longitudinally). See Fig. 5-15. On the corner, adjacent to the rabbet, *cut off* the corner at 45 degrees. *Taper* both *ends*, on the side below the rabbets, starting at 2 1/2 in. from the ends. Taper so that the ends are 3/4 in. wide as shown in Fig. 5-15.

3. *Cut* the *legs* to squared dimensions. *Lay out* a fullsize pattern of one end of the table. *Mark* the appropriate *angle* by referring to Fig. 5-15, and *cut* corresponding angles on the ends of legs. *Drill* two shank holes in one end for oval-head brass screws No. 10-2 in.
4. *Glue* and *assemble* with the screws mentioned above.

NIGHT TABLE

The night table of Fig. 5-16 has been designed with specific space allotments, each space to perform a certain function. Function and design usually go together. Craftsmen should be thinking about design as they fashion objects of wood. They should constantly be asking themselves how the project they are constructing could be designed to function better for their own use. Also, they should consider how it could be designed to save material.

Material:

Materials needed to complete a nightstand are listed in Table 5-16.

Table 5-16.

Quantity	Description	Thick	Width	Length	Wood
1	Top (lamp, clock)	3/4	10 1/2	16	Maple
2	Sides	3/4	15	23 1/4	Maple
1	Telephone shelf	3/4	14	15	Maple
2	Doors	3/4	7	7 3/4	Maple
1	Under drawer shelf	3/4	14	15	Maple
1	Bottom (general storage)	3/4	14	15	Maple
2	1-1-inch Dowels for door handles			4	
1	Dust panel	1/4	15	24	Masonite, hardboard , or plywood
1	Drawer front (Kleenex, medicine)	3/4	3 1/2	14	Maple
2	Drawer sides	1/2	3	13 1/4	Birch, maple. or pine
1	Drawer back	1/2	3	13	Birch, maple. or pine
1	Drawer partition	1/4	2 1/4	13	Birch, maple, or pine
1	Drawer bottom	1/4	12 3/4	13	Masonite, hardboard, or plywood
1	3/4-inch Dowel, long for drawer pull			4	
4	2-inch Brass hinges				
2	Magnetic catches, door				

Note: Measurements in inches

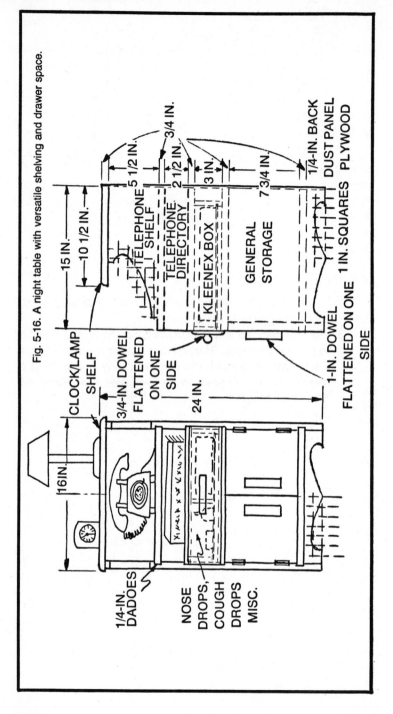

Fig. 5-16. A night table with versatile shelving and drawer space.

CLOCK/LAMP SHELF

TELEPHONE SHELF

TELEPHONE DIRECTORY

KLEENEX BOX

GENERAL STORAGE

15 IN.

10 1/2 IN.

5 1/2 IN.

3/4 IN.

2 1/2 IN.

3 IN.

7 3/4 IN.

1/4-IN. BACK DUST PANEL PLYWOOD

1 IN. SQUARES

3/4-IN. DOWEL FLATTENED ON ONE SIDE

24 IN.

1-IN. DOWEL FLATTENED ON ONE SIDE

16 IN.

1/4-IN. DADOES

NOSE DROPS, COUGH DROPS MISC.

Procedure:

1. *Glue up stock* and *cut* the *top* (clock/lamp) *shelf* to size. Roll the front and end edges with a plane and sandpaper.

2. *Glue up stock* and *cut* the *sides* to squared dimension. *Make* paper *patterns* for the curved portion. *Mark* the curved portions with the patterns. *Cut* the *curved* portions with a band saw. *Cut* the four *dadoes* 1/4 in. deep, 3/4 in. wide.

3. *Glue up stock* for all four shelves and bottom (telephone shelf, telephone directory shelf, Kleenex-medicine drawer shelf and bottom general storage shelf). *Cut* all *shelves* and *bottom* to the same size.

4. *Cut* the *bottom front rail* to squared dimensions. *Make* a paper *pattern* for the curved parts. *Mark* the curved portions with the pattern. *Saw* the curved portions with the bandsaw.

5. *Cut* the *doors* to size. *Cut* a *hinge gain* and *install* the hinges. *Cut* the *dowel handles* and install.

6. *Glue, assemble* and *clamp* the *sides* and the four *shelves*.

7. *Fit* the *doors* and install with the other half of the hinges. *Install* magnetic catches.

8. To construct the medicine drawer, *cut* the *drawer front* to outside dimensions. Measure the drawer opening and *cut drawer rabbets* accordingly (approximately 1/4 in. × 1/2 in.) Roll the front edges of the drawer front with a plane and sandpaper. *Cut a dowel* (3/4 in. × 4 in.) for the drawer pull. *Cut* 1/4 in. × 1/4 in. dadoes one-quarter inch in from the rabbet. *Cut* 1/4 in. × 1/4 in. approximately 7 in. from the rabbet (or a little wider than the Kleenex box generally used). *Cut* the *drawer back* to dimensions. *Cut* the *drawer partition* to size. *Cut* the *bottom groove* 1/4 in. × 1/4 in. near the bottom (3/8 in. up from the bottom edge) on the drawer front, drawer sides and drawer back. *Temporarily assemble* the drawer (no glue) and measure for the bottom. *Cut* the *bottom* to size. *Glue, assemble* and *clamp* the drawer parts together. Flatten one side of the dowel pull and attach it to the drawer front with FHB screws from the back of the drawer front.

9. *Attach* the top (clock/lamp) with dowel-covered FHB screws or with support blocks 1 1/4 in. × 1 1/4 in. × 7 in. and screws.

10. *Cut* a *dust panel* to size and *attach* it with small brads or nails and glue.

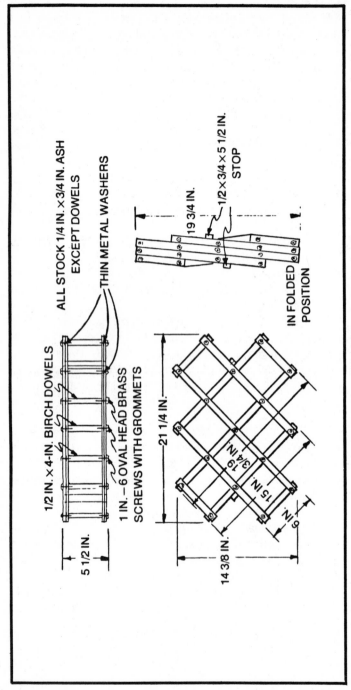

ALL STOCK 1/4 IN. × 3/4 IN. ASH
EXCEPT DOWELS

THIN METAL WASHERS

1/2 IN. × 4-IN. BIRCH DOWELS

1 IN. – 6 OVAL HEAD BRASS
SCREWS WITH GROMMETS

5 1/2 IN.

19 3/4 IN.

1/2 × 3/4 × 5 1/2 IN.
STOP

IN FOLDED
POSITION

21 1/4 IN.

19 3/4 IN.

15 IN.

6 IN.

14 3/8 IN.

Fig. 5-17. A wine rack that folds for easy storage.

WINE RACK

When not in use the wine rack sketched in Fig. 5-17 can be folded and stored away. For those who do not drink wine, this type of rack is being used frequently by the knitters in the family for storing skeins of yarn.

Material:

Table 5-17 lists materials needed to complete a wine rack.

Table 5-17.

Quantity	Description	Thick	Width	Length	Wood
4	Short members	1/4	3/4	6	Ash
4	Intermediate members	1/4	3/4	15	Ash
2	Long members	1/4	3/4	19 3/4	Ash
17	1/2- inch Dowels			4	
34	Oval head brass screws # 6-1 inch				
34	Gromets				
34	Thin metal washers, hole slightly larger than shank of screw				

Note: Measurements in inches

Procedure:

1. *Cut* all *members* to dimensions.
2. *Drill holes*, slightly larger than the shank of the screws, in the center of each member, 3/8 in. in from the end.
3. *Cut dowels* to length. *Drill pilot holes* in the end of the dowels slightly smaller in diameter than the spiral part of oval-head brass screws 6-1 in.
4. *Assemble members, screws, grommets* and *washers*. If the rack is hard to open or close, back off the screws slightly.

Index

Index